Rebel Brothers

TEXAS A&M UNIVERSITY
MILITARY HISTORY SERIES
44

Rebel Brothers

*The Civil War Letters
of
the Truehearts*

Edited by Edward B. Williams

TEXAS A&M UNIVERSITY PRESS
College Station

The paper used in this book meets the minimum requirements
of the American National Standard for Permanence
of Paper for Printed Library Materials, Z39.48–1984.
Binding materials have been chosen for durability.

Library of Congress Cataloging-in-Publication Data

Trueheart, Charles William.
    Rebel brothers : the Civil War letters of the Truehearts / edited by
Edward B. Williams — 1st ed.
        p.   cm. — (Military history series)
    Includes bibliographical references and index.
    ISBN 0-89096-656-7 (alk. paper)
        1. United States—History—Civil War, 1861–1865—Personal
narratives, Confederate.   2. United States—History—Civil War,
1861–1865—Campaigns.   3. Confederate States of America.   Army.
McNeill Partisan Rangers—History.   4. Trueheart, Charles
William—Correspondence.   5. Trueheart, Henry Martyn—
Correspondence.   6. Soldiers—Texas—Galveston—
Correspondence.   7. Galveston (Tex.)—History.   I. Trueheart,
Henry Martyn.   II. Williams, Edward B., 1935–   .   III. Series.
E605T78   1995
973.7'82—dc20   95-13098
                                                            CIP

For Judith Ann,
with love

Contents

List of Illustrations   ix

Preface   xi

Introduction: The Truehearts of Galveston   3

BOOK I:

Selected Letters of Charles William Trueheart, 1861–65   13

1. "These Troublesome Times," 1861   15

2. "A Band of Southerners," 1862   41

3. "This Fearful War," 1863   71

4. "That Much Dreaded Place—The Field," 1864   86

5. "That All Important Arm of the Service," 1865   136

BOOK II:

Selected Letters of Henry Martyn Trueheart, 1862–65   151

6. "Prepare Quietly to Evacuate the Place," 1862   153

7. "A Texan and Possessing 'Winning Ways,'" 1863   158

8. "The Wild and Ever Changeful Life," 1864   186

9. "People Are *Blue, Blue*," 1865   211

Epilogue   215

Notes   221

Selected References   265

Index   269

Illustrations

Charles W. and Mary Bryan Trueheart   17

Four Napoleon guns, 1st Rockbridge Artillery   30

Henry M. Trueheart   155

MAPS

The Confederate States of America   145

Virginia, 1861–1865   146

Shenandoah Valley   147

The Romney Expedition   148

Seven Days' Battles   149

Preface

The Civil War–era letters of Henry Martyn Trueheart (1832–1914) and Charles William Trueheart (1837–1914) are part of the Trueheart Family Collection in the History Center of the Rosenberg Library, Galveston, Texas. The collection contains materials relating to the Trueheart family's history and business affairs during the years 1822–1904.

There are three major subgroups within the collection. The first contains the papers of Charles W. Trueheart, M.D. A second subgroup consists largely of letters written by Charles's older brother, Henry Martyn Trueheart. The third subgroup contains records and correspondence of H. M. Trueheart & Company of Galveston, Texas. Smaller subgroups contain the papers of Anne Tompkins Minor Trueheart and John Overton Trueheart, Henry's and Charles's parents; and the papers of James Lawrence Trueheart, John Overton Trueheart's brother and the boys' uncle.

The papers of Charles W. Trueheart consist largely of two sets of letters written to family members and friends. Charles wrote one group while he was a medical student at the University of Virginia in 1860–61. The second group was composed during Charles's military service, first in the Army of the Valley, 1861–62, and then in the Army of Northern Virginia, 1864–65.

Henry's letters recount his experiences first as a participant in the battle of Galveston, Texas, in January 1863, and later as a cavalryman and as a partisan ranger in the Virginia theater from mid–1863 through 1865.

Those Civil War–era letters and journals that have been edited to date were written mainly by infantry soldiers. Few were written by cavalrymen and fewer still by artillerists. As for letters or journals of military doctors (not to mention doctors with prior experience as infantrymen and also as artillerists), research turned up only a handful. Charles Trueheart, M.D., C.S.A., entered the war as an infantry-man in a University of Virginia student military company in 1861. From October 1861 through September 1862, he served as an artil-lerist in the soon-to-be famous 1st Rockbridge Artillery, "Stonewall" Brigade, Army of the Valley, commanded by Maj. Gen. Thomas J. "Stonewall" Jackson. During the Seven Days campaign in the sum-mer of 1862, the brigade became part of the Army of Northern Vir-ginia, with Gen. Robert E. Lee commanding. From April 1864 to Appomattox, April 1865, he served as a regimental assistant surgeon, first with the 8th Alabama Infantry and finally with the 1st Regi-ment, Confederate Engineers. Henry Trueheart's letters, mainly those of a partisan ranger, provide less conventional glimpses of the conflict.

The brothers' letters invite modern readers to become ac-quainted with them, with their family, and with their times. These men were socially prominent in Galveston and knew most of the locally influential people of the day. When the war broke out in 1861, Henry was serving as the elected tax assessor-collector of Gal-veston County, and Charles was in Virginia studying to become a medical doctor. Their father was a local businessman. Their sister, Mary Minor Trueheart, was the wife of Thomas M. Joseph, mayor of Galveston in the early 1860s.

The Truehearts were Virginia-bred and were quite conscious of that aristocratic fact. Charles counseled one of his sisters not to have anything to do with soldiers who were her "social inferiors." The Truehearts owned slaves and took slaveholding for granted.

The brothers were life-long Presbyterians. Of the two, Charles was the more religious, evangelically reminding correspondents of their religious obligations. Henry's faith was more inwardly directed, although probably it was no less important to him.

Both men reacted to their war experiences in what strikes us to-day as an oddly clinical manner. They saw considerable action and bloodshed, yet neither expressed the revulsion typically felt upon witnessing such scenes of carnage. Their descriptions of body-strewn battlefields do not convey any special sense of horror. This is not unusual, however. The letters of other Civil War soldiers dis-play a similar detachment. George R. Stewart notes: "Nothing is more striking . . . generally than the absence of gloom. The armies suffered casualties such as few modern armies have endured, but the men did not seem to feel sorry for themselves."[1] Similarly, Ed-win B. Coddington observes: "It was a strange war, the bloodiest in our history; yet often the participants seemed to treat it as nothing but a rough game played according to established rules."[2] As Gerald F. Linderman points out, "Often the most powerful fear was that one's fear would be revealed—and that meant a prohibition on discussion, frequently even among comrades, of the topic of greatest concern to each soldier. Fear was not an anxiety to be shared but a weakness to be stifled."[3]

Perhaps, among other things, stoicism was the Trueheart brothers' way of sparing their family the anguish of worrying about their safety. Nonetheless, they were devoted to the Southern "cause" and willing to risk their lives for it. Charles felt that the family at all times should have someone in the "fighting department." In the latter stages of the war, when serving with the Engineers, he indicated that he missed the excitement of the "line." Once Henry, ever the flamboyant horseman, while on a raid into Maryland with his partisan unit, passed up a chance to bring out a spare horse. He reasoned that leading a horse would place him at the rear of the column, effectively removing him from the action and excitement. These were men of action.

* * *

The original letters are, by and large, in remarkably good condition—a testimonial to the quality of stationery of that period. A salute must also go to Sally Trueheart Williams, Henry's daughter, who—probably early in the twentieth century, judging from the typewriter used—undertook the painstaking task of transcribing the letters. Comparing the transcriptions with the original letters revealed only minor discrepancies, all of which have been corrected.

The letters of Henry and Charles Trueheart were written from the perspective of mature men, they being about ages twenty-nine and twenty-four, respectively, in 1861. The two brothers had been educated privately but well in Virginia, and their letters are well-written. Their penmanship is good. One can overlook some informality of form and punctuation, given the military field conditions under which most of the letters were composed.

The letters are addressed mainly to family members. There are gaps in continuity, and the letters do not weave a continuous story, as a journal might. Such gaps may be attributable partly to the South's loss of the Mississippi River in 1863 and the consequent disruption of Confederate mail service to the Trans-Mississippi theater. The Confederate mail service was not terribly reliable even before that time, however. Of course, some of the letters were probably discarded and others lost over time.

The introduction to this book supplies historical background material, and extensive chapter notes provide further explication. The letters included in this volume have been selected for their historical relevance. Most of the letters contain the soldier's traditional endless plaint, "Why aren't you writing more often?" Some letters, addressed to different people, recount the same event. Unless they provide additional information, such repetitious letters generally have been omitted. Some letters relate to matters of family interest only and have been excluded. It would be difficult, from some letters, to detect the fact that a terrible war was in progress and that many people were suffering horribly. Those letters, too, were excluded.

This work is not intended as a guide to Trueheart family genealogy. Except where necessary, no attempt has been made to identify all the aunts, uncles, cousins, and the like alluded to in the letters.

The letters are presented largely as they were written, including misspelled words, grammatical errors, and minor vulgarities. In cases where words are indecipherable, they generally are omitted; where indecipherable but obvious, words are added in brackets. The placement of the opening and closing elements of the letters, such as the date line, address, greeting, and signature line, has been standardized for the reader's convenience.

A literary work is never completed without assistance. I would like to thank, the Rosenberg Library, John Hyatt, former head librarian, and the Board of Directors for permission to edit the letters. Special thanks go to Lisa Shippee Lambert, head of special collections, and to her colleagues, Casey Greene, assistant archivist, and Margaret Schlanky and Julia Dunn, archival assistants.

Thanks to Edward Cotham, Jr., of Houston, Texas, for help in determining the locations of various historical sites around Galveston. It was my pleasure to interview Mrs. Marjorie Trueheart Williams McCullough and Mrs. Edward McCullough Futch of Galveston, Texas, granddaughter and great-granddaughter, respectively, of Henry Martyn Trueheart. They supplied the photographs of Charles and Mary Trueheart. These women reflect their heritage; my special thanks go to them both. Thanks also to Mr. Joseph C. Brown and Mrs. Mary Hill Brown Whitcomb of Houston, Texas, grandson and grandaughter, respectively, of Henry M. Trueheart, for their help and photograph of their grandfather.

Thanks to Perry Jamieson, who read the manuscript and made recommendations and constructive suggestions for its improvement.

Finally, thanks to my wife and friend for over thirty-two years, Judith Ann Fisher Williams. A truly dedicated Texas elementary school educator and administrator, she has been a constant example and inspiration.

Edward B. Williams

Rebel Brothers

INTRODUCTION

≈

The Truehearts of Galveston

In Galveston, Texas, a large old cemetery lies nestled between 40th and 43rd streets, fronting on Broadway Avenue. Known by various names, it is sometimes referred to as the "Old City Cemetery." The cemetery is divided into sections. A wrought-iron fence guards the perimeter but is breached by gates on the eastern and western sides. From gate to gate, a narrow paved lane traverses the grounds, allowing access to visitor and vandal alike. The cemetery has long survived, if in less than immaculate condition, the ravages of hurricanes and the unrelenting Texas sun.

While no true "greats" are interred here, the near-great slumber side by side with the humble beneath the rough surface. In the Episcopal section, an obelisk-topped monument marks the grave of Maj. Gen. John B. Magruder, C.S.A. An early hero of Southern arms in Virginia, he quickly fell into disfavor and was exiled to Texas. Nearby, marked by State of Texas granite, is the place of Louis T. Wigfall—U.S. Senator, secessionist firebrand, Confederate senator, and one-time confidante of Jefferson Davis. The list could go on: Gen. Sydney Sherman; Lt. Comdr. Edward Lea, U.S.N.; Samuel May Williams; Confederates killed in the battle of Galveston.

The Evergreen section is located on the western corner of the grounds. Few trees provide shady solace here, and the unpaved gravesites are thick with grass burrs. Near the southwestern edge of the section, just off 43rd Street, one aisle removed, a plain stone monument bears the family name *Trueheart*. The homeliness of the site is relieved only by a Texas state marker briefly identifying John Overton Trueheart as an early settler of the state who served as a

Texas Ranger in the 1840s. Perhaps this somber scene is appropriately symbolic of frontier Texas in the 1830s and 1840s, when the first of this clan ventured into its confines.[1]

The first Truehearts came to the Lone Star State from Virginia. Their family history in Texas began in 1838, when John Overton Trueheart, traveling with his brother James Lawrence Trueheart and a French man-servant, arrived in the fledgling nation by one-horse wagon.[2] The Trueheart brothers, sons of Washington Trueheart, were descended from Scotch and French Huguenot ancestors.

John O. Trueheart, patriarch of the Galveston clan-to-be, was born in Hanover County, Virginia, in 1802. According to a family historical sketch written many years later by his eldest son, Henry Martyn Trueheart, John came from a good family. A graduate of Princeton College and a lawyer by training, he apparently was of modest means. It seems likely that the chance to win his fortune brought him, at age thirty-six, to the frontier. By the time of his death in 1876, at age seventy-four, he had realized that goal, having become a well-to-do, respected member of the Galveston community.

In 1824, John Trueheart had made an excellent match. His bride, Ann Tompkins Minor, was a daughter of Col. Launcelot Minor of "Minor's Folly," Louisa County, Virginia.[3] The Minor family boasted distinguished lineage. Colonel Minor's sister Diana was the wife of Richard Maury of Spotsylvania and the mother of Commodore Matthew Fontaine Maury, U.S.N., the outstanding oceanographer of the age.[4] Ann Tompkins Minor's brothers were men of attainment—Lucian, professor of law at William and Mary College; Charles, a physician of Albemarle County, Virginia; William, a physician of Huntsville, Alabama; John, professor of law at the University of Virginia; and Launcelot, a prosperous farmer of Amherst County, Virginia.[5]

In the 1830s, Texas offered opportunities for enterprising young men, and for five years after his arrival in 1838, John Trueheart remained in the environs of San Antonio, Bexar County.[6] Land was available in abundance, and during that time he, like many others, supported himself working as a surveyor.

The work was not without dangers. Much of the land available was in territory roamed by the dreaded Comanche and still claimed by Mexico, which refused still to recognize the outcome of the Texas Revolution of 1836. Under the circumstances, it was customary that "surveyors worked heavily armed or under the protection of a military escort. . . . [I]t was quite natural for a surveyor to divide his time between frontier patrol and surveying."[7] From June to October 1841, John Trueheart served in a frontier military company commanded by the famous Texas Ranger captain, John Coffee "Jack" Hays.[8]

Apparently John adapted well to his new environment, for, as a Ranger recruit, one had to meet rigorous standards. An applicant "had to possess good character, courage and skill in marksmanship and horsemanship, and [had to] own a horse worth at least a hundred dollars. . . . A Ranger also [had to furnish] his own arms and other equipment."[9] Although there is no family record of John Trueheart's military activities, it can be assumed that he saw some action, given the agitated state of Indian affairs and the ongoing disputes over the Mexican border during that period prior to the Mexican War of 1846–48.[10]

It was during this era, Henry Martyn states, that his father acquired about twenty thousand acres of land as a result of his surveying activities. Ultimately, however, most of that land was lost while John was in Virginia in 1843–45. He emerged with only a few small tracts to show for his first five years in Texas.

In 1843, John Trueheart returned to the Old Dominion for his family.[11] His odyssey had an epic beginning. After John sailed from Galveston for New Orleans on the sloop *Dream*, the vessel foundered in a severe storm. Such storms were not uncommon in the Gulf of Mexico, given the occasional summer hurricanes and frequent winter "northers." Rescued by a passing vessel, he was able to save only the clothing he had worn into the water. In New Orleans, by luck or by plan (Henry does not say which), John met his half-uncle, William Overton of Louisa County, Virginia, from whom he was able to borrow enough money to complete his journey.[12]

The stay in Virginia extended to two years. John returned to Texas in May 1845, about the same time the Republic of Texas was annexed by the United States. John's second arrival in Texas must have been a far happier occasion than his first. Since the 1824 union, eight children had been born, and most of them—Henry Martyn, Fanny Overton, Mildred, Charles William, Elvira Susan, and Caroline Hill—accompanied him and his wife to Texas. Two offspring—Mary Minor and Lucian Minor—remained in Virginia.[13] Both came to Texas at a later date.

John Trueheart's original intention had been to bring his family to the San Antonio area. However, once landed in Galveston, they found it suited them, and they decided to make their new home on the island. Soon thereafter, a ten-acre plot was purchased with money given Mrs. Trueheart by her brother, Lucian Minor. Over time, the property came to be known as the "Trueheart block." It was bounded by 33rd and 35th streets between avenues Q and R.[14]

The Galveston that greeted the Truehearts in 1845 was only eight years old. The founder of the city, Michel B. Menard, was a Canadian who had drifted to Texas in 1829. He had gained control of the site through a series of convoluted financial and political maneuvers during the years 1833–36. His first efforts to acquire the property had been stymied by the fact that only Mexican-born citizens could purchase land; prior to the Texas Revolution of 1836, the area was still a part of Mexico. To circumvent this requirement, Menard had utilized the Mexican citizenship of an acquaintance, Juan N. Seguin, to apply for a "headright." Meanwhile, the Texas Revolution intervened. Afterward, Menard, now with nine associates, petitioned the Republic of Texas for confirmation of the pending Mexican claim. Finally, on 9 December 1836 the petition was granted, in exchange for fifty thousand dollars, payable within the following four months.

With the claim secured, the group in 1837 hired John D. Groesbeck to survey the site and divide it into lots. Groesbeck's survey took a gridiron form similar to the plans of Philadelphia and New York—a pattern that persists in Galveston to this day.[15] In 1839, "the Texas Congress granted incorporation to the city with a charter which specified the election of a mayor, recorder, treasurer, and eight aldermen."[16] By the time of the Truehearts' arrival, the foundation had been established upon which the city could grow and prosper.

Surveys and political organization notwithstanding, Galveston in 1845 was very much a frontier settlement. In most respects, it must have struck the cultured, newly arrived Virginian immigrants as distressingly crude and vulgar. A few years earlier, one Francis C. Sheridan, a British diplomat, had arrived for the first time on the Texas coast. Recording his impression from the harbor, he described the scene spread before him as "singularly dreary." The only laudable feature he could find was the beaches, which he thought were composed of the most beautiful sand he had ever seen.[17] Another early arrival described Galveston as something an entrepreneur would not care to advertise in a "full-color brouchure, . . . a low, flat, incredibly desolate stretch of sand that flooded with every violent tide and . . . [was] virtually useless for agriculture. [It] was solitary and monotonous, . . . a hotbed of disease and pestilence. . . . [T]he harbor was [seen to be] as dreary as a West Texas stock pond, without definition or landmarks."[18]

If these dismal physical descriptions of Galveston in 1845 were accurate, then the rustic inhabitants of the settlement had adapted admirably to their environment. The men were described as typically wearing "boots, trousers, and frock coats made from blankets [and] carrying pen knives for cutting tobacco, trimming their nails, and picking their teeth. For more violent purposes they carried pistols and Bowie knives. . . . Business took place in the bars, and every new friendship had to be 'wetted' as soon as possible. . . . There was also the benefit of the 'spitting box.'. . . [and] where the spitting box was missing, floors and fireplaces suffered."[19] John Trueheart had prior frontier experience and knew what to expect. He and his family, if they witnessed such scenes, refused to allow them to interfere with their plans. They stayed and prospered; their descendants, under vastly improved circumstances, remain on the island to the present.

In the years intervening prior to the onset of the Civil War in 1861, the family became firmly established. The group had a large truck garden on its property, and Henry and younger brother Charles worked there to raise melons and vegetables to sell around town. They also gathered oysters and sold them "by the boatload" at the local wharves.

During the 1850s, conditions gradually improved, as Galveston became the first genuine city in the state. "Merchants [had begun] importing ornate iron fronts for their buildings, and the town council [had] constructed sidewalks, installed gaslights, and paved primary streets with shell."[20] The Truehearts' circumstances similarly improved. John Trueheart continued his work as a surveyor and eventually opened a real estate office in the city. The census of 1860 lists his occupation as "surveyor."[21]

Henry accumulated a herd of cattle and in the process developed into a skillful horseman. He said that he "delighted to ride wild horses, and would buy them just for the fun of breaking them. . . . [He roped] wild cattle, and could, with ease, pick up a dollar from the ground while riding at a gallop."[22] In 1851, he sold his beef herd, used the proceeds to purchase a dairy herd, and opened a dairy. In 1857, he sold the dairy operation and worked for a time as a clerk in his father's real estate office. Later that year, he was appointed to fill a vacancy as assessor and collector of taxes for Galveston County. He was reelected to the post several times and continued in the office until 1862–63.

In 1858–59, Charles began to study medicine in Galveston under the direction of Dr. S. B. Hurlbut. In 1860, he went to Charlottesville, Virginia, to continue his medical studies at the University of Virginia. He was there when the war overtook him.

* * *

The sectional conflict that engulfed the nation in 1861 had been brewing for decades. Tensions flared between dissimilar neighbors—an agrarian South whose economy was based on ownership of black slaves, and an industrializing North where slaves were rare. The election of the "Black Republican," Abraham Lincoln, to the presidency of the United States in November 1860 precipitated the final crisis. On 20 December 1860 a secession convention in Columbia, South Carolina, took that state out of the Union. In the months that followed, South Carolina's action was duplicated in other Southern states, until a total of eleven states banded together to form the Confederate States of America, with its first capitol at Montgomery, Alabama.

The effect upon the Truehearts was swift. Texas seceded on 1 February 1861. On 12 April 1861 the Federal garrison at Fort Sumter, in the harbor at Charleston, South Carolina, was surrendered to besieging South Carolina forces. In response to these acts of open rebellion to federal authority, the newly elected president of the United States resolutely called for 75,000 volunteers to suppress the insurrection. The war was on. Five days later, on 17 April 1861, Virginia declared for the Confederacy. The course for the Truehearts was clear; they were Virginians and Texans—Southerners—and would help defend their native land. Their fiery ordeal was beginning.

At the University of Virginia, as war appeared more likely, students had petitioned the faculty to be allowed to organize military companies. As early as 1860, the "Sons of Liberty," a company composed of seventy-four student members, was organized. In January 1861, the one-hundred-member "Southern Guards" was organized, with Charles Trueheart as one of its number. Another member and friend was Robert E. Lee, Jr., son of Gen. Robert E. Lee, at that time commander of all Virginia troops. In April or May 1861, a third company, the "University Volunteers," was organized.[23]

Initiation into active campaigning came on 16 April 1861, when Gov. John Letcher ordered Shenandoah Valley militia companies to capture and occupy the key position to control the valley at Harper's Ferry, Virginia. In Charlottesville, two militia units, the Monticello Guards and the Albemarle Rifles, invited the Southern Guards and the Sons of Liberty to join them on the foray. Collectively, the four groups were known as the Charlottesville and University Battalion.[24]

Charles described the experience in a letter to brother Henry— the train ride in box cars to Strasburg, the march from that place to Winchester, another train ride from Winchester to Harper's Ferry. This was heady stuff for a bunch of college students. Alas, they arrived too late to prevent the small Federal garrison from firing the arsenal and partially destroying it. For the next ten days, the student companies were kept occupied on guard. When finally sent back to Charlottesville on 21 April, they had not fired a round in anger. Back on campus, the two student companies were disbanded.

For the next six months, Charles remained at the university, continuing his studies as circumstances allowed and learning military arts part-time in a "military school" run by graduates of the Virginia Military Institute (VMI). Meanwhile, the first big battle of the war was fought on the plains of Manassas, yielding a victory for the South.

As a result of his military training, Charles felt qualified to command. He attempted to recruit volunteer companies but was unsuccessful, mainly because he had no influence and was relatively unknown in the region. He considered returning to Texas for the same purpose but decided against it. In October 1861, he decided to join a unit in the field as a private soldier. The unit he chose to join was the 1st Rockbridge Artillery, a part of Gen. Joseph E. Johnston's army, then concentrated near the site of the first battle at Manassas. The unit—also known as Pendleton's Battery, after its first commander, William Nelson Pendleton—already had distinguished itself as part of the newly famous "Stonewall Brigade" and was destined to become one of the fabled fighting units in a fabled army. Its ranks included Robert E. Lee, Jr., and two sons of a former president of the United States, John Tyler.

For the next year, Charles shared the dangers and triumphs of the unit. He participated in "Stonewall" Jackson's winter campaign of 1861–62, taking part in expeditions to destroy Dam Number 5 on the Potomac River and forays against Bath and Romney in north-western Virginia. He participated in the famous Valley campaign in the spring of 1862—Kernstown, McDowell, Front Royal, Winchester, and the crowning triumph at Cross Keys and Port Republic on 8–9 June. He went with the "Stonewall Brigade" into the inferno of the Seven Day's battle before Richmond in early summer of 1862. Although no letters confirm it, the record indicates that he was at Second Manassas in August 1862 and went into Maryland for the war's single bloodiest day along the banks of Antietam Creek near the sleepy little village of Sharpsburg. Charles pens no lengthy accounts of his experiences at Sharpsburg, but, in a letter to his sister Cally, he does mention that he was there. A kinsman, W. W. Blackford, in his classic work *War Years with Jeb Stuart,* mentions seeing him at Sharpsburg with his battery.[25]

Shortly after Antietam, on 24 September 1862, Charles—suffering from scurvy and presumably because of his medical background—was detailed to duty in a Winchester, Virginia, hospital. On 18 February 1863 he was appointed a hospital steward and transferred to a hospital in Lynchburg, Virginia. He served there until September 1863, at which time he went to Richmond to complete his medical studies.

Having completed those studies and then passed examinations in March 1864, he was assigned as assistant surgeon, 8th Alabama Volunteer Infantry Regiment. He served with the regiment in the Wilderness, at Spotsylvania Court House, Cold Harbor, and in the lines defending Petersburg, Virginia. In December 1864, he transferred to the 1st Regiment of Confederate Engineers on the Petersburg line. It was with this regiment that he surrendered at Appomattox Court House on 9 April 1865.[26]

Meanwhile, in Texas, Galveston had fallen to Federal forces late in 1862. Brother Henry was among the troops defending the island. He participated in the battle of Galveston, fought on 1 January 1863, that resulted in the recapture of the city. Afterward, he was appointed captain and assistant provost marshal of the city by the Confederate commander, Maj. Gen. John B. Magruder.

In June 1863, he went to Virginia, serving first with the 7th Virginia Cavalry Regiment of Maj. Gen. J. E. B. Stuart's Cavalry Division. In a skirmish with Federal forces near Orange Court House in the fall of 1863, he suffered an accidental, self-inflicted saber wound to the knee. Fearful of having his leg amputated against his will, he took matters into his own hands. Painfully, he made his way first to his Uncle John Minor's home in Charlottesville and, finally, to his Uncle John Overton's home, where he recuperated.

Upon recovering from his wound, he became a member of McNeill's Rangers, a partisan unit serving primarily on the northwestern Virginia—Maryland border. He took part in the unit's many exciting and dangerous forays into enemy territory, including Lt. Gen. Jubal A. Early's raid into Maryland in July 1864, reaching the outskirts of the city of Washington. Perhaps the most exciting adventure in which he participated took place in February 1865. A volunteer force of about sixty-six McNeill men raided Cumberland, Maryland, capturing Union Generals Kelley and Crook. They then spirited them back across Confederate lines in Virginia.

During this period, Henry met his future wife, Annie Van Meter Cunningham, the daughter of William and Sally Cunningham of Hardy County, Virginia. Against Charles' advice, he continued to serve with McNeill's Rangers until the end of the war. He was paroled at New Creek, Virginia, on 5 May 1865.[27]

The selected Civil War letters of Henry Martyn Trueheart and Charles William Trueheart follow.

BOOK I

Selected Letters of
Charles William Trueheart, 1861–65

~

CHAPTER I

"These Troublesome Times," 1861

University of Virginia
January 14, 1861

Dear Father:

I congratulate you on your safe arrival from the Country. What amount of land and money did you make by the trip?

I am anxious to know your politics in these troublesome times. Can't you sit down on receipt of this, and give me your views on the subject. I am not sufficiently informed to have an opinion hardly; but as far as I am able to judge, I must say that I cant see what we of the South can do as things have turned out, the position that near all our States have taken being such that they cant honorably recede from it until the North have complied with at least a part of their demands; which they seem not at all disposed to do, if we may judge by the tone of their meetings, Congressmen and press; I say I don't see what they can do less than secede from the Union—Tho' I don't believe in the right of Secession, as I think it contrary to the spirit if not the letter of the compact entered into on the formation and adoption of the present Constitution. I think this is clear from the tone of the debates that occurred soon after, and at the time of its adoption. So I would substitute the word Revolution, for that of Secession. In view of the fact that our section of the Union is much the weakest in point of numbers, and on account [of] the slave population in our midst; and the fact that our treasuries are empty; and we cant borrow abroad or at home enough money to support an army, carry on war, erect forts, and use other means for protection; and the fact that our peoples' source of wealth would be gone without the ability to produce and export their produce; and direct taxation to raise such an amt would be impracticable; it seems to me that disunion, with the inevitable war, immediate or growing out of the many questions that would come up for settlement by the two sections, then become rival nations for supremacy on this Continent, would prove most disasterous to all our best interests. And yet it seems that there is no other alternative left us, unless we come down from the high ground that we have taken, and humble our heads in the dust at the feet of Black Republican masters; disgraced in our own eyes and before the whole world. I dont know what would be best for us to do; our help can come from God alone—I hope Texas will never consent to go into a Southern Confederacy acknowledging the right of the States forming it to secede when it suited them. Such a government would not be worth a button— liable to disruption at any day, or at the whim of a dissatisfied State it would not have the credit to buy a loaf of bread without the cash. And capitalists would not be willing to make investments under it; there would be no security for property or any thing else worth having[.] But here I have been flourishing away as if I knew anything about it.

It is hard to say what Va will do. People here are very bitter against S.C. [South Carolina] for her conduct; and don't seem willing to have anything to do with her.

Affectionately yr. son,
C. W. T.

University of Virginia
February 20th, 1861

Dear Henry

You have been rather remiss in writing to me of late; whats the matter? Are you in love? Or are you overrun with business?

I dont believe I have ever told you how I am pleased with my Professors here; and as it may serve to interest you somewhat; I will devote this sheet of foolscap to them and their merits. Dr. Howard, our Prof. of Practices Obstetrics and Medical Jurisprudence is the one I like least of all; I think I can say with truth that he is the most unmitigated bore I have ever had the misfortune to come across.[1] Fortunately for his class, the Textbooks in his department are unexceptionable, so we dont have to rely on his Lectures for obtaining a

Rebel Brothers

∽

Dr. Charles W. Trueheart and first wife Mary Bryan, circa 1866. (Courtesy Mrs. Sally McCullough Futch)

knowledge of them. During the first part of the Session I concientiously; i.e. I made it a matter of concience to listen carefully to all that fell from his lips; but I have come to the conclusion that its time thrown away so as soon he begins to lecture, I begin to prepare another subject from a text book that I bring with me. He delivers his lectures—said to be the same he used ten years ago, through his nose, and in the most monotinous ding dong tone, that you can well imagine of; never or seldom looking up from his manuscript. Sometimes diversifies it by attempting to get off what in college parlance we term a "curl," i.e. an attempt at eloquence wit etc. One of his favorite steroptypes is delivered when lecturing on a disease of the stomach. Its something after this fashion. "Gentlemen, this is the disease of which the great Napoleon died;—some call him great, but I care not what others may say; it is the opinion of *this* chair that true greatness consists alone in moral goodness!!!" Some time ago he got off the following when speaking of certain things as aids in diagnosing disease. "Gentlemen; with these guides you would be like the mariner on the trackless deep without his compass." On such occasions the students applaud loud and long with their feet. The old gentleman smiles too, as tho. he had done some thing great, and was very well pleased with the achievement.

Dr. Cabell, Lecturer in Physiology, Surgery and Comparative Anatomy, is unexceptionable in every respect.[2] He is a most admirable lecturer;—very dignified, and keeps good order.

Dr. Allen, Demonstrator of Anatomy is also as good as could be desired;—said by good judges to be the best demonstrator in this country—But here must stop for tonight, as its half past eleven.

Thursday 21st–12 at night—Its past 12 but I must do something towards completing this sheet of foolscap;—so heres at you!

Dr. Maupin, lecturer on Chemistry, is a very dry and uninteresting lecturer, and he bores me no little.[3] The course that we "Meds" have to swallow, is the full academics, which contains a vast deal of stuff that is of no sort of use to us, and is only an additional burden to our already too heavy and extensive course. The Doctor is a good old soul, but a very indifferent teacher. Doctor Davis is my favorite,—indeed he is a favorite with all the students in college, both "Meds" Academics & Law.[4] In giving Colithurups [?] . . . etc, the students always treat him and Uncle Jno. [John Minor, Professor of Law] with the greatest respect, and dont come near their houses to make a noise etc. Although Anatomy is perhaps the dryest thing in the whole course, he makes it by far the most interesting. Without a doubt he has the most facinating, clear and happy faculty of imparting knowledge of any man that I have ever met with. He takes the most difficult subject and makes them as clear as daylight; the dryest, and most uninteresting, and by his inimitable nack of blending his wit humor and anecdote makes them charming. I wish I could remember some of his sayings so as to let you have a specimen of them. I had some of them set down in my notes but reading them over I concluded that they afforded us pleasure rather by their connection and manner in which they were told by him than in their intrinsic worth.

One day where on . . . Medicine & Therapeutics he was lecturing on Enumata and held forth in something like the following strain;—it was the only occassion when he has made any approach to being vulgar. "Gentlemen—Injections are in much better . . . in Europe than with us; there a young lady or gentleman does not consider wardrobes complete till it is furnished with an injecting apparatus;—and they take their daily to promote evacuations etc. But how different is it with us;—why there is nothing so shocking to ears polite; and one you young gentlemen would think your moral character forever ruined were you to receive one. In former times, even in England, this was thought to be rather "low practice"; a regular Doctor would not be found giving one, but confined themselves to cathartics per mouth, leaving the injections to the Apothecaries, quacks etc. This state of things is well exemplified by a poet of the day on the subject of recovering a ring that had been swallowed by a pet bird.

> *The* doctor *used his oily art,*
> *Of strong emetic kind*
> *The* Apothecary *play[ed] his part*
> *And engineered behind.*

But I can give you no idea of the character of his lectures.

We have two military companies formed here by the students; the "Southern Guards" and the "Sons of Liberty." I am a member of the former. We spend an hour every afternoon in drilling. Our officers are graduates of the V.M.I (Virginia Military Institute). I am improving very fast in the drill, and hope to be in a condition to take charge of the Texian forces by the end of the Session.

I am getting on quite well in my medical studies; and think I shall find myself greatly benefited by my stay here. I think it was without doubt the course that I could have fixed upon for getting a medical education. But turning to another sheet of paper—I want to start home just as soon as the lectures on Medicine here are completed; not waiting to witness the "Celebration of the Commencement." I dont think I shall have time to do any visiting among our relations in these parts, either;—it takes too much time and money. I shall want to go out to Uncle Charles' [Dr. Charles Minor] and Cousin Wm Minor's to take leave of them; stay a day in Lynchburg, and one or two with Uncle Lanty [Minor, Ann Minor Trueheart's brother]. If I go down to see Uncle Wm Overton, I should be obliged to visit a number of other people in Louisa;—and indeed in Hanover too, for Mac. Fleming and Berkley Minor, two of our Cousins with whom I . . . and am very well acquainted, would never hear of my going in that direction without paying them a visit, but as I said before, it takes too much time and money for me to afford it. My plan is to hurry back to Galveston and try to see some practice in our Hospital with [Drs.] Burk and Hurlbut during the summer and then would be from June to the middle of November when the New Orleans Medical school opens, that I could spend to great advantage in that way, I think. Cant you keep your eyes open to my interests; throw out intimations to Hurlbut or Burk on the subject?

Certainly this is a most egotistical and lengthy letter; and I suspect it has numerous mistakes of orthography and diction in it; but you may make the most of them; I have'nt the time to read it over and make corrections.

The Washington Society's [Jefferson and Washington Literary Society] celebration came off tonight; it was a grand affair I hear. Large numbers of people were here to witness it. The [Public] Hall was most beautifully decorated with wreaths of evergreen etc. A Mr. Weddel was the orator of the occassion; he is said to have made a very pretty speech. Not only was the feed off, but arcade was lit up [with] numerous colored burners. I should have liked to attend, but I had some hard lectures to prepare for tomorrow. It is 1 oclock at night so I must stop. Just hear company of seranadirs come in hearing so I must slip out and have a sing with them. They are first waking up the ladies (three or four or five staying here at Uncle Jno's) with a very spirited song.

Come boys, come and we'l sing tonight;
The moon is up and the stars shine bright;
The girls, the girls, our hearts delight;—
We'l sing for them tonight.
Chorus—Hurrah! hurrah! hurrah for the girls hurrah

Rebel Brothers

The night is really a splendid one; the air is cool and bracing, and the moon & stars are indeed shining bright–2 Papers and yours of the 6th inst are received. Tell Mother I will answer her letter in a day or two—

Charles

University of Virginia
March 1st, 1861

Dear Cally [Sister Caroline]:

Your big foolscap letter of the 28th ultimo has been sticking up among my letters to be answered for some weeks; calling loudly for an answer. Money and letter paper are both scarce commodities in this part of the world, so I shall take the liberty of writing on big foolscap:—tho' I wont promise to write more than two pages of it. The fact of the matter is, I have nothing to write about: we poor hard worked students never go anywhere but to lecture rooms, etc., so we have no opportunity of collecting material for writing interesting letters. Well, you will just have to put up with anything that comes uppermost; but on paper without much regard to penmanship, orthography and diction.

My Chum, who has been sitting on the other side of the big fire place, has gotten sleepy and is now reclining on the bed with his pipe in his mouth, fast asleep. He is a good-natured obliging fellow, and suits me very well as a room mate. His Father and Mother came in today. The latter dined with us upstairs today. They are both very warm Secessionists, and declare that in the event of Virginia's refusing to secede they are going South,—that they have no idea of living in this State with their negroes (of which they have some one hundred and odd—March 7th—Just a week has elapsed since the above was indited; but it was positively, comparatively super[l]atively stale when it was penned; a weeks keeping has not improved its merits, I reckon. It's past 12 at night and I still have a lecture to prepare for tomorrow before going to bed, so I shall not write much more.

Ere this you all have doubtless received Lincoln's Inaugural. What do you think of it? Don't it crown all; and just what we might have anticipated;—a downright declaration of Coercion. I am for *Resistance to the death.* It has produced a most tremendous sensation here. The Virginia students have had a meeting in wh were made strong Secession speeches; and strong resolutions to the same effect were adopted unanimously,—I should not say unanimously either for there was one fellow from Western Virginia who dissented. That's the quarter from which the Secession movement has to expect trouble in this State. Numbers of the members of the State Convention, now sitting in Richmond, hitherto warm Union men have come out strongly for immediate Secession. But it's hard to say what Virginia will do in the matter. One thing I know, vast numbers will leave the State if she does go with the North, Uncle Charles among the number. All our friends hereabout are well. Best love to all—Tell H. [Henry] I have enjoyed the numerous papers he has sent me, very much indeed.

Your brother, Charles

March 25th, 1861
At the University of Va.

Dear Henry

On the 19th inst. I received a letter from [Sister] Cally, one from [Sister] Fanny and a short P.S. from yourself. Todays mail brought me a letter from Mother, and one from Minny. On the 14th wrote to Mother, but having been quite busy with my intermediate examinations, I dont remember to have written a letter since. Tonight I shall put you off with one that will be sufficiently short to suit your fastidious taste;—or do you remember having found fault with the length of a letter—or rather two of them, one to you, and one to Father? If this should not prove of the proper brevity, just let me know in your next.

In addition to the above letters, I have received numerous papers; which have afforded me much information and pleasure. Some of them were most decidedly stale tho' having been loitering on the way some of them, since December the 3rd, 5th etc. But I read them all; in some cases even the advertisments. I had made a resolution that I would not read any paper but the Presbyterian and papers from home, depending on Bill Minor and Uncle Jno. [Minor] for the news political. (I did so because I found that I was following in the footsteps of many of my fellow students and devoting more time to the Subject of Politics than to Medicine). So I found much in the "News" and "Civilian" that was new to me in regard to Texas politics and people. By the way, who is "Capt Howard, of the Wigfall Guards"?

Tell Mother that Cousin Betty Hill must be as much attached to her as ever, for she never sees me without asking specially after her and hers, sending love etc; which I fully intended to deliver;—thought I had done so; and that as to taking an interest in me, she . . . me up salt ... every time she comes across me, for not coming to her. I have been to see her and the Doctor once, if not oftener, but I am under bonds not to visit unmarried ladies during my stay in Virginia, and I believe she comes under that head. I am afraid my young affections might get engaged in this miserable land of anti-Southern sentiment; so I am careful to keep clear of the soft influence—to avoid Misses.

One morning, a few weeks since the Union people (Anti-southern) hereabouts were terribly shocked, by discovering a large Secession flag floating from the cupola of the Rotunda; having been put up there in the night by some *Maryland* and *Virginia* students; they accomplished this feat by cutting through one of the doors below, and then climbing to the top. Dr. Maupin and the rest of the Union Profs made them take it down tho'; indeed all the Faculty disapproved of its being put up there. A majority of the Profs. are Secessionists; and I dont think that there are over a half doz. Union men to be found among the students. Secession flags now wave from all parts of College, reared on flag poles 50, 60, & 70 feet high. Last Friday afternoon, the military company [Southern Guards] to which I belong was invited down to a Mr Harris' near here to witness the raising of a beautiful flag. A fine band of music was sent up to escort us down. Reaching the ground, we were drawn up alongside the flag pole and fired several salutes on the flags being hoisted up by the little daughter of the gentleman, dressed in a dress made of another flag. We have 86 men in our company;—as handsom[e] a set of fellows as can be started anywhere. Have for officers Graduates of the V.M.I.—There is another company of equal size here [Sons of Liberty]—both composed entirely of students. Love to all

Yrs. Chas.

University of Virginia
April 13th, 1861

Dear [Sister] Elvira:

I very much regret not having received either letter or message from you, for so long a time. I think you might put yourself to the trouble to write me occasionally, letting me know how you and yours were getting along in the world; but both you and Sister Mary have quite slighted, and treated me shabbily; you in particular. Sister Mary has written me only once, and you not at all.

When I left home, the understanding was, that all of you should open correspondence with me, and keep me posted on family af-

Troublesome Times

fairs; instead of my writing first, as I would have so much to occupy me, while at college; but neither you nor Mother did so. I wrote to Mother *first*, and have been waiting for you to write, but in vain.

Today is the anniversary of Mr. Jefferson's birth-day, and the literary society here named after him, gives a celebration in honor of it. The University grounds are brilliantly illuminated, a band of musicians are located on the Lawn to discourse National airs (i.e. Dixie, etc.); one of the society delivers an oration, etc. It's looked upon as one of the grand days hereabouts; large numbers of people come to witness the doings;—parents, brothers, sisters, and friends generally, to see the display of the acquirements of the youths in whom they feel interested. The young ladies of the country are on exhibition too—to see, and be seen by, the numerous young men collected here. It's really surprising to see what an attraction the young men have for the young ladies. I begin to think they have fully as much of human nature, if not more, than the young men.

Our military company, the Southern Guard, had a grand turnout today, together with two companies from Charlottesville [probably the Monticello Guards and the Albemarle Rifles]. All of our company, and the greater part of the other two companies, refused to march under the Stars and Stripes, so they had to substitute the flag of Va. The Southern Guard is as handsome set of soldiers as can be started any where; having good officers, and fellows anxious and able to learn, they have made fine progress in drilling. I look upon drilling as one of the most important tickets I take; tho' I do not slight anything else on account of it. We spend the time that we would otherwise spend in exercise, in drilling; so we lose no time from our studies.

While on drill this afternoon, our Captain received a special telegraphic dispatch telling us of the cannonading & surrender of Ft. Sumter, that the C. S. [Confederate States] flag floated from its walls, etc. We immediately fired salutes, and did no little hurrahing, in honor thereof. With love to Brother[-in-law] Bob [Howard], I conclude,—begging you will write me at an early period.

Yr. affectionate bro:
C. W. Trueheart.

Harper's Ferry.
April 20, 1861.

Dear Henry:

You will no doubt feel great surprise at the heading of this letter. Lincoln's hordes have invaded the soil of Va. I felt it my duty to take arms in defence of this the state of my birth—more particularly since she has taken such a noble stand, tho' late, for the rights of the South, so I am here, expecting and hoping to have a brush with the Yankees (if fight we must our Northern brethern). Our company, the Southern Guard composed entirely of students, left the University on the 17th inst. and after a tiresome ride, crowded together in dirty freight cars, and a fast march of 18 or 20 miles, we reached this point,—just in time to witness the destruction by fire & explosion of the U.S. arsenal and 16,000 or 17,000 stand of arms; the vile enemy having retreated in all haste at hearing of our approach; i.e., of some 300 Virginians, among whom were the two University companies of about 75 each. We got under way in a few hours after hearing that we were needed. There are now some 3,000 men under arms at this point. Our company is to be armed with Minnie muskets tomorrow; and we expect to be ordered to some other place, where I can't say, but I hope to some place where we shall be called into action.

The S.G. [Southern Guard] are the admiration of everyone that sees them. All the Officers here acknowledge our superiority in discipline, drilling, etc., & I am anxious to see how we will stand an encounter with the enemy. Since reaching here we have been on service continually, night & day,—standing guard,—searching the houses, etc., for arms. On inspection we found trains of powder laid for blowing up the bridge connecting Va & Md. here; but we succeeded in removing the powder before it exploded, thus saving the machinery for the manufacture of arms, etc.

I don't know when I shall return to the University; but to get back in time to receive a certificate of having taken a full course in Medicine, & so be entitled to graduate in one session. Direct all letters as formerly. Send the money for coming home at the close of the session. Lights will have to be put out in a little while, (at the beat of the drum, so I must close; asking with best love to all, write soon.

Your bro, Ch W. Trueheart

University of Virginia
August 25th, 1861.

Dear [Unnamed Person]:

For some time past I have contemplated writing you a letter; but press of work, etc., have heretofore prevented me from doing so. What mighty changes have taken place since I last saw you! I can

Troublesome Times
~

scarce realize they have occurred. A gigantic revolution has been set on foot; a Nation has been born, or rather is being born; and the world holds its breath while it watches the throes. Certainly we people of the South have a great deal to be thankful to God for. We have been blessed with an almost unanimous people in the struggle for national liberty, that we have undertaken; with plentiful crops—with glorious victories over our invading enemies;—in short, with near everything we could desire, and more than we had any right to expect. The "King of Kings" is certainly smiling on our cause; and if we do but do our duty, will continue to do so.

Since the first of June I have been diligently engaged in learning "Military," at a military school that has been established here;—for some five or six months previously, I had been drilled daily, in a company made up of students, officered by graduates of the V.M.I. You doubtless heard through our family of my going on the expedition to take Harper's Ferry. For some weeks previous to entering this Military School, I had spent all the time I could spare from lectures, and the study of medicine, in drilling the volunteer companies stationed hereabouts, and getting them ready for service. I feel very anxious to hear from you all, as in the last accounts I had, by letter and newspapers, Galveston was expecting to be bombarded, and an attempt on the part of the enemy to land a force to take possession of our island home, was daily looked for. Indeed, in one of the papers, I saw it stated that a number of shell, etc., had been thrown into the city; and threats made by the Commander of the blockading fleet to burn the whole town, if two Yankee boats were not given up by some parties in the city, I should be glad if you would send me Galveston papers occasionally.[5]

We have quite a flourishing Corps of Cadets. I am Captain of one of the companies; a son of General Lee [Robert E. Lee, Jr.], a youth of 18, is Captain of the other. I am rather at a loss to decide positively, what course to take when I leave this school in October. It is the opinion hereabouts that the enemy will give us a trial down South, after it gets too cold up here to operate; or rather, after it is cool enough for them to venture a descent, with their troops, into our hot climate. Certainly they could easily do it, having at their command such numbers of vessels for transportation of troops by sea.

How do you think it would do for me to return to Texas, and try to raise a company for service? I have had several Lieutenancies & Sergeantcies offered me up here; but declined them all, as I wished

Rebel Brothers

∿

to remain at this school, & be free to do as seems best on the 1st of October next. I am thoroughly drilled in the musket and rifle manuals, squad & company drill, pretty well posted in Betallion drill;— and shall be fully so by October, as also in skirmish drill. We are also learning something of Artillery drill. I am also pretty well posted in camp duty; in guard mounting, dress parade, inspection, etc. etc. What chance do you think I would stand for getting up a company? Or getting a position in the military service in Texas? Make inquiries about it & let me know in your reply to this.

I've been in the habit of sending numerous papers to Elvira, Mary M. J.[his sister, Mary M. Joseph, wife of Thomas Joseph] & other friends; do you know if they were ever received?

My best love to Bow [Elvira] and the children tell her I have looked long, and in vain, for an answer to my letters to her.

Love to [Brother-in-law] Mr. Joseph, [Sister Mary M. Joseph] M. M. J., and family. As it is getting late I must conclude and go to my duties.

Yours affectionately,
Chas. W.

Names in letters at such times as these ought to be avoided as much as possible.

Chas.

University of Virginia
October . . . , 1861[6]

Dear Mother:

I write just on the eve of st[arting for] Manassas to join a company of Art[illery] called [the] Rockbridge Artillery, but it is mo[re widely] known as Pendleton's Battery. It [was] formerly commanded by the Rev[erend Pendle]ton of Lexington, Va., an Episcopal min[ister] and a graduate of West Point.[7] This ba[ttery has] already become quite famous. It now [has] . . . picked men; and is to be increased to 200 men and to have two more cannon [added to] the six it now has. A large num[ber of my] college mates belong to it. Among [them are] Lanty Blackford and Berkeley Mi[nor] . . . Lucius boy. Charles Minor Jr. and . . . Maury are going to join too. So I [have] a number of friends and kin to [keep me] company. There are some 50 edu[cated] men of the better class; four A.M.s of [the] University, and a number of young men who are studying for the Ministry. The remainder of the company is composed of hardy mountaineers from Rockbridge [County]. The Battery is com-

manded by Wm McLauchlin [William McLaughlin], a lawyer of
Lexington. Young Brokenborough, [John B. Brokenbrough] [son] of
Judge Brokenborough, is 1st Lieut. [I am disappointed] to have to
go as a private after [having p]repared myself so thoroughly for . . .
a higher capacity. Uncle Wm [Overton] . . . [and] other friends advised me . . . not to go as a private, but wait [and app]ly to the Confederate Government [for a c]ommission as Capt or Lieut. But . . .
course would be attended with [m]uch delay and uncertainty; and
[I am] very impatient to get into service . . . and participate in some
of the [fi]ghts. The Artillery service is by far the most preferable for
a private as he is [exempted] from piquet, and guard duty; [also]
from the long marches with [k]napsack[s]. . . . If Henry should come
on to [Virginia, I]would advise him to join the . . . Artillery, by all
means. But, . . . he will give over the idea of leaving [Galve]ston,
as his services are more need[ed] there than any where else. The
[en]terprise of getting up a Battalion of Artillery, that myself and
some ten or twelve other young men were engaged in, since the
Military school closed, proved a failure; as it was impossible to get
the requisite number of men to enlist, Just on the eve of a winter's
campaign. For six weeks past, I have been [rid]ing and riding almost
incess[antly on] recruiting tours in Bucking[ham] and Nelson [coun-
ties]. But all to very [little result]. I called to see the Blackfords . . .
Lanty while in their vicinity. . . . B. treated me with the greatest
[courtesy] and all the family with much [hospit]ality. . . . She sends
her love to you . . . a charming visit of a day . . . half at Uncle Lanty's.
His is . . . delightful—a happy family . . . his girls are hard to beat.
Fanny is [a] splendid looking woman. If she we[re] not a first cousin
there's no [telling] what would be to pay. All [of them] sing well
and play . . . instruments too. Family prayer . . . reminded me very
strongly . . . Uncle, Aunt Mary Ann and . . . girls joining in singing
the hym[n].

You ask that I will tell you [some]thing of our kin who are in the
army. Now I know little or nothing about them. However, I can tell
you as to the Blackford boys, Willie is Adj. of a Regiment, Lewis,
Lieut. in a corps of engineers, stationed in the vicinity of Norfolk,
Charles is Capt . . . a fine company of Cavalry, . . . Capt of Infantry,
and Lanty . . . private in Pendleton's Artillery. . . . Lewis are at Manassas . . . L. C. Minor is private in a . . . company. Willie Overton . . .
[L]ieut in the Regular army & is . . . Western Va. Jno Harris . . . a
short time since. . . . I have received several letters from . . . lately;
one from Cally & Henry, one from you and H, one from Sister . . .

Rebel Brothers

∾

28

which gave me especial pleasure . . . from H. by himself. Contin[ue to d]irect to the University, and they w[ill] . . . sen[d] on to me at Manassas or . . . where. Tell H that Uncle Wm . . . supplied me with all the money I stood in need of.

Best love to all,
Your aff[ectionate] son,
C. W. Trueheart

Thursday, Oct. 31st, 1861
Camp at Centerville, Va.,
Rockbridge Artillery, 1st
Brigade (Gen'l T. J. Jackson)
2d Corps (Gen'l G. W. Smith)
C.S. Army of the Potomac

Dear Father:

Having become tired and disgusted with raising volunteer companies, and seeking commissions in the Army in Virginia, I have joined this Battery of Light Artillery. I was too much afraid that another fight would come off without my being in it, to remain out of active service any longer. I am sorry to have to enter as a Private, only because I have spent months of precious time, money, and no small ammount of diligence and patience in fitting myself for a higher position. And then too competent judges pronounced me very capable of acting in the capacity of an officer; either field or company—but it was useless to attempt any longer to get a commission, unless by raising a volunteer company; which it proved utterly impossible for me to do, stranger as I am to the men whom I had to recruit amongst. I have I think succeeded in getting into one of the best Arms of the service, and into one of the best Corps of the Arm. Our battery (the Rockbridge, more familiarly known as Pendleton's Battery) contains one hundred and sixty men; about half of whom are of the better class. Some 25 or 30 of the number are former University students; 3 or 4 of them A.M.'s of that institution; one Presbyterian preacher, a Mr. Gould, who performs the duty of Chaplain for our company; a man of reputation, good education and natural ability; and a number of students for the University.[8] Our Corps has its own surgeon, Quarter Master, etc. We have six first rate pieces and two more expected from Richmond shortly. We have pretty good officers. Our Capt. and 1st Lieut. are lawyers from Lexington, Va.[9] We have prayers while in ranks, morning and night, Mr. Gould officiating. I have heard less profanity and blackguardism

Four Napoleon guns used by the 1st Rockbridge Artillery are overlooked by a statue of "Stonewall" Jackson at the Virginia Military Institute. (1993 photo by author)

among our numbers, than among any body of men of equal number that I have ever had the pleasure of meeting with in any State. I am comfortably fitted out with winter uniform. Have a good tent, and am now forming a mess, all the desirable messes here, being full. Uncle Charles' [Minor] son, Chas., Cousin Mat. Maury's son, Jno and several other agreable young men, will be in it with me. I have sent off for camp cooking utensils, etc. to Charlottesville—but here I must stop writing for a while, as I have to get ready for a grand Review, to be had of all the troops by some of the big Generals. Yesterday we had one of all the Va. forces, before Gov. Letcher, who presented, in the name of the Convention a beautiful Va. flag to each of the Va. Regiments. 'Twas a beautiful spectacle, some 7 or 8,000 Va. troops (all in this immediate vicinity, of the Army of the Potomac).[10]

Having just returned from the Review, I resume writing. The Review of this afternoon was of Va. troops only. I have had the pleasure of seeing a number of our great Generals. Among the number, [Pierre G. T.] Beauregard, [Joseph E.] Johnston, [Earl] Van Dorn, G. W. Smith, and [Thomas J.] Jackson. A reorganization of the army has been lately made. The description is not familiar to me, so I will wait till one of my comrades comes in. We are throwing up earth forts, and breast works as fast as possible; as the Enemy may make an attack on us any day. It is the belief in these parts that we shall certainly have a fight ere long. But the fact of the matter is, that very little is known about the matter. The enemy at present are some ten or twelve miles off; rumor says closer. My term of enlistment will expire the 11th of May next [1862]. If the war is in a fair way to be concluded, or if the necessity for men is not very great at that time, I think I shall go at the study of Medicine again—that is, if I can by any means. . . . I went down from Charlottesville to see Uncle Wm. Overton to get some money to get an outfit for service. All the family were well. Uncle Wm. had just had his smoke house broken open and a quantity of bacon and flour [taken out]—a very important loss in these times. Willie is over in Western Virginia, in Gilham's Regt. of Regulars, as a 2d Lieut. In getting the money from Uncle Wm, I proposed to return the amount out of the wages I receive, and the twenty five dollars I shall get at the time of my first payment, an amount, that is allowed to each soldier for clothing every six months. It would be unnecessary for you all to send me money; as I have a good outfit, and enough pocket money. I feel very anxious to hear from you all. More particularly as the Yankees are about you, and as the Yankee expeditions fitted out to be sent South, have not all yet reached their destined points of invasion, and I fear they may undertake to occupy Galveston.

Uncle Jno. Minor and family are well. He has a fine little girl, named after his former wife. Aunt Nannie and Mary L. who have both been very sick with typhoid fever, have both gotten well. The latter weighs 140 pounds. The weather here is getting very cold; we have to keep good fires in our tents most all the time. I have attracted a good deal of attention by building a chimney of turf. We construct a flue in this way—We cut a little trench entirely across our tents, from the door back; dig a good size hole in the center of the tent; cover the entire trench over with flat rocks with a layer of dirt on over the top. At the highest end, (the uphill end) of the trench we set a barrel or build a turf chimney—make the fire in the hole in the center of the tent and use as a cover a large flat rock. This makes the tent quite comfortable. If we are to have a fight before going into winter quarters, I wish the Yankees would come on at once.

I hope you are sticking to your resolutions about not using tobacco. I find it very tempting when all the soldiers smoke, and it seems to be a source of great comfort to them. If you meet with errors on any kind in this letter you must overlook them, as I have not the time to read it over.

Give my best love to Mother, Henry & all the children—also to sister M.[ary] & Elvira & families.

Tell Cally, Minnie and Fanny to write me and slip their letters into one of Henry's—

Your affectionate son,
Chas W. Trueheart

Thursday, Nov. 20th 1861
Camp near Winchester, Va.
Army of the "Valley
District" under command
Major Gen'l T. J. Jackson[11]

Dear Minny:

I write you this morning in pursuance of a plan of correspondence I have determined on within the last month. It is this; to write to some one of our family three times a month on or about the 1st, 10th & 30th of each month. In this way you all will be enabled to hear from me with regularity. And it is to be hoped that you all will thereby be induced to let me hear from home with more regularity than heretofore. It seems to me that you all happen to be seized with the notion of "writing to Chas" at the same time. And that you all equally concur in neglecting to write to me. So that in the course of a single week, perhaps, I get several letters from different members of our tribe, and then too, they all contain pretty much the same matter while again for weeks & weeks at a time I am left in total ignorance of what is passing. Now if you all will observe some degree of method in the time and subjects of your epistles, they will prove much more interesting to me; and will spur me up to writing with punctuality and interest. I, at any rate, will give my plan a trial. My facilities for writing are, as you see, very poor. Nothing but a lead pencil can be carried conveniently, and we are at a loss to get something to write on. Boards are seldom to be had, so place the paper on a blanket spread out on the tent floor; or write on a newspaper, pamphlet, or the like spread on the knee. I very much fear you may find it hard to read my letters, written as they are in pencil, after they have made the long journey to Texas. If such be the case some of you all must let me know it; and I will try my best to get some pens and ink. However, Chas Minor tells me that if the writing

Rebel Brothers

be dipped into water, it will be as legible as if written with ink. I think I shall try it.

We are encamped just outside of Winchester; just beyond Senator Mason's residence, in a most luxuriant field of clover and grass, which is a great treat to the hard marched horses of our Battery.[12] The land is very rolling and here and there may be seen ledges of rocks jutting out of the well sod soil. These ledges of rocks serve a very good purpose for hiding our mess fires behind; and for sitting on while eating, etc. We have succeeded in getting a supply of wheat straw for beds, which adds much to our comfort. The ground has been frozen for some days past, and it is quite cold. I have only one pair of single blankets, but manage to keep warm by sleeping with my great coat all on. I don't know what I shall do when we have snow and ice in real good earnest. Hope to be able to get another pair ere long. I have had some difficulty in getting winter clothes. The tailor at Charlottesville sent me a suit, a few days since, but it proved too small for me; so I had to sell it at a loss of $3.00; and buy another suit at $18.00. Clothes of all kinds are very dear here. A suit (pants and jacket) of the coarsest heavy negro cloth, such as our uniforms are made [at a] cost [of] $21.00 if made by a tailor. I succeeded in getting one at $18.00 by having it cut only by a tailor, and made by a seamstress. I'm very well pleased with what I have seen of this vicinity. The society is good; people quite sociable, and easy to get acquainted with. I made one call in town a day or two ago, but it is hard to get a pass to go to town; and when we go we are limited to two-hours stay.[13] Only three can be absent from Camp at once, so not more than six or seven of us get off daily. And as there are some 140 in the company, all anxious to get off to town, it is seldom I get there. We have fine opportunities, however, on Sunday; as we are allowed to go to Church, as many of us as wish, in squads, in charge of a Sergeant or Corporal. Last Sunday morning I went to the Episcopal Church to hear a Rev. Mr. Meredith. We had Communion which [was] enjoyed no little. I had not enjoyed the privilege for a long time. But I must stop for a time, as a battery drill takes place this afternoon. I have just returned from the above mentioned drill. A large concourse of ladies, several of the "big officers" and a number of others were spectators. Our Captain gave us a hard drill of some hour and a half. By the way, one of our Trueheart cousins (a son of Mr. Daniel Trueheart) is on Genl Jackson's staff as Chief of Artillery.[14] After the drill, a large number of ladies (many of them having acquaintances in the company) came to our encampment to see what was to be seen. After strolling around for some time, examining our tents, mess ground, etc., with considerable minuteness they accepted an invitation to take supper with us. As it happened the mess that invited had a box of good things just sent them, so that quite an array of eatables could be mustered for the occasion. I was acquainted with only two of them, and spent some 15 or 20 minutes in their company. But I did not like to circulate among them where they would be on all sides of me, as I had a big hole in my breeches—A frequent misfortune with us poor privates in Camp. But here I must close. I will not look this letter over but leave you to do so, and send me a list of mistakes in your reply. Love to all.

Your affectionate brother,
C. W. Trueheart

Martinsburg, Va.,
December 12th, 1861

Dear Mother:

I wrote Henry a letter four or five days ago from Winchester; since then we have been on the go almost incessantly. On Monday night at about 8 o'clock, we received orders to report at a certain place in town with blankets, haversacks and great coats; and as much cooked provisions as we could get.[15] In three quarters of an hour after the orders were received, we were at the appointed place, with two of our rifled guns.[16] We were carried to Charlestown, (the place where old Jno Brown was hung in the beginning of the present terrible war) on the cars, together with four cos. of Infantry. We could form no idea as to the object or destination of the troops forming our party. We left Winchester at about 1 o'clock in the night, it having taken several hours to get our horses, cannon, etc., aboard the train, and reached Chastwn at daylight.[17] Spent the day there and started out on another tramp at 1 o'clock that night. While at Charlestown, I made the acquaintance of some pleasant ladies, with whom I took tea by invitation and spent a pleasant evening. I made the acquaintance of the family, as we soldiers of the South feel priviledged to do by finding a house with good exterior, and walking in asking for a drink of water; or using some similar device to get into conversation with the fair inmates. If they invite us in and make themselves agreeable, we spend some time with them, and if invited to do so, call again during our stay, or when we happen to be at the place again. If they are not of the stripe to suit our taste, or are too dull of perception to discover that we are gentlemen accustomed to good society and treat us cooly, why we make a short stay, and fail to call again. I have made some very pleasant acquaintances, spent pleasant spare hours, and got some comfortable meals by making these sans ceremonious calls among strangers. When near the place of our destination (the 4th dam on the Potomac) we discovered that the object of the expedition was to destroy some seventy odd boats with their cargoes of supplies for Washington, on the way down the Canal, which were reported to be near a little town called Hardscrabble or Scrabbletown.[18] Soon after our arrival the Yankees made their appearance on the opposite side of the river in some force, and sent over a boat with a Capt, one Sergeant, and six privates to reconnoiter but we discovered them and after a short fight, in which we lost one man mortally wounded, we captured the entire party. The Yankees from the other side the river (some 150 or 200 feet wide at this point) keeping up an incessant and galling fire on us all the while. On a hill some distance back from the river, was another party of the enemy, in charge of a large U.S. flag. A few shots from one of our rifled cannon, however, made them let fall their flag to the ground, and scamper off as fast as their legs would carry them. Colonel Ashby, the greatly celebrated partizan leader, was in command of the expedition.[19] We found no boats to capture so started off for this place with our Yankee prisoners which we reached a little after dark, having been on the march except during the skirmish, or when we stopped to breathe our horses since one o'clock the previous night; making in all a distance of thirty miles. Colonel Ashby is a fine looking fellow, rides most gracefully, is as brave as a lion, and the dread of the Yankees.[20] He has a body of mounted riflemen under his command; acts as scout and gives protection to border people.[21] We shall probably start again tomorrow morning—where to I can't say, as our officers, very properly, keep all their plans to themselves. We are now quartered very comfortably in the house of a Union family that ran off to Maryland at the beginning of the war. It is furnished in good style, and affords us very comfortable lodgings. When I last heard from the U.V. [University of Virginia], all of our friends there were well. Lanty Blackford is standing guard over our guns, etc., on one of which I am sitting to write, and sends love to you—says all at his home were well. I think I informed you in a previous letter that Chas and Wm were Capt in the Cavalry service; Eugene, Captain of an Ala company of Infantry; Lanty, a Private in this Artillery; and Lewis, Lieut. in the engineers department. Eu-

Troublesome Times

~

35

us, there stood a house in an old field, near which the Col had discovered eight of the enemy, armed to the teeth. A fence, some four or five feet high stood between our position and the house; he cleared the fence with the greatest ease, and outstripping all his men dashed up to the Yankees, who fired volley after volley at him as they retreated toward the house, where they at last took refuge and kept up the fire on our troopers. But it soon became too warm for them, and they rushed out of the house and they made an attempt to get to the river. But Ashby with a loud voice and his six-shooter leveled at the Yankee Captain's head, commanded them to surrender. They sang out loudly for quarters. And in a minute or two the whole party, Capt. and all were astride behind our troopers, and borne in triumph down to where we were stationed, amid the shouts of our men. One of the prisoners a six-foot-four fellow and large in proportion, who proved to be a Kentuckian, was mounted on a small horse behind a diminutive boy of fifteen, and cut a most ridiculous figure, his legs hanging down near the ground, and head reaching far above the little fellow's head. Numerous were the questions put to the Yankees, who seemed not at all put out at what had befallen them;—one of the rascals with a good-natured laugh, called for a chew of tobacco before he would do any talking. Only the Captain seemed at all gruff.

While at Martinsburg, I made some very agreable acquaintances; particularly among the young ladies. I became well acquainted with Mr. Holmes Conrad's family A man noted for his piety, hospitality, etc. He lost two most charming sons in the Battle of Manassas. They were much admired and beloved by our University friends. They were fighting side by side, were shot down by the same volley from the enemy, and actually fell clasped in each other's arms, and thus expired.[22] How remarkable, how beautiful was their death. They were both characterized in an eminent degree, by a fervent piety, amiability of temper and manliness. In a word they were such young men—such Christians as are seldom met with. They were much admired and beloved by their professors and college mates of the U.V.; and idolized by their good Father and Mother and sweet sisters. And was touchingly beautiful to witness the Christian resignation with which all that interesting family bore up under their great affliction. The old man spoke frequently and affectionately of his dead "boys"; the sisters, of "our brothers." It might be most appropriately said of Tucker and Holmes Conrad they "were lovely and pleasant in their lives, and in their death they were not divided."

Troublesome Times

≈

37

'Twas not my privilege to know them personally, as they were at the U.V. before my time; but Lanty B., Charles Minor, and others of my friends, were intimates with them. One of the young men was a student of Law and the other, Divinity. Of Col. Ashby and his beautiful black, I must say that they are noble animals. The Col. is not a man of much intellectuality, or capacity for command in scientific warfare, or with a larger force. But he is as brave and noble as a lion, and fully as much dreaded by the Yankees.

At dam [Number 5] . . . which it was our mission to break down, and thus make the [Chesapeake and Ohio] canal useless in the transportation of supplies to Washington City, and the "Grand Army of the Yankees," we had continuous skirmishing with riflemen and Artillery across the Potomac. We lost one man killed and one or two wounded.[23] I shall give Henry a fuller account of our Dam No. 5 expedition.

I am truly sorry to hear that Galveston is considered untenable and you all have to leave your home. Give my best love to all the dear ones of home—And understand, all of you, that the term "love to all" embraces Father, Mother, sisters (married and single), brother, and Brothers-in-Law. I have met a pretty and particularly appropriate piece of versification for the present wartimes, which I can't refrain from enclosing, even if it make the letter cost an additional 5 cents.[24] But here I must close and go to work on my tent which the wind has torn.

Affectionately your son
C. W. Trueheart

Winchester, Va.
December 26th. 1861.[25]

Dear Cally:

I have just finished a letter to Mother but [as] I did not quite get through with what I had to say, thought I would write this half sheet full to you. I was giving Mother an account of expedition to Dam No. 5 on the Potomac etc., which I will continue in this to you, for the want of something better to write about. An expedition under command of one of our Cols. But it did not succeed—the Yankee sharpshooters across the river making it too hot for our men to work on the destruction of the Dam; so our forces had to withdraw, one of our men being killed and one wounded. The gun to which I am attached was not in this first expedition, four other guns being the Artillery attached to it. Old Jack [Maj. Gen. Thomas J. "Stonewall"

Jackson] not being satisfied with the doings of his underlings took the matter into his own hands; had a number of boats built for crossing the river if it should prove necessary; took up his march with his "Stonewall" Brigade 35,000 strong ten pieces of Artillery, and a Brigade of Militia, 1500 strong under command of Militia General Carson. We regulated march so as to reach a woods in the neighborhood of the Dam where we bivouaced for the night on the bare ground with our blankets only. The upper blankets were stiff with frost when we arose at daybreak in morning. During the night a large force of the Infantry, under cover of the darkness, threw up a stone wall, that entirely protected them from the riflemen of the enemy; besides doing a large amt. of work in the destruction of the Dam. We remained at the work of pulling down the dam some five or six days. And we did the work pretty effectively too. We were engaged in skirmishing with the enemy every day, both with Artillery and riflemen. Genl Jackson by his admirable strategic movements, entirely deceived the Yankees, making them think he had a large force some six miles down the river, by sending the 1500 Militia down there and making them keep up a large number of fires during the night and attempt to cross the river during the day. But at last, just as we were completing the work on the dam, they brought up some of their Artillery from below to play upon us, and a large force of Infantry. But here again Old Jack fooled them completely. He had the wagons with the boats (Old Jack's fleet, as the soldiers called it) brought in sight on their way up the river to a point of some five or six miles above the Dam, conducted by a considerable display of troops as tho' we were going to effect a crossing up there. No sooner did the out witted Yankees discover this new and apparently formidable and important movement, than off they posted with their whole force up the river leaving us just where we wanted to be left. Without opposition, to prosecute our designs on the Dam.

The Yankees tried hard to shell our Camp, but Jack had out a strong piquet so that no spies could approach and discover our positions. And then he made us move our positions once or twice during the 24 hours; had fires kindled in different positions, of a night, so as to entirely deceive the rascals. Many were the iron messengers sent over to discover our location to them; some of which burst quite near us, so that we picked up the fragments of shell etc. But thanks Almighty God they did us no harm. We lost only one man killed and one or two slightly wounded.

Troublesome Times

∽

and be ready to march by daylight in the morning. We started on our present tramp, with a force of about 12,000 men; regulars, volunteers and Militia.[2] We first marched on Bath, in Morgan Co., Va., where a considerable force of the enemy held sway.[3] We found the roads as we approached the mountains (spurs of the Alleghenies) almost impassable from the steepness and deep mud. On our second days march, it began blowing, and was extremely cold. On the 3rd day it began snowing. We were now within four miles of the Yankees. Met with one of their scouting parties. Had a skirmish in which we lost one killed and several wounded.[4] The Yankees loss was about the same. That night we went to bed without anything to eat since breakfast at eight in the morning. Our waggons were behind some miles, stalled; so we had nothing to eat and no blankets to sleep on. The most of us spent the night around the fires. Myself and a dozen of my friends slept, or rather tried to sleep on the floor of a room in an old house that had a fireplace in it, with a crowd of lousy, dirty fellows, in a like fix with ourselves. Our waggons came up at 3 or 4 in the morning, and we then cooked and ate to our hearts content, as we expected certainly to have a big fight. Genl Jackson ordered us to tie a badge of white cloth on our right arms. When within three miles of the place the previous evening we had a skirmish in which we lost 4 wounded, one of whom afterwards died. We did not discover whether we killed any of the Yanks or not, as it was dark, but we captured eight prisoners. Again today we had a skirmish with them on the streets of Bath between opposing forces of Cavalry. We killed three of their horses, and probably wounded one or two men. The dismounted Yanks were borne off behind the cavalrymen. We lost none. The Yankees evacuated the place, and retreated in two columns, by two different roads, to the river. We pushed on after them; but they proved too fleet for us, and crossed the river into Md., leaving behind them, however, in their hasty retreat, some $40,000 worth of military stores, which fell into our hands; only a part of which we could bring away, as we were scarce of transportation, and the roads so mountainous and slippery with sleet as to be almost impassable. We burnt about $10,000 worth on leaving the river. We were situated directly opposite Hancock, Md. Old Jack amused the Yankees for a day or two by making a formal demand for the unconditional and immediate surrender of the place; making feints at crossing the river, etc. while the real object of our being at this point was to destroy the R.R. and R.R. bridges as it is generally believed in the army.[5] And while we were going

Rebel Brothers

◦

42

through the motion of shelling Hancock and preparations to take the place, thereby making the Yankees concentrate all their forces at this point, our column under Gilham was effecting the destruction of Big Capon [Cacapon] Bridge and the railroad in that vicinity, the bridges across St. John's River, and some water tanks and depot warehouses.[6] We have been out on this expedition for 16 days. Have suffered no little from cold and hunger. Several times we had nothing to eat for 18 or 20 hours, our waggons having been left far behind in our rapid march, and owing to the bad condition of the roads. Our horses fared even worse than we. I am sure they did not average more than one feed in 24 hours for 5 or 6 days. Once they had nothing to eat for 36 hours. The Yankees had made away with all provender, and feed was not to be had. So famished were the poor creatures that I saw them hunting about in the snow after dry sticks and weeds, within range of their halters. One was found with its bridle 1/2 down its throat; another ate up a silk flag & the staff (a stick 3 or 4 feet long by 1 inch in diameter), the cannon wheels were quite disfigured by their gnawing the woodwork. The roads were so slippery with sleet, that the poor things could not keep their feet in pulling the cannon & waggons, but fell continually—sometimes 3 out of 4 of a team would be down at once. Splotches & puddles of blood frequently marked the places where they fell. The poor soldiers too fell. In going down one hill over a slippery space of 20 yards I saw full a 1/4 or a 1/3 of a regt. slip up in passing along the road. I got several severe falls. Many of us got our feet and hands frostbitten. My feet were so badly bitten that I could scarcely walk. They are now better—of nights bivouaced in the snow.

You have doubtless been informed by Uncle Jno. or some of our kin of Uncle Chas' death. I am not in possession of the circumstances connected with it. In my next, which shall be to Thos M. [Joseph] and Elvira, I will give some further accounts of the movements of Old Jack and his army—as to how he came to be in possession of Romney, the stronghold of the Yanks in this part of Va.

Love to all,
Yrs, Charles

Camp Romney, Va.
January 20, 1862.

Dear Thomas M [Joseph]:

Yours enclosed with one from Henry, came to hand in due time. It afforded me real pleasure, I can assure you. It was the first that I have received from you since leaving Galveston a year and a half ago. I was sorry you so slighted me, in not writing to me, and scarcely sending a message. But I can readily understand how friends can apparently be forgotten in a long silence, thrown as you have been, in trying and strange scenes, by the distressing condition of our city. I hope however, you will not forget your good resolutions for the new year 1862, in regard to following the bent of your inclination and writing frequently to me. You wish me a Happy Christmas; I spent that day in standing guard over our guns, cooking and eating bull beef, and white leather bread. As to being merry, that is a thing out of the question. Who could be merry when our beloved country is in its present condition? True we have much to be thankful for to a merciful and just God—a united South, continued victories, plentiful crops, warm and good clothes to wear, and last but not least, the sympathies of the civilized world. But an order to prepare two days cooked rations, and be ready to march as soon as possible, has been read. The mud is very deep, its been raining & snowing by turns for six days, the rivers and creeks are swollen to overflowing, it's still raining and snowing, and we are called on to march against the enemy, and to destroy railroad, tunnels, bridges, etc. Good by—after an hour's hustle and preparation, the unwellcomed order alluded to above, was countermanded; as the rain and snow, and the condition of the rivers, would not admit of an advance movement.

In a letter to Henry, a few days since, I was narrating the incident of our expedition. As I am not in a position to communicate any thing but army news, I shall continue it. After having destroyed the railroad bridges across St. John's River and Big Capon [Cacapon] River, several water tanks, depot ware houses etc., and some miles of the road,—all works recently rebuilt by the Yanks; having been destroyed by Genl Johnston last spring—we fell back to the crossing of the road, leading from Winchester to Romney, where we remained three days to recruit soldiers and horses. Both of which were badly used up by hard marches over mountains and rivers, through snow and ice, by turns through mud, snow, etc., and again over roads made as slick as glass by sleet, or impacted snow. It was (thought to be) Old Jacks intention to march on Romney, and drive out the enemy who were 7,000 strong and well fortified, and supplied with 18 or 20 pieces of artillery; but, they became panic struck at our movement on this left flank (which I believe was a preconceived plan, or rather manouvre of Old Jacks); and thinking we were going to surround them, evacuated the place in the greatest haste, leaving behind them a number of tents, stores, etc., besides a large quantity of baggage, ammunition, tents, etc. that they destroyed. We found quantities of ammunition etc., thrown into the wells, rendering them unfit for supplying the inhabitants and army with water.

The Yankees have been permitting the most barbarous and wanton outrages in this quarter 40 or 50 houses have been burnt in the county of Hampshire, (so I am told by several residents)—I counted twelve different establishments immediately on the road, in the space of 4 or 5 miles, burnt to the ground. Some of the houses were two, and three storied buildings with 4 or 5 chimneys. 9 of the establishments I saw were dwelling houses. All of the outhouses, fences, etc. were burnt also. 2 were mills, and one was a large tannery establishment, with a fine new steam engine attached. The families were driven out of some of the houses, tho' most of them were vacant. One house was inhabited by a shoe maker; his body was found and dragged out by our troops, who came up a little after the Yanks had been at their honorable work. He was said to have been shot by the vile savages while in his own house, (he was a non-combattant) and then they set fire to it, and left him to his fate. The Yankees fully intended to burn Romney, but were deterred from it by something or other. Some say Genl [Benjamin F.] Kelley (a Virginian in the Yankee army) interceded for it. A strong guard was posted to prevent its destruction, as the wretches evacuated the place, so I was told by the residents of the place. Even tho they did not burn, they have made the once beautiful little town look desolate indeed. Old Dr. Foote, a Presbyterian divine, the owner and principal of a once flourishing and large institute, who preached to us last Sunday, at the end of his sermon told us, with his eyes full of tears, and his voice tremulous with suppressed emotion, that he 'prayed God to forgive him, if he had displayed a vindictive spirit the day before when he walked through his once handsome establishment, now ruined by the fell hands of the ruthless invader, when he entered his library once filled and beautified by 3500 choice & valuable volumes, of which only 500 defaced books remained when he found of innumerable manuscripts, and valuable papers and relics, that it took a long life time to accumulate, all destroyed. When he saw the loved and once beautiful home, the abode of his wife & his children, now in ruins; when he saw the homes of his friends and neighbors laid waste; and the town that they left flourishing, beautiful, a few months before, when they had fled before the invader; when he saw

Band of Southerners

〜

etc! Can't the power creating a law—making a constitution, abrogate the same at pleasure. Why its this very principle that constitutes a part of the bone of contention twixt the North and South. But, however all this may be, rest assured that I shall most certainly write to some of the dear ones at home, at least three times a month, unless something serious should prevent. Mess No. 19 has lately had to turn off the cook employed, as he proved worthless and dirty; two of our number are in Winchester sick. The ground has been covered with snow, and the weather quite damp and bad for several weeks past, so we have had anything but a pleasant time of it. We are negotiating for another cook, a free negro, whom we hope to get. We pay Fifteen Dollars a month for a man to cook for a mess of eight men.[9]

Henry, it would make your blood boil to see what I have seen of Yankee vandalism, since I have been over in this part of Va. I counted immediately on the road from Martinsburg to Romney and from Winchester to Romney, no less than twenty-eight different establishments. Five of the number were mills, one church, and one large tannery—the rest were dwelling houses, many of which were two story buildings, with several outhouses and large barns, stables etc., attached. I saw large numbers of hogs of all sizes lying about in the corners of the fences. In some places whole pens of fattening hogs were killed, and lay dead in large puddles of blood. All this was just on the road. It was snowing and raining while we were passing this portion of country, so I could not look about me much. I was told by several residents that I conversed with, that the Yankees destroyed hogs, cattle, sheep, dogs, & horses (that were unfit for use)—besides carrying off all the horses, etc. they wanted. We are now quartered at the foot of a mountain some five miles northwest of Winchester, in a body of timber. An order has been issued that we shall forthwith erect winter quarters and make ourselves comfortable. February is rather late in the season to build winter quarters; don't you think so? My mess has been very busy for a day or two past cutting down and dragging through the snow, ice, and mud fifteen and eighteen foot logs, to construct a place 12 x 15 feet for eight of us to eat, cook, and sleep in. Don't you want to take a berth with us? I feel confident that we shall be called off on another expedition just as we get snugly fixed in our huts, as the Yankees will be very apt to undertake a movement against Romney, or some of the places we have just driven them from.

Within the past few days we, the first [Stonewall] Brigade, have

Band of Southerners

been very much distresed by something that has unfortunately happened. Genl Jackson had stationed Genl Loring and his command of 6,000 men, to hold Romney and winter in that region. Genl [Loring] displayed considerable temper thereupon, and made some belittling and contemptuous remarks about Jackson and his generalship in the hearing of one of Jacks Aides, and several other officers. He has since made such representations to the War Department as to the utter impossibility of holding the place with his force, etc, etc., that the Department (as we think very unwisely) has ordered him to return to Winchester, evacuating Romney to be occupied again by the enemy. This you see is done over Jacks head, and contrary to his wishes; so he has very properly sent in his resignation. We dont know what will come of it.[10] I enclose you some letters from Uncle Jno, Aunt Nannie, and Mary L. Also some clippings from the newspapers. Best love to all.

Yours, Charles

Camp 5 miles from
Strausburg [Strasburg].
March 14, 1862

Dear Henry:

My last letter was addressed to Cally, but intended for all my kith and kin as is the case with most of my epistles. I was forced to compose that letter very hastily, by intelligence that the Yanks were advancing on us. For eight or ten days previously they had been in considerable force at Harper's Ferry, Charlestown, & Martinsburg, besides several regiments they had stationed at Berryville, and at Bunker Hill (the latter a little village on the turnpike between Winchester and Martinsburg & 10 miles from the former place).[11] They also had a force of several thousand men under the late General Lauder (now under General Shields) in the direction of Romney.[12] In all, amounting to some twenty odd thousand men. By consulting the map you will see that our little army reduced to only 5 or 6 thousand men, by furloughs, sickness, etc., was hemmed in on three sides by a superior force of the enemy. But Genl Jackson held his position at Winchester with that skill and daring determination that has always characterized the "Stonewall" Genl. To avoid surprise and capture by a superior force, he kept a large force of mounted, well armed scouts, continually hovering around the enemy to watch his every movement, & communicate with him by means of rockets or couriers. At the same time his entire army was kept in a continual

Rebel Brothers

☙

state of readiness to move in fifteen or twenty minutes after the alarm was [given]. Then to blind the enemy as to his intentions [and to] make him think we would make [no] resistance to hold Winchester he had us [drawn up] in line of battle. . . . But while by strategy he kept a superior force of the enemy at bay . . . the greatest activity prevailed in all departments, in removing all the Government stores. The 13 large and valuable siege guns from the fortification,—besides getting all the rolling stock of the r.r. ready for destruction by fire on our evacuation, and giving those of the people who wished to fly from the city, ample time to carry off their valuables, negroes, etc. At nightfall on the 11th [of March], after having been drawn up in line of battle, making the most formidable and imposing demonstrations for fight, all day, we very quietly began our retrograde movement towards this place. In two hours after, our entire force was in full retreat up the Strausburg turnpike, not a man remaining behind but scouts to watch the Yanks, and a few stragglers who stayed to enjoy for the last time, the hospitalities of the inhabitants; or perhaps some devoted lover to steal a parting kiss from the lips of his terrified but hopeful lady love. As we passed through the streets, in many places, the windows, balconies, front gates, or corners of the streets, were ornamented by Virginia's daughters, who waved their handerkerchiefs, or kissed their adieux to their "favorite Battery" while many a bright eye was bedimmed by tears of regret at the military necessity that caused a band of Southerners to *retreat,* leaving to the mercies of the vile Northerners a rich and beautiful district of country, and in most part a loyal and defenseless population of women & children—and many a sweet voice grew tremulous with emotion, and fair face was flushed with indignation at the thoughts of what they would have to bear from the meanspirited invaders. . . . My feelings were anything but . . . I could not for the life of me divest myself. . . . better judgement told me retreat was. . . . [13]

[Unsigned]

Bivouac of the 1st
Brigade in the woods,
Shenandoah, Rockbridge
Co., Va. Apr. 4" 1862.

Dear Cally:
A letter from you with an annexed P.S. from Mother, both of the 6th Ultimo, and a long and truly agreable letter from Mother,

Band of Southerners

⤳

49

H[enry] and Sister Mary, conjointly, both came to hand a day or two since; after taking a tedious long time to make the 2,000 mile trip. A few days prior to their reception, I dispatched a hastily written, and brief letter to H. to inform you all of the fact of our having had quite a severe little battle near Winchester. I propose to give you in this letter, a somewhat detailed account of the fight; which I hope will prove in some degree interesting to you.

For some days past we have been exposed in our bivouac to real April weather;—as capricious as a woman. It has rained, sleeted, hailed, etc., and blustered generally—But today however, is really beautiful and delightful. Not a cloud is to be seen to obscure the welcome and genial rays of a Spring sun; and the wind is as gentle and balmy as a zephyr in midsummer. This morning when 'roused at dawn by the call for Reveille, I found that a heavy dew (the first of the season) had wetted my outter blanket, and that my face and hair were really "dewy with Nature's tear drops". Even the birds seemed charmed and delighted by this first lovely spring morning weather; and after a dreary long winter of almost profound silence they broke forth in the merriest warblings—as if their little hearts were overflowing with gratitude to their Maker for this return of spring. But how strange it sounded to hear martial music mingled with the songs of the birds! The latter brought to my remembrance our Sunny South, and "happy days gone by," that I have spent in Texas. For a moment, my eyes were suffused with tears, but it was only momentary, for the drums, etc., quickly disspelled these soft emotions, and caused the fearfully stern realities of life to intrude their unwelcome form upon me. Truly, our lots have fallen in troublous times; in times that severely try men's souls. God grant that we have abundant grace given us for this our time of need; and for every new trial that we may be called, as individuals, or as a Nation, to pass through. And that we may come forth from the fiery ordeal a better people, fitted for the formation of a great and happy Nation, that shall be the instrument of greatly advancing the interests of Christianity and Civilization.

Saturday the 5th. Camp duties prevented the completion of this epistle yesterday, so I resume it today. Last night it rained heavily and gave our Brigade a disagreable ablution—something the dirty scamps stood in need of doubtless—but it was rather a low temperature, and not as well calculated to improve their tempers, as bodily cleanliness. I was considerably surprised to hear of Kate Bulkley's marriage. I had gotten into the habit of looking upon her and my "little sisters" as young ladies not yet arrived at a marriageable age. *I* have been growing old very fast; but I somehow forgot that my . . . friends were also. How old it makes me feel to hear that one of you are married! I was a quarter of a century old on the 27th of February last. My hair is beginning to be sprinkled with grey hairs, of which I send you a fair sample that you may keep for my sake. My kindest regards to Mrs. Bulkley and Kate. Tell Mrs. B. that I frequently look back from my present life of toil and dangers, to the times that I spent at her "Sea Island Cotton Farm" as a part of the bright spot in my past existence. But if nothing happens, Cally, when this cruel war terminates, I shall return to Galveston, and we can have some of those pleasant times over again. I hope that you, Minny, and Fanny G will not fail to write me frequently. All of your letters afford me much pleasure—more pleasure than anything that I enjoy here in the army. Our Battery, which had increased to 240 men, has recently been divided into three companies of 4 guns each. I will send you a copy of the roll of the one to which I belong as soon as its organization shall be completed, & our officers and cos accepted by the C. S. War Dept—We have had a good many desirable acquisitions to our co. lately; among the number, five or six Presbyterian Students of Divinity and young ministers without charges.

Your affectionate
bro, Charles.

P.S. Finding that I shall not have time to carry out my plan in regard to a description of the battle of Kernstown for the want of time, I postpone.[14] Love to all,

Yrs,
Charles

Rockingham Co. near the
Green Line, Apr. 19" 1862

Dear Father:

I drop you a few lines from this point to keep you all easy as to my welfare. The Yankees, some twenty five or thirty thousand strong, have been slowly advancing up the Valley, and our army falling back before their superior force. (We have about 7,000 or 8,000 men.) Where we shall get reinforcements and give them battle I can't say. It seems that we have a large force somewhere over towards Gordonsville, which is held in readiness to reinforce Jackson, or Johnson [Johnston], as the case may require.[15] It seems that we are waiting for the Yanks to show their hand. So far, as usual, "Old

Jack" has managed his retreat, and all connected with it, most admirably well. We have brought off all military stores, etc.,—pretty thoroughly draining the country of horses, cattle, fighting men, Union people, and eatables, as we withdrew—not leaving much for the invaders. Our advance guard have had several skirmishes—indeed on about every other day—with the enemy. Men killed and wounded on both sides. One day last week, one of the guns of my Battery threw some shell amongst the Yanks, (a baggage train) killing 15 horses, and killing and wounding 8 men. A few days prior to this we caught the Yankee boys at a game of ball on a field near this encampment. We threw them a "Secesh" ball from one of our rifled 10 pdrs.; but they didn't seem to fancy it, and dropped their bats and scampered off. Some ten days since I sent you all a hastily written description of the battle of Kernstown. From all we can learn the Yankees lost from 1,500 to 1,700 in killed and wounded.[16] Our loss was 587, 230 of whom were taken prisoner—(95 of the 230 were wounded men).[17]

No letters from any of you all of a later date than the 10th March (from Cally & Mother). Wish very much you would write me occasionally at least. It wd. give me great pleasure. All our Va. friends & kin, as far as I have heard from them, are well.

Best love to all. I am somewhat troubled with sore throat, but am comfortably housed for once. Shall be out tomorrow if the weather is good.

Your son,
C. W. Trueheart

P.S. We retreated up the Valley as far as Harrisonburg where we struck across the mountains towards Green. Hair for Cally.

[Unsigned]

Tuesday morning, Apr. 22, 1862. H.Q.
Army of the Valley.
Rockingham Co. Va. (At
foot of the Blue Ridge Mts.)

My dear sisters:

I have not written to you for a long time—but then you have no right to complain, as you have not written to me either.

For no less than three days and a half, it has rained almost continuously. Our poor soldiers are without tents, and hence exposed to the whole of this inclement weather. They have been drenched to the skin; scarcely able to keep up enough fire to cook their meals, much less to warm by. Today however, the sun shows its wellcomed face through the masses of clouds that still envelope the little Valley that we are in; and the "fellows" are lying about sunning themselves, like so many snakes, or turtles, of a spring day. I fortunately for my dry jacket and health, happened to be on the "sick list," with a sore throat (my voice entirely gone); so our Surgeon gave me permission to get quarters in a neighboring house. Being fond of good company, I took up my abode in the same house with Our Maj Genl [Jackson] and Staff. Two of my college mates being on the Staff and the inmates of the house being very hospitably disposed toward the soldiers, I have spent an agreable three days. My throat, after the free use of oil of turpentine externally and internally, has gotten almost well. As soon as the weather clears up, I shall join my company again. This is the first time that I have been sick enough to take to a house since I have been in service. I have so far been blessed with the most exuberant health; first rate appetite, and sound sleep, for which I am truly thankful to the Giver of all good things. Our Army of the Valley has seen a very hard time since it came over from Manassas last fall. How much I do want to see you all. It seems an age since I left Texas. I have reenlisted, "for two years or the war." As soon as we shall have succeeded in driving the Yankees back, and in getting our new armies into the field, and well organized, I expect to get detailed for Hospital service at the University Hospital, under Doctors Cabell or Davis.[18] In the present condition of the country, with such an inadequate force in the field, I cannot think of going out of the fighting department; tho' I believe I could do much better service among the sick and wounded, than as a mere private in the ranks. The passage of the Conscription Act in the Confederate Congress, seems to have caused some dissatisfaction among the men of these parts, who have been forced into service by its workings—But nothing better could have been expected of such men—men who were willing to remain at home, while such a struggle as we are engaged in, is going on, and leave their countrymen to defend their common liberties and property.[19] You all have doubtless seen something in the papers of the Rockingham Militia having mutinied etc.? They had been drafted, and were on their way to join Jackson's command, when the mutiny first showed itself. Some two hundred men deserted and were led off under the guidance of a Dutch doctor (somebody). They took a position in the mountains between this county and Albemarle, and made pretty active demonstration for resistance, and threatened to

Band of Southerners

⁓

53

Since the battle of Kernstown, the Army of the Valley has fought two pitched battles, besides frequent and severe skirmishes with the Yanks. In the battle of McDowell, fought in Highland Co., Western Va., 4,000 Confeds were engaged with about 6,000 Feds. The fight lasted till 9 o'clock at night—(3 hours)—we routed the enemy, captured some prisoners, and a large quantity of stores, a few wagons and several hundred Enfield rifles. We lost about 75 killed, and 225 wounded. The enemy's loss is not certainly known, as they had all their dead and wounded, carried off after our army left the field and came into camp. The Yanks hid their dead about in the mountains, by burying some of them, covering others up with leaves, rock, or cedar and pine boughs, etc. The wounded they carried off with them. We saw a number of fresh graves, which were attempted to be concealed by cedar and pine brush.[22] In the battle of Winchester, which occurred yesterday, we repulsed the enemy, driving him through Winchester, capturing a number of prisoners, and some stores. Within the past three days, in the skirmishes, and the battle of yesterday, we have taken from 2500 to 3000 prisoners, a large number of waggons, horses, negroes, two trains of cars, a few pieces of Artillery, and a large quantit[y] of ammunition, commisary and medical stores. We have driven the Yankees from the Valley. God has seen fit to very greatly bless our arms in this district. Our Battery suffered severely in yesterday's fight. We lost 18 or 20 killed and wounded. When I feel more like writing than I do this evening, I will give you a fuller account of the doings of our little Army of the Valley. Thanks be to God, I have escaped unhurt in all the fights we have had. Berkeley Minor was slightly wounded yesterday.

Men and horses were shot down on all sides around me—shells burst in a few feet of me, but I have sustained no injury.[23]

All our Va. friends are well, I believe. Best love to all.

Address your letters for the future to the U.V. to Uncle Jno's care. He will forward to me.

Yr brother,
Charles W. T.

(Probably) June 1862.

Dear Henry:

I write to say that our little army has had quite a bloody engagement with the enemy.[24] I am happy to say that none of our friends are among the killed, wounded, or prisoners.

After our evacuation and admirable retreat, the enemy followed us with a large force for 25 or 30 miles. But they, very suddenly, began a rapid retrograde movement towards Winchester. On Friday afternoon last we began to advance on them. After a very fatiguing forced march, we came upon the enemy at 12 m. on Sunday. Our Cavalry had been skirmishing with them all morning. At about 1 p.m., the fight was opened by the Artillery on both sides. The fight lasted 5 or 6 hours. Our men fought as well as men could be expected to fight after a heavy march; but the enemy was 12,000 or 15,000 strong—three or four to our one. We fought them till night came on, when we retreated. Our loss is estimated at 300, killed, wounded and missing. My company of Artillery, (200 strong) lost one man killed, & 12 wounded. We also lost one brass 6 pounder, and 2 caissons, and had one rifled 10 pounder disabled, several horses wounded and four [or] five killed. None of our men were taken prisoners, that I am aware of. Lanty, Berkeley M. [and] myself were in the thickest of the fights, but we escaped unharmed, thanks be to God. Our Battery was charged by the enemy. They are some ten or twelve miles from us. I must close, as we shall have to take our line of march (retreat), in a short time. Best love to all.

> *Yours,*
> *Charles W. Trueheart*

Direct to the *University* till I say otherwise.

Near Richmond, Va.,
[Summer, 1862][25] . . .
[Mrs. Jno. O. Trueheart
Galveston, Texas.]

A Yankee prisoner on being asked why McClellan did'nt go "on to Richd.," replied that "there were two Hills," (A. P. and D. H., both Maj Genls) & a Stone Wall to pass over, and a Longstreet to go through; so that McClellan couldn't begin to get there.[26]

A prisoner over in the Valley, on one of our fellows saying to him, as he was being marched under guard to the rear, "well we euchered you Yankees this time"; replied, "No wonder, you held the Jack," (and he might have added, "& a hand of trump cards"). The battle (or battles) of Richmond [the Seven Days] lasted for 6 days; and frequently some times into the night. Night putting an end to a day's fighting, the boastful McClellan would retreat during the night.[27] Next day bright and early we would be in pursuit, and succeed in overtaking him and cornering him by noon or early in the afternoon. A bloody, but comparatively short fight would then ensue; the Yankees being whipped and driven back at every point, in spite of their formidable earthworks and fortifications, extending *for miles* across our path; in many places, both above and below Richmond. Every day's operations added new trophies of Batteries, prisoners, colors, small arms, and fortifications; besides tents, baggage, and stores of all kind—and horses and mules.[28] Day after day, for six long, long days, we slept, [ate], prayed, marched and fought amidst the roar of Artillery, the roar & rattle of small arms, the explosion of the enemy's magazines; surrounded by the dead and dying horses and men, and suffocated by the stench of the battle fields. Day after day, was the picture, as above described, repeated, till the stoutest heart sickened of the sight of carnage and the spoils of war.

Tuesday, the last day's fight, [Malvern Hill] was the only time that our battery did any firing. On this day we were very hotly engaged, and lost two men killed, and 10 or 12 wounded. On today I received a slight sting on the shoulder from a very small fragment of shell. It's surprising that of all the pitched battles and skirmishes, that I have so escaped without even a rent garment. At the battle of Port Republic, when the Yankees charged and took my gun, five out of the six of us that stood to their posts were shot, and 3 out of 4 of the horses; I only escaping unhurt. Surely, we ought all to feel deeply thankful to Almighty God for His merciful preservation of my worthless life, amid so many dangers. Of the result of the truly glorious victory that we have achieved before Richmond, by the help of God, the newspapers will doubtless afford you very full and accurate accounts, before this reaches you. We captured about 10,000 prisoners, 55 or 60 pieces of Artillery, a large quantity of all kinds of military stores, horses, mules, etc. And caused the enemy to destroy millions of dollars worth of stores. The last heard of the "Young Napoleon" ... and his splendid army, they were huddled down together on the swampy bank of the James, (their "new base of operations") under cover of their gunboats.[29] I hope they may fully enjoy all the beauties of the situation, mosquitoes, chills & fever, etc. Our Army of the Valley is now lying in the vicinity of Orange C.H.[30] Tomorrow I expect to return to the Battery. I have been suffering for some 10 days past with diarrhoea, and torpidity of the liver. Where our Army of the Valley will move to, of course, I know not; but wherever it goes I fully believe that under the guidance of that God-fearing Genl [Jackson] it will be victorious. I shall be glad if you will favor me with a letter at an early period. Uncle Wm. sends love. Best love to all, both great and small. I haven't time to look this letter over, and put in words left out, etc. so excuse it.

Affectionately your son,
Charles W. Trueheart.

Chas. City Co. 26 miles
S.E. of our Capitol.
July 4th, 1862.[31]

Dear Mother:

I was much delighted at the reception of a letter from your dear hand, of the 31st inst. It reached me day before yesterday. Continue to direct your letters to Uncle Jno's care. Henry in his last says "so you have actually been under fire?"—alluding to the battle of Kernstown—I had been "under fire" on several occasions before that fight, in skirmishes on the Potomac. Since the battle of Kernstown (or Barton's Mills) the Army of the Valley has been marching and fighting continually; crossed the Blue Ridge Mts. 4 times, and whipped the Yankees in four pitched battles, and three combats. In the space of thirty-seven days (from the 3rd of May to the 10th of June inclusive) it marched 425 miles (11 1/2 miles per day), fought four pitched battles and three combats, defeated three Yankee armies under Fremont, the one under Shields and that under Banks. Fremont's was whipped twice; at McDowell on the 8th of May, and in the Battle of Stone Church, or "Cross Keys," 15 miles from Port Republic, on the 9th of June. After that most bloody and brilliant fight at Kernstown, in which Jackson, under orders from the Powers that be at Richmond, to hold Banks & Shields in the Valley, and prevent their sending reinforcements to McClellan, or attacking Johnson's [Johnston's] rear in the retrograde movement of the Army of the Potomac; we retreated up the Valley with the most dogged obstinancy fighting them as we went. The army, when it had reached Harrisonburg, cut across to the left, and took a strong position in the pass of Swift Run Gap. Our little army of 3000, with which we attacked, and held at bay, about 15,000 Yankees for 5 hours at Kernstown; killing and wounding 1,700 of them, with our loss of 768 killed, wounded and prisoners, had now been recruited up to 8,000. The Yankees thought they had the whole Valley & Jackson to boot; but by this splendid movement to the left, the enemy was completely nonplussed. He could not get at our army, and was affraid to go on to Staunton, leaving us in his rear. Here, [Richard

S.] Ewell[']s Division of some 12,000 men moved up from about Culpepper C. H., crossed over & took our positions while we made a rapid movement up the Valley to Port Republic, where we crossed over into Albemarle, through Brown's Gap; then into the Valley again, through Rockfish Gap, and on past Staunton, out into Western Va. by forced marches. While at Meechum's River Depot, ten miles from the U.V., Uncle Jno [Minor], Dr. [Socrates] Maupin, and other kind friends, came over to see us—'twas Sunday the 3rd of May. Lanty [Blackford], Berkeley [Minor], Chas M[inor] and myself spent the night at Mr. Colston[']s hospitable mansion, Hillandale. Forming a juncture with Brig. Edward [Allegheny] Johnson's army of 4,000, we made a rapid movement against the enemy at McDowell, Highland Co. (a part of Fremont's army under Millroy) who were threatening Staunton; and after a severe battle, in which both sides lost heavily, routed him, capturing, or causing him to destroy large quantities of stores, and drove him out into Pendleton Co. After a days rest, we pushed back towards Staunton, turning off to the left passing through Harrisonburg, and New Market, Shenandoah Co.— (the Yankee army thereabout had fallen back down the Valley, Banks remaining at Strasburg, while Shields moved across towards Fredsbrg., to cooperate with McClellan) over into the little Valley in wh. Luray, Page Co., & Front Royal, lie. Moving rapidly down this Valley (having been joined by Major [General] Ewell's Division;) by forced marches, we completely surprised a portion of Banks' army, at Front Royal;—capturing after a short fight, one stand of colors, two ten-pound [P]arrott-rifled cannon, 600 prisoners (three field officers, a number of Capts and Lts), 2 trains of cars, and a large quantity of stores military. On this day we made a forced march of 31 miles—early the next day we pushed on across to the Strasburg and Winchester turnpike, broke through and cut off the rear of Banks' column as it retreated down the road towards Winchester, capturing after a short fight, a large number of prisoners, horses, ambulances, waggons, and medical & commissary stores. Banks was retreating as fast as he could; but we kept close upon his heels, fighting & pursuing all day, we captured numbers of prisoners, wagons, etc. We continued the march all that night, reached within two miles of Winchester just before day, found the enemy drawn up in line of battle in a strong position ready to receive us. We pitched into them, and after a battle of two & a half hours, routed them, driving them through the streets of Winchester, capturing a large number of prisoners, etc. To the day of my death I shall never forget the scene that greeted our delighted eyes, created in us the wildest enthusiasm, and nerved us for the fray. On all sides,—from windows, on the side walks, and porches were throngs of the fair young ladies, and hospitable matrons, old men and children, hurrahing and shouting for joy; waving handerkerchiefs, bonnets and hats; and some of the fair ones even weeping and laughing by turns, for joy at our arrival, and their being rid of the detested Yankee rule. As we passed up the streets, waiters loaded with eatables and drinkables, were handed to us by the ladies and servants, altho' we were going at a double quick. And most refreshing they were to us too, hungry, tired and sleepy as we were. The Yanks had set fire to two blocks of large 2 & 3 storied buildings, regardless of the safety of the city. They had even set fire to a large building containing their ordnance stores, tho' one of their hospitals, containing 300 of their wounded, was so near, that had not the fire been extinguished, numbers of them must have perished by the explosion and burning of the wooden hospital. The ordnance and medical stores captured here were of the greatest importance to us, from our need, and their real value. We pursued the flying vandals for 6 or 8 miles, capturing large numbers; and then halted to rest, eat & sleep. The Yankees, officers and all, marched into Winchester, when they heard that the army at Strasburg had been routed, and told the slaves & free negroes that Jackson was coming, and that he was going to shell and burn the town and butcher every black person in the place. The negroes, slave & free, were panic stricken, took flight with the vile Yankees. Men, women and children, in large numbers, fled towards Harper's Ferry, taking with them what effects they could haul off with their master's vehicles, etc. All along the road for miles were strewn women's & children's clothing, that they threw away in their flight; some even left their little babies behind them. One of the officers in our battery found, while in search of something to eat, in a Yankee waggon, a negro baby only a few days old. There were a few Union people in Winchester before the Yankees came, but their love was soon turned into hate, so abominably did the Yankees behave themselves. Next day we marched to the Ferry to make a demonstration at crossing into Md., and going towards Washington. And it had the desired effect. Yankeedom trembled in its boots. Lincoln immediately called on the Yankee Govs. to send on the State Militia to protect the "Capitol"—but I must postpone the rest for another letter. In the Valley we whipped the armies of Shields, Banks & Fremont—captured some 4,000 prisoners, 350

wall" and his veteran Legion! No wonder he called upon the Yankee Govs. to send on the Militia. That unconscionable liar, Major General Banks in his report to Secty Staunton [Secretary of War Edwin M. Stanton], says he lost only 30 waggons, captured, and a few that had to be burnt to prevent their falling into the hands of the enemy. I saw with my own eyes at least fifty waggons, besides three large pontoon bridge boats with their appurtenances that they had burned. The N.Y. Herald dubbs Halleck [Maj. Gen. Henry Halleck] the "Maj Gen Liar of the West." Banks should be dubbed "Lieut. Gen'l Liar." We took no less than 3,000 well men, besides several hundred sick and wounded that we paroled. But at this juncture, Shields, with a column of 8,000 moved rapidly across from toward Fredericksburg, while Fremont with an army of 25,000 [to] 30,000 moved over from Franklin[,] Pendleton Co. to form a juncture with him to cut off our retreat. They thought they had "Old Jack" completely. No time must be lost. "Jack" must lead back his fatigued & bleeding army of veterans by forced marches, up the Valley again, or be cut off and overpowered by an enraged & superior force of the Yanks. We only had 24,000 men when we started down this brillant successful movement. The Yankees had fought well but had lost many a good soldier by our balls & skill. Our Battery lost 19 men killed and wounded in the battle of Winchester, & 2 wounded in the fight of the day previous. Probably our whole loss was 500 killed & wounded in that battle. The Yankee loss was not as great, owing to their being posted behind stone fences & breast works & their Batteries being on elevated ground. We made 30 miles on the 1st day's march—by noon the next day our whole army was at Strasburg, (a distance of some 44 miles), drawn up in line of battle to repel the attack, & hold in check the hordes of Eastern men under that black villian, [John C.] Fremont. We succeeded in getting all our waggons past, loaded with Yankee spoils, and our tired army, except some 250 who exhausted by fatigue and heat, sank down in their tracks, or crept under the shade of the trees along the road, and fell asleep. For several hours might be heard the roar of artillery with an occasional volleys of musketry on our right. The deepest anxiety was felt lest the heavy column of the enemy should arrive in our path on the right, & penetrate our retreating column; but soon the welcome news came, the firing continued to recede till the white smoke of the batteries could no longer be seen for the intervening woods and mountains. Thanks to God our army is safe. The enemy is driven back at every point. We, or a part of our army, remained in

Rebel Brothers

line of battle till night fall, so as to enable the stragglers to come up, & the waggons to get a good start. A little after dark we were all under march again, about 100 stragglers having come in before we started. We marched six miles beyond Strasburg & halted about 11 o'clock at night; although it rained hard never did men sleep more soundly or enjoy rest more. Before next morning we were under arms and on the [Valley] turnpike. Today we moved on quite leisurely—part of the army being pushed ahead to guard Massanuthen [Massanutton] Gap in the[B]lue [R]idge, so as to prevent Shields, who[,] foiled in his attempt to get in our rear by the timely burning of the large bridge at Front Royal (across the Shenandoah), had moved to Massanuthen [Massanutton] to try to get in our rear. Not a day passed when on this retrograde movement that we did not have a skirmish, & sometimes our rear guard & the enemy's advance were fighting all day. At Harrisonburg our army turned off to the right taking the Port Republic road. We halted & went into Bivouac in a few miles of Port [Republic]. This was on Thursday. The next day the enemy's advance came up & a severe skirmish ensued. 'Twas here that the lamented & Gallant Ashby fell while leading a charge against the vile Yankees. He had just been made Brig. Gen of Cavalry. He was in command of the advance and was leading a charge. His horse being shot under him, he extricated himself from the fallen animal, & proceeded on foot, waving his sabre over his head, calling on his men to follow him. But he had not proceeded far when he fell, a corpse, pierced through the breast by the destroying Minnie, & in him fell one of the Noblest & bravest of Va['s] sons. He was strictly moral and temperate; read & revered the Bible which he always carried with him. He seldom if ever, made use of profane language; was highly polished in his manners, & admired & respected by everyone. Few men, even those in higher sphere, have rendered more efficient service in the field of our cause. No man has killed with his own hand as many of the enemy. A splendid rider, swordsman, & pistol shot, in every encounter he dashed into the thickest of the fight and felled the enemy on all sides. He never said "Men, go on" but it was "Men, follow me." When I heard of his death I could scarcely keep back a gush of tears! The *poor* fellow was interred in the U.V. Cemetary surrounded by his weeping comrades of his "Old company," & a sorrow stricken throng from different parts of the country, his favorite horse came first after the hearse in the procession; his "old company" next. The horse stood quitely by the grave during the whole of the service. I had enjoyed many opportunities of becoming acquainted with him, from [being] under his command on piquet guard, & the advance rear guard. On such occasions he would laugh and talk with the men, with great urbanity and freedom, & made himself most agreeable too—but to return to my story.[32]

Saturday was spent in reconnoitering & skirmishing. On Sunday morning, the Fremont column being fallen back, Old Jack gave orders for preaching to be held at 10. Many of the men were down at the [river] washing, etc., and others getting ready for preaching, and some fast asleep, & others sitting about in squads chatting. It was about 8 o'clock that we were roused from our different occupations, by the fire of cannon in our rear, and the passage of singing shells far over our heads.[33] The enemy under Shields had surprised, or in some effectual manner disposed of, our piquets (on the 2nd page of this sheet I have made a very rough sketch of the surroundings, etc, of the battle fields of Cross Keys & Port Republic, or as we called them "Sunday's & Monday's fights") And then by an admirably bold dash had gotten possession of the Port and the bridge over the deep, broad, and rapid North Branch, capturing a number of prisoners—Col. Crutchfield (one of the General's aides) among the number.[34] They came near getting the old General himself—he only made his escape by taking across the fields on foot, & crossed the bridge just before the Yankees brought up & planted two pieces of Artillery, so as to take the bridge. He picked up a steed somewhere, & came dashing into our camp, and ordered our Battery to hitch up & run down to the bridge as quickly as possible, & open on the enemy at once. Never were horses harnessed up as fast before. In fifteen minutes we were at the bridge, & in position on the hills, pouring a deadly fire of canister & shell into the Yankee's Artillery and Cavalry. (They had not been able to get their Infantry up as quickly). In 20 mts we had driven them from their guns & back across S. Branch leaving behind them in their haste, all their prisoners.[35] In a little while several other batteries took position along side of us. The columns of Shield's infantry now began to immerge from the woods, moving in double quick with colors flying. We immediately opened a deadly fire on them with some 16 or 18 guns. The fire was so deadly they could only advance a short distance, when the columns . . . begin to break and be led back. Time after Time did they repeat the attempt, but in vain. All who witnessed the firing of our guns, declared they never saw such firing done before. We burst our shells directly in their faces & in the midst of them. Their ambulances were continually engaged in carrying off their dead & wounded, but the next day a considerable number remained, some with their heads shot off, and some who had lost a leg or an arm. One or two were pierced directly through the breast with a cannon ball. For two and a half hours they endeavored to pass the fire of our guns, but all to no purpose. The only two cannon that they succeeded in getting into position had the cannoneers driven from them by our fire and fell into our hands. When we had gotten well engaged with Shield's column, we heard the storming of Fremont's guns in our rear, near X Keys.[36] In this quarter the battle lasted from 9 or 9 1/2 a.m. till 4 or 5 p.m. Fremont, although in superior numbers (25 to 30,000 to our 16 or 18,000) was defeated & driven back at every point, leaving the greater portion of his dead, and wounded in our hands. We occupied the battle ground till near midnight when we all fell back to the South side of the N Branch, our wounded, etc., having been removed from the battlefield. Betimes next morning [Monday, June 9] . . . 4 brigades advanced against Shield's column which lay 3 or 4 miles below Port [Republic near Lewiston]— Fremont undertaking to come to his relief. The long bridge was burnt, which entirely frustrated his purpose. In a short time his [Fremont's] whole force was drawn up in line of battle to witness the entire overthrow, and discomfiture of Shield[']s army without being able to raise a hand to help him. I seldom enjoyed any military success, whether gained by the strategy of our Genls or that . . . to the hard fighting of our men, as I did, in seeing the army of this mean spirited renegade outwitted and outgeneraled, with the bridge burning under their very noses. This bringing of the entire army over the river, burning the bridge, and leaving Gen. Fremont and his army to their own pleasant reflections was a very wise movement. In the worn down condition of our men & horses, it would not have been safe to have given Fremont a chance to wrest from us the decided victory of the previous day; 'twas better thus to take the armies in detail. The fight [Port Republic] lasted from about 7 a.m. to 12 p.m. In point of numbers we were about equally matched—we may have had a few more than they had. They fought most obstinately; at one time, our whole left wing was driven back about half a mile. 'Twas here our battery was charged; we fired until they came within 300 yards. The infantry giving way, we were ordered to limber up & fall back. We had done so in the midst of a storm of grape and Minnies (not a well directed fire though[, as] the wheat & swells in the ground prevented their getting a view of us)

Band of Southerners

~

all anyhow? On the 16th [of] August I wrote to you, on [the] 6th of Sept. to Minny—on [the] 21st to Fanny, on [the] 8th [of] October to Henry, and on [the] 7th of Nov. to Mother. And there were others that I have written and forgot to set them down. How many of these have reached their destination? I do hope they will come to hand eventually, as they contain accounts of many matters of interest, descriptions of battles, etc. Did I ever tell you of what a narrow escape I made at the battle of Port Republic? Our Battery was posted on the left wing of our line of battle. The Yanks by concentrating their forces on this wing, succeeded in driving it back. Our Battery was moving to the rear, the infantry having been driven back in some confusion. My gun was behind and Gen'l. Winder (acting Maj Gen'l) ordered me to halt, unlimber, and give the advancing enemy canister to hold him in check, while our disorganized infantry was being rallied and reformed. I was just having the first load rammed down when orders came to limber up and fall back as quickly as possible, the Infantry having given way entirely. I had just got my gun under way again when the Lieut. of Section two drivers and two cannoneers and their horses were shot down. The Lieut. asked me to lift him down, as he was dying. I had tried to get the gun off but to no purpose—I lifted the Lieut. down and put him to one side in the wheat. The Yanks had gotten within fifty or sixty yards of me. There was a perfect storm of Minnies and grape flying around me. Five out of six of us that had stayed behind to work the gun, and three out of four horses, were already shot. I at first determined to feign being badly wounded, and got down under the gun carriage, but upon reconsideration determined to attempt to escape at all hazards. I crept from under the gun, and bending down half double so as to be below the heads of the wheat, struck off as fast as my legs would carry me in an oblique direction from the Yankee line, towards an orchard. But no sooner had I gotten from under the gun than the scamps spied me and began shooting at me—but I reached the orchard under a lively fire and by dodging from tree to tree, managed to elude the pursuing Yanks and their bullets; and getting down close to the bank of the Shenandoah ran up it and soon rejoined the rest of the Battery. In twenty minutes time, reinforcements had arrived and we were in hot pursuit of the flying enemy. But they got my gun and carried off one of my wounded comrades. In this, the battle of Port Republic, besides killing and wounding large numbers, we took 500 prisoners, 8 pieces of Artillery, small arms, etc, and pursued them 7 or 8 miles. I am very sorry

Cally—make at least this one resolve—"I will no longer slight my Maker's offers of mercy, of pardon and reconciliation. I will lay hold of & accept Jesus Christ as He is freely offered to me in the Gospel—I will by God's help be a Christian." Will you not at least try by prayer and reading of God's word to become a Christian? Do not postpone longer a preparation for a future state of existence; life is too uncertain, the interests at stake are too vastly important to be postponed, or to be trifled with. Now is the accepted time, today is the day of Salvation.

I enclose some poetical productions which I think will please you. Rhodes' [Brig. Gen. Robert E. Rodes'] Brigade is the one that Eugene Blackford is in. It's Genl is a Virginian, a native of this city. Few commands have more distinguished themselves in this war. And our Texas Brigade too, stands among the first, I am proud to say, for it's behavior on the battlefield, and under all circumstances.[41] I think I told you how much Uncle Jno Minor (and indeed all my friends at the U.V.) was pleased with it; with the appearance and gentlemanly, soldierly deportment of the men, while the Brigade's bivouaced on the Lawn and under the arcades of the College;—It was when Jackson's army was enroute for Richmond last summer. I have had the pleasure of fighting alongside of them on several occasions, and witnessing their cool determination and unsurpassed bravery. At the battle of Sharpsburg [Antietam] I saw them make a splendid charge, putting the enemy to flight. If there is one thing that I am proud of, it is being a Virginian, and a Texan! The ladies of this city, besides their many other patriotic and charitable acts, gave the several thousand soldiers in hospital here, a first-rate Christmas dinner. The steward, (of this Hospital), called me down to see the table as it was being prepared yesterday. Basket after basket of good things—substantials and niceties—were received from the liberal donors, brought in by their house servants—and our convalescents sat down to a plentiful repast of excellent soup, roast turkey, duck, corned round of beef, chicken pie, spare ribs, & Irish potatoes; and dessert of cake, pies, etc. I have seldom seen men enjoy anything of the sort more than the poor fellows seemed to do. For those patients not able to go to the table, various little delicacies were sent round. I ate my Xmas dinner with our affectionate relatives the Blackfords; found Charles & Lewis both home on a flying visit. The former has recently been made Judge Advocate to Jackson's Corps d'arm. The former is in command of a Corps of Engineers, engaged in making surveys (military) in Louisa Co. Dr. Minor is absent just now for a few days, so I am kept specially busy. I have a good many cases of pneumonia in my ward, and other important cases, so I am called up frequently out of my warm bed to see them, or to patients in the other two wards (Dr. Minor's & Dr. Tucker's wards). It gives me a slight foretaste of what I shall have inflicted on me, when I get into private practice.

Tell me if you all see the newspapers regularly. All at Uncle Jno Minor's are well also at Dr. Pendleton's so Lewis B. tells me. You all both great and small, must try to write to me more frequently. Tell me something about Elvira's and sister M's children. Who of my Galveston friends have taken refuge in the part of the country you all are in? Give me your views on the enclosed pieces of poetry— don't be bashful; write away, just what comes uppermost.

My best love to all and by "all" I mean all the children (of my dear Mother and Father), and Mr. Joseph and Mr. Howard.

Your affectionate brother,
Charles W. Trueheart.

Cousin Mary Blackford sends love to Mother.

is on another of his raids to the enemy's rear; and people are naturally in expectation of important results.[6] Do you all get the news pretty regularly? Do our Texas papers copy pretty freely from Virginia sheets? In a recent letter to Cally, I enclosed a number of clippings, etc., which I intended for the perusal of all the family.

I have made but few acquaintances in this burg, and should have rather a dull time of it, were I not kept closely employed by my hospital duties, and medical studies. On New Year's day the ladies of the place gave our patients, etc., another splendid dinner—six large turkeys, numerous geese, ducks, chickens, hams, round of beef, etc., sponge cakes, pies, custards, etc., and apples, pickles, milk, hominy, stewed fruit, cabbage, etc., were among the articles that we feasted on. After furnishing all this to the patients, they sent down a dinner especially for myself and Dr. Turner, the other Asst. Surgeon in this hospital.[7] We had Dr. Minor, and several other Surgeons to dine with us. I am so much charmed with Lynchburg women in general that I think I must try to fall in love with, and captivate, one of the dear creatures. How would you like a Virginia sister? Or have you and Cally some one picked out for me in Texas?

Do you all go to preaching nowadays? Tell me all about your manner of life, etc., now that you are thrown out into the country.[8] Where is Mr. Sydnor's family, and Mr. Cole's? We have an uncommonly fine preacher in chg of the Presbyterian Church in this place; a Mr. Ramsey—today we had Communion which I enjoyed no little.[9] Minnie, do you ever think seriously of that world—that life beyond the grave, to which we are all hastening?—of that awful day, the Day of Judgement, when we shall be obliged to give an account to God, our Maker, as to how we have used these lives—these talents that he has given us? If you have not, it is high time that you were considering this important subject. Do not put it off for even a day. Life is too uncertain—the interests at stake too valuable.

Does Mother hear from Cousin Lucy Byars now, as formerly? How are the negroes in Texas behaving themselves? We are having a good deal of smallpox in the hospitals here—and even about in the city among the residents some cases have occured. Two have occured in my ward, indeed, I fear I have another one there today. I sometimes vaccinate fifty or sixty soldiers at one time.[10] A few days since a rather suspicious looking eruption made its appearance on my face, hands, etc., and for a time I thought I had the much dreaded disease. I should not much object to having it, as it would only be in a mild form—varioloid, and then I should be forever exempt from the veritable smallpox, and save the trouble of vaccination. But I must come to a close—I am not afraid of being made uglier.

Best love to all. Respects to Mary R. Write to me immediately on receipt of this. If you all don't write more regularly than heretofore I shall stop writing altogether.

Your affectionate brother,
Charles W. Trueheart

February 9, 1863

Dear Henry:

I am still at Lynchburg, that city of steep hills, nasty sticky mud, and all sorts of tobacco.[11] No letters from any of my Texas friends since one from you of the 22nd December, containing an enclosure from Mother of the 20th December, received January 14th. You all haven't written to me since last year; this is too bad I declare! I shall be tempted to renounce and disinherit the whole . . . of you if you don't do better. Ever since first hearing of the gallant little achievement in Galveston Bay, I have been anxiously looking for letters from some of you, giving me an account of it, telling me what part you took in it, and if you and those in whom I feel an interest, came out safe. I would have given something pretty to have participated in it. I have seen enough hard service and hard fighting in pitched battles between large armies—and dozens of skirmishes too, for that matter, to satisfy any one man; but then there is something specially pleasurable, to my notion, in a fight on water, on Galveston Bay, in immediate defense of our Island home. Indeed I think I should like it hugely to have a berth on one of our C.S naval vessels. Were it not for this thing of medicine, I think I should offer my services to the C.S. government for service in the Navy; for instance, join one of the crews they are making up to go to England to man one of the new vessels now being built there. How would you like it old fellow? You know you and me are crack sailors. When you write give me a full account of the *battle of Galveston*. Something different and more than what the newspapers give—go into minutia. I am anxious to hear who of my friends distinguished themselves, what amount of injury the city sustained from the cannon balls of the enemy, etc, etc. Have many families returned to live on the Island, since we have gotten possession of it again? What has become of Mr. Joseph and Mr. Howard? I hope they are in the fighting department. I want to see our tribe well represented in that department. What company

This Fearful War

∼

and regiment do you belong to? And by the way, tell me exactly how many regiments of infantry, and of cavalry, and how many batteries has our State put in the field? And how many has she in the field now?

There is but little army news of interest from the Army of the Potomac. They say the mud is ankle deep in our encampments and the roads in vicinity almost impassable.[12] Supposing that you hear through public channels all the news that transpires in these parts, I refrain from giving what I derive from the newspapers. The opinion that the prospects for peace are daily improving seems to be gaining ground with the people with whom I come in contact. The opinion as far as I can learn is based on the fact of our military successes, the rapidly growing and spreading spirit of dissatisfaction among the people of the North—particularly those of the Northwest.

Give warmest regards to Cousin Sarah and Cousin John Sydnor when you see them.

The Small Pox is decidely on the decrease in this city of Hospitals, I am happy to say.[13] We had two cases occurring in one day in this Hospital last week but have had none since. I believe I told you in my last that I was no longer acting as Asst. Surgeon as I have been for some months past; there were several commissioned Assts. out of employment here, so I had to give place. Cousin Jno gave me up rather unwillingly. I am at present performing the duties of a sort of house surgeon, and have no longer charge of a ward. Best love to all. Uncle Jno Minor has been quite sick, but is now better—as also Uncle Lanty—the latter with erysipelas, the former with bronchitis.[14]

Aff your loving brother,
C. W. Trueheart

(Horrid Confederate paper this!)

Lynchburg, Virginia
February 21st, 1863.

Dear Mother:

Two months of the New Year, 1863, have nearly passed, and I am in receipt of only two letters from home; one enclosure from you and Henry jointly received Jan 14th, and one from Fanny Garland received Feby 15th, the last that I have received. Fanny is really deserving of commendation for this last letter of hers. It gave me much pleasure. I, one individual, have written three letters to you

Rebel Brothers

~

all, and you, the whole family of you, have written me only two. On the 4th Jany I dispatched one to Minny, on the 17th one to Fanny, and on the 9th Feby, one to Henry. The latter, a trifling dog, has been unusually remiss in writing of late. He has not written to tell me of his first smell of gunpowder, that gallant little affair at Galveston. I felt no small degree of anxiety on the subject until Fanny's last arrived; as I saw in the newspaper that a number of our Texans had been killed and wounded in the action, but the accounts did not give the names of the fallen.[15] I was sorry to see that our infantry did not behave very creditably in the affair—i.e., from what Henry tells in his letter to Fanny which she forwarded to me. Our Texas troops serving in this state, have on all occasions shown themselves unflinchingly brave, steady, and dashing. I am glad that Major Gen'l Magruder is so much liked by our Texans; and really he seems to deserve no little credit for the energy and enterprise displayed at his new post.[16] He is not one of our great generals. In these parts he is considered only a second-rate gen'l ; not comparable to Lee, Jackson, Bragg [or] Longstreet. Does he let whiskey alone now? That was a very serious failing with him while in command on the Peninsula. Speaking of able Gen'ls, I for my part, tho' not a competent judge I confess, can't help being half of the opinion that we haven't any military geniuses among our Generals; that is, any comparable to Marlborough, Wellington, Napoleon Bonaparte, or even our own Gen'l Washington. I am rather inclined to the opinion that our soldiers are better than our Gen'ls in their respective spheres; and deserving of more credit for the victories won than they—tho' the praise all goes to the Generals. I believe that with such *soldiers* as we have composing our Southern army, and a truly great military head to direct them, that we should have conquered a peace months ago; that instead of the almost barren victories of Manassas, No 1 and No. 2, Sharpsburg, and Fredericksburg, etc., [should] have utterly routed and demoralized, making large captures from, if not annihilating the Yankees; that we should be today carrying desolation to Yankee homes, dictating terms of peace to them, instead of squatting down on our own soil, and having our land despoiled by the invading enemy right here under our noses. But we ought to feel deeply thankful to God for the successes with which He has crowned our efforts in defence of our liberties so far. Today's telegrams bring us news of the capture of the Yankee gunboat "Queen of the West," by our Batteries on Red River.[17] I have heretofore refrained giving you all any of the news culled from the newspapers,

This Fearful War

boat etc has to my regret never made its appearance. Can't you send on a duplicate? Your letters are read with the greatest avidity by our Blackford friends as well as by myself. Mr. B[lackford] invariably asks if I have any recent letters from home, in meeting me, and gets me to let him see them. Tell Mother that she is the frequent theme of Cousin Mary B[lackford]'s conversation. She regrets that the state of her health will not admit of her writing to Mother. She is still obliged to lie down the greater portion of the time, and suffers much pain. With all her "Minor failings," she is an admirable woman, a beautiful character and an affectionate kinswoman, and one that is very kind and attentive to me, and whose society I am very fond of, tell Mother.

You don't mention having received any of my letters written while I was at Winchester, Va. Or perhaps none of them reach[ed] you at all. I was detailed and sent there for hospital duty in the latter part of Sept, and remained there until the middle of November. I performed the duties of Asst. Surg, having entire charge of the Small Pox Hospital two & half miles out of the city, and a Hospital with from seventy five to 150 patients in town. This suited me to a T, as you may well imagine. Since coming here I have acted Asst. Surgeon in this Hospital, from the latter part of November to the middle of Jan., at which time a commissioned Asst. was assigned to the ward I had charge. Since that time I have been performing the duties of house Surg; occasionally when Dr. Minor or one of the Asst. Surgs were sick or absent I have had a ward to myself. For the past week Dr. Galt being absent on a 7 or 8 days furlough, I had the pleasure of having charge of a ward; and now Cousin Jno. is off on a week's furlough to see his family, who are staying in Halifax Co., so I still have charge of a ward.[20] Have you ever met with him? He is a very affectionate relation; has shown me every attention in his power. He is a man of uncommonly good sense and vigorous mind, naturally, and he has been untiring in perfecting himself in his profession. He is looked upon as one of the very first medical men in point of skill and attainments. I could not possibly have gotten in a better school I think. Did I tell you of a visit made to Hanover Co., of a week in January? I went to Dundee, Dr. Lucian Price's, for the sake of making, or rather renewing the acquaintances of the charming young ladies of the family, and to see Aunt Livy Minor, who is now living there. She happened to be absent in Richmond, but I had a charming time of it with the young people. I found that Cousin Lizzie had, but a few days previously, been married to Doct. Fontaine, a

This Fearful War

~

77

son of Col. Fontaine. Maj Gen'l Stewart [Stuart], Brig. Gen'l Fitzhugh Lee, and several other military gentlemen were among the guests present. The former [Jeb Stuart], though a married man, is very fond of the young ladies generally, and takes the liberty of kissing all the pretty ones I notice. He and his staff rode forty miles through the mud to attend this wedding. He is a brave, dashing fellow, and sticks his men into the hottest kind of places. I have fought under him on two occassions.

Uncle Jno. Minor and Aunt Nannie were here on a visit to the Blackfords, a week or two since. He was better of the bronchial affection from which he has been suffering during the earlier part of the winter. Uncle Lanty, I am happy to say, has nearly recovered from an attack of Erysipelas that he has been laid up with several weeks past.

What is the reason that you all write so seldom? I am the only absentee and yet scarcely average two letters a month from the whole of you. Give my best love to all. Excuse any errors that you may discover in this letter, I haven't time to read it over. Cousin Mary Blackford sends love to Mother and you.

> Your affectionate brother
> Charles Trueheart.

Lynchburg,
September 24, 1863.

My darling Brother:

Uncle Jno's telegram, dated 9 o'clock 23rd inst. and a letter from Tom Joseph, have been handed me.

Twas only this morning that I was wishing that in the event of your getting sick, or wounded, that you might be able to get to the University, where I knew you would meet with a hearty welcome, and have the best of nursing, and Medical skill bestowed on you. How thankful am I to Almighty God, that you are only "slightly wounded," and in such good hands. I shall be able to come over Monday or Tuesday probably, and remain with you two or three days. I have seen the Medical "Powers that be," and they speak favorably of granting me a short leave. I could not come at an earlier period, as I have charge of a large ward, and have some 6 or 7 severe and very troublesome surgical cases on hand, and as I have no good dresser on hand to attend to their wounds, I am doing so myself. By Monday, I hope to be able to make some other arrangement, temporarily.

Rebel Brothers

The enclosed letter is the first that has come for you. I had sent you sundry papers by yesterday's, and a letter from myself by today's mail, directing to your company & regiment as usual. My best love to Uncle Jno, Aunt N[annie] and Mary L[auncelot].

Affectionately your only brother,
C. W. Trueheart

P/S. If you desire it and will let me know by telegraph, I will strain a point and come at once; I can slip over and stay with you a day without getting a formal leave, upon a pinch, tho 'twould be rather risky.

Yours,
Charles.

11 1/2 p.m.
This letter will be sent to the cars in the morning. Many thanks to Uncle Jno for his telegram.

Chimborazo Hospital[21]
Richmond, Va.
Nov. 18, 1863.

My darling Mother

How I long to see you and the other dear ones at home! But I'm even deprived of the pleasure of hearing from you. Neither Henry nor myself have had letters from Texas since one from Mr. Joseph to H[enry] written some time in the latter part of July or August. We have both been in the habit of writing and sending letters every few weeks by private hand for mailing in different points in the Trans Mississippi country; and I see no reason why you should not have received a considerable portion, at least, of them. How is it? How many have come to hand since Henry left home?

When I last heard from the dear fellow he was in the neighborhood of Harrisonburg, Va. A ride of eighteen or twenty miles had caused his wounded leg to become inflamed, and the wound to open again; so he had to lie by for a day or so to let it get better. He had just purchased a very fine riding horse at six hundred and fifty dollars, and left his old steed at Cousin Patsy . . . to be fattened up at thirty dollars a month. No doubt he has given in some of his letters a full account of his having joined McNeill's company of Partizan Rangers. Since my last letter home written from Lynchburg, I have by request, been transferred to this place with a view to attending the winter course of medical lectures, so as to enable me to graduate. I was sorry to leave Lynchburg, where I had formed some pleasant

This Fearful War
~
79

acquaintances, and made warm and very kind friends. Then too, I was enjoying very admirable advantages for practice and study. I had charge of a fine ward accomodating eighty odd patients, which I had gone to considerable trouble to have thoroughly renovated and fixed up for winter, and the Hospital guard to attend on. I had a pleasant room, well fitted up; and messed with my kind friend Cousin John Minor. When I left there last week all of our kith and kin thereabouts were as well as usual. Cousin Mary B[lackford] had just returned from a visit to Edge Hill in Hanover. Her brother Lucius had just died. [Lannie] Minor returned with her and has gone to live at Mr. Holcomb's in Bedford County, to teach school for him. Uncle Jno. had gone to Edge Hill to assist in arranging the affairs of the now orphaned family of children. Uncle Lanty, generous soul, had also offered to go down to lend his aid, tho' he has his own farm and large family to care for. Just before leaving Lynchburg, I paid him a visit of a day or two; was very affectionately and kindly received and treated by all the family. He seems to have an abundant supply of eatables etc., and set a first rate table. Aunt Mary Ann seems to be a fine housekeeper and manager. Cousin William Swan's family were well. Fanny Minor was married to Robert Berkley, of Hanover, some months since. He is an A.M. of the University and a worthy fellow. On my way down by the Central road, I called to see Uncle Wm. Overton; all there are well. He has made good crops this year. I also stopped in Dr. Pendleton's neighborhood—Cousin Betty's health is very precarious. I am comfortably housed and fed here in Richmond; and shall enjoy a good chance for attending lectures, and improving myself in my profession. Today I called to see Cousin Cornelia Dabney, and Cousin Overton Steger. Was affectionately received at both places. Aunt Livy's Clara is living at Mr. Dabney's and going to school nearby. I saw Aunt Livy at Uncle Wm's, where she has been staying for some weeks past. She and the children are well. They are an affectionate and interesting set. Lucian is living at Uncle Lanty's, and going to school to an old Mr. Tompkins, who by the way, is I believe a kinsman of ours. Lucian stammers as badly as ever; is an amiable boy, and very good.

Direct all letters for me or Henry to this place; 5th Division, Chimborazo Hospital, Richmond.[22] I understand that a private mail has been established between this and the Trans-Mississippi country. Do get Father and Mr. Joseph to exert themselves to get letters through to us. By getting some friend in Houston or Austin to allow you to send letters to them to be retained and sent across the Miss. river by the first chance, you all can accomplish it.

Best love to Father, Cally, Minny, sister M[ary], and Elvira, and Mr. Joseph and Mr. Howard, and accept a large share for yourself.

Your affectionate son.
Chas. W. Trueheart

Richmond, Va,
December 6, 1863.

Dear Sister Mary:

It's 10 o'clock Sunday night. I've just returned from Church; Dr. Moore's.[23] Went to hear Dr. Moses Hoge this morning.[24] I got a transfer to this city for the winter, so as to be able to attend the medical school here, with a view to graduation. I have been acting Asst. Surg in Winchester, and more recently in Lynchburg, as you have doubtless seen from my letters home. The illcontrived old Surg Genl [Samuel P. Moore], refused to commission me, so I determined to graduate at once, and put myself in way of advancement.[25] I am very comfortably fixed in every respect in my present situation; have little or nothing to do, so that I have a plenty of time to devote [to] medical studies, etc. Have a pleasant room and room mate, and fare quite well in the eating line for these war times. I am stationed at Chimborazo Hospital, beyond Church Hill; a long walk into town it is too. All of our friends in Va. are about as usual. There are no marriages, births or deaths, among those you feel an interest in; unless it be the death of Cousin Lucius Minor of Hanover. He died about a month ago. Just before coming down here I made Uncle Lanty, and Uncle Wm. Overton, each a visit. The former has an interesting, warm hearted, affectionate family of 9 daughters. Uncle Wm's son, William, is a Capt. in the P.A.C.S. [Provisional Army of the Confederate States], & Polly is a sensible affectionate girl. Henry, when I last heard from him, was still suffering from his wound in the knee; he is now over in the Valley with McNeill's Partizan Rangers, a service that will suit him very well I think. He has not written to me recently. Why under the sun don't some of you all write and get your letters brought through by private hand? There is a mail established now across the Miss river, and by paying 40 [cents] postage, letters come through by it. Urge Mr. Joseph to exert himself in getting letters through to us. Tis bad enough to be separated from [you], but not to hear from you either is hard to bear.

This Fearful War

~

If Mr. Joseph will get some friend in Houston, Austin or Shreveport to take charge of letters, and forward as they have chances, we can get them through quite often. My best love to him, father, mother and the girls, as also to Mr. Howard and Elvira. Best respects to Mrs. Joseph, and kiss the children for [me]. This is by the politeness of a Maj Hill of the P.M. [Provost Marshal's] Department.

Your loving brother,
C. W. Trueheart

Richmond, Va.
December 25, 1863.

Dear Henry

I am at a loss to know where to direct this letter to you, as you spoke in your last of coming over this side the Ridge to spend your Christmas with Uncle Wm. Overton's people; so I shall enclose this to him, asking him to forward to you if you are not in, or shortly expected in, the Green Springs neighborhood. I hope however, that you may have been able to have come over on a furlough, so as to visit me and your other friends. In your last letter received by me (which I forwarded to Father) you ask if I can accomodate you with lodging, etc. Yes, very conveniently. I have a large room and a bed large enough for both of us to occupy it in this cold weather. As to eating, I can give you pretty good fare. So come over and spend a good portion of time with me. I have not as yet become acquainted with "Mrs. Street and Daughters", but have written to Mary Launcelot to get her to send me a letter of introduction to them; and I will devote a part of my spare time to finding out what they are made of, and ingratiate myself into their good graces, for your sake; not for my own—am I not a disinterested, good brother?

I am visiting by rule, confining myself to an afternoon and a night out of the 6 week days, to society generally. I only go visiting one evening in the week. Sunday I go to Church with some of the women of course; but not with the view to leading any of them to the alter; only to keep my hand in till "this cruel war is over," and for the sake of my manners. Last week, among others, I went to see the Misses Mason from Winchester, and was very cordially welcomed. Mrs. Mason received a box some months ago, from Mr. M[ason], by a blockade runner, which she, supposing to contain some wines and liquors which he had promised sending, and wishing to save them for a time of sickness, had them stowed away without mentioning its reception to any of the family. A few days since hav-

from their friends through the mail established by Cushing of the Houston Telegraph, only yesterday. Then too, there's the 40 [cent] mail via Brandon or Meridian, Miss., established and under the control of the P.O. Department; Why dont you send letters by that route? If only one in three or four that you start, reach us, that would be infinitely better than not getting any at all. Both Henry and myself, do most earnestly beg and entreat that you all will leave no stone unturned to get letters on to us. We have both been in the habit of dispatching letters every few weeks—sometimes every week—by private hand, or the C.S. mail alluded to above. Henry, is for one thing, very anxious to hear from Mr. Joseph as to how his Assessor's business is coming on. It is very consoling to us to know that you all are in a land of plenty; and not seriously molested by the Yankees. But my fears have been somewhat aroused by hearing that Banks had gotten a foot hold on Texas soil; and had been burning etc., as is usual with the invaders. I have not heard from Henry recently; he was well and hearty by last accounts tho' I am expecting him over to spend a short time with me, during the bad weather of next month, when military operations will necessarily come to a stand still. I have informed you all in former letters that my application for commission as Asst. Surgeon having been refused by the Surg Genl on the newly taken ground that I was not an M.D., I have gotten a transfer to this place with the view to attending medical lectures and graduating. I am pleasantly located out on Church Hill nominally on duty at Chimborazo Hospital. I have all my time to devote to lectures, etc. All our kith and kin are well as far as I know. Uncle Lanty, dear generous fellow, wrote me one of his affectionate warmhearted letters a short time since, enclosing me a hundred and forty odd dollars, as a present, which was most acceptable to me in the present low state of my finances. Henry too, is hard run for money, he writes me. I am in the habit of devoting an evening or two every week to society; it's very necessary to prevent one from relapsing into a half civilized state of habits and manners. I am in the habit of visiting Mrs. Mason's family, now here, refugees, from Winchester; Professor Gibson's family; Cousin Broadie Herndon's; Cousin Overton Steger's; and some others that you all don't know anything about. Henry writes me word to get acquainted with, and cultivate Mrs. Street and daughters, for his sake. I have written to Mary Launcelot Minor, who is a friend of theirs, to send me a letter of introduction to them, so as to enable me to comply with H's request. I am enjoying a rich treat in hearing the sermons of such men as Doctors Moore, Hoge, & Minnegrode. Who is preaching for you all now? I have not indulged in Xmas farther than eating a good dinner, and visiting a few friends. Military operations on the Line of the Rapid Ann have come to a stand still. Indeed there is no news of any kind just now. I saw Genl Lee in town a few days ago; he is a fine looking old gentleman; and looks bright and cheerful. Congress has so far failed to bring anything to a head on the great questions before them; the Currency, and Recruiting the Army. We get very little news from you Trans-Miss. people—hope you may be able to hold your own as well as heretofore; but fear you may be worsted, on the coast, at least.

My best love to Father and Mother, Minny, Fanny, Sisters Mary and Elvira, Mr. Howard and Tom Joseph, and kiss all their dear little ones for me.

Don't forget to pray to Almighty God in behalf of yourself and Country, and me and others dear to you.

Your affectionate brother,
C. W. Trueheart

CHAPTER 4

≈

"That Much Dreaded Place—the Field,"
1864

Richmond, Va;
Jan. 3d, 1864.

Dear Minny:

Last week I wrote to Cally, so this week its your turn for a letter. I dispatched the one to C[ally] through the mail, but don't know how I will send this. Last week I received a note from Henry, enclosed with a letter of four pages closely written large sized letter paper to Cally, which I forwarded by private hand. So you see, H[enry] and myself keep writing, sending by every chance with hope that you all may get a few of our letters. Were you all to do likewise, I think probably we [could] get an occassional letter; as it is have not heard a word from any of you, since sometime in August last—now more than four months. Henry, according to last accounts, had been exposed to a good many of the hardships of war, while on a rapid movement to intercept a body of the enemy. In a charge his horse fell on the ice, bruising him a little, but fortunately, inflicting no serious injury. His health was good. Wherever he has been, he seems to have made kind friends who have shown their liking in very substantial forms. He seems to be an especial favorite with the ladies, who present him with socks, gloves, etc.—mend and make clothes for him, dress his wounds, and bruises with a sisterly tenderness, and sweeter, dearer than all, sigh soft accents of regret at his departure. I wonder at all this tho' for he's a sweet fellow, and as good as he's sweet. How would you like for H[enry] and myself to bring out two sisters for you when we come home, after "this cruel war is over";—in other words, when the Yankees have been thrashed into peace? Or have you got some fair Texas damsel in store for us? If so, keep her in store; I at least will want a Texas wife.

The Confederate Congress now in session has just enacted a law doing away with substitutes, and bringing into service all who have heretofore been exempted by having substitutes. The bill seems to afford infinite satisfaction to such as have not put in substitutes, but is as might be expected, very unpopular with those who have.[1] So far, no decided action has been taken on the Currency question; tho' it has been discussed in all its various aspects for months past by the people and the Press. There is no news of any import afloat just now. Gen'l Lee's Army remains still in position on the line of the Rapidan.[2] The recent raid made by a body of Yankee cavalry under [Bvt. Maj.]Gen'l [William W. Averell] Averill, into Roanoke and adjoining counties, has been driven off, and several hundred of them captured, or killed and wounded. Unfortunately, for our side not till they had inflicted heavy losses upon us by destroying bridges, railroad, etc. on the Va. and Tenn. road, gov't stores, etc. to a considerable amount.[3] In spite of all the various reverses we have sustained, however, the people here seem doubly nerved to resistance to the death. Of course, now and then, we meet with a miserable croaker who talks of our being "overwhelmed, overrun" etc.; such are few and far between, and not listened to with any patience by people. Prices as you will see by the enclosed price-current, are very high, but so is labor, and money is as plentiful as blackberries. From all I can learn I am inclined to believe that none of the people have suffered seriously for the want of food, unless it be in those portions of the country overrun by the enemy. I am very comfortably and agreeably situated here in Richmond, with what is equivalent to a furlough for the winter, to enable me to attend medical lectures, and complete my medical education.[4] Our relations and friends in this State are well as far as I have heard from them. I think I told you that Uncle Charles' daughter Lucy Ridgeway, was married to a Mr. Abbot a few weeks ago. He is poor, but well educated, of good family, steady and industrious. Uncle Lanty's Fanny was married some months ago to one Robert Berkley of Hanover, Co., an A.M. of the University, steady, good and industrious, but poor. Both Mr. Berkeley & Mr. Abbot were school teachers before the war. I knew them

Much Dreaded Place

officers, counting the medical staff with the Regt. It numbers 220. Sixty odd have been killed, wounded or captured since the commencement of this fight with Mr. Grant, on Thursday last. I am tired and dirty, and rather disposed to wish myself back again to Lynchburg, and its ease and luxuries, as they now seem to me when I compare them with what I now endure. My clothes are blood stained from the handling of the wounded in performing my duties; and the hot weather etc makes my garments smell anything but sweet. I have, contrary to my expectations, and the general rule with field assistants, seen and performed a number of operations. Among the most important, taken off a leg just below the knee, and another half way between the knee and hip. Another recommendation to this Brigade is that Henry and Peter Minor are both in it; the former Surgeon, and the latter private in the 9th Ala. They are affectionate, whole souled fellows, and have shown me every attention in their power.

My feet are blistered from walking, and it has worried me no little to keep up with the soldiers. My place on the march is in the rear of the Regt. and whenever a man gets sick, or is wounded, I have to stop, attend to his wants, see to getting him off on an ambulance, or litter, write him a permit to go to the rear and into the hospital; and by that time the Regt is far before me, and I have to double quick to overtake it.[8] But I shall have to get used to it, as buying a horse on Asst. Surgeon's pay is quite out of the question. An Asst. Surgeon's pay is $110.00 per month, his privilege, to draw ration (1/4 lb. of bacon and 1/4 lb. of flour—sometimes a little coffee and sugar) per day, and *one* suit of clothes *per year.* I should not dislike it so much were it not that I am the only Asst. in the Brigade if not in the Division, who is afoot; and then worse still, being afoot prevents me from associating with my equals in rank, military and social. But "what can't be cured must be endured"; so you shall not be troubled with a farther narration of my trouble on this score. Just then a 12 pd. shot struck the breast work of logs behind which I am seated writing, and threw the dirt over me.

As to these battles, upon which so much depends, I can give you but a meager account as to details. The battles opened on Thursday last some 15 or 20 miles from Orange to the left of the Plank road leading to Fredericksburg.[9] Our troops have repulsed them and driven them back day after day, and still they return to the attack. Our losses have been insignificant so far. The enemy's very heavy; probably from five to ten to our one. This disparity in our favor is

Much Dreaded Place

∾

mainly due to the fact that we fought in the woods of the Wilderness (a very continuously and densely wooded poverty stricken section in Spotsylvania Co. in which the Battle of Chancellorsville was fought) where the Yankees could not bring to bear their artillery. Then too we threw a breastwork of logs on all occassions, waited for the enemy's attack, and let him come close up, when a well directed fire was poured on to him. The destructiveness of our fire was terrorable. Grant played the same game here in contending with Lee that he tried with, for a Yankee, remarkable success, in the West against Bragg, et al, and massed his troops from three to seven lines deep, and hurled them upon us regardless of the sacrifice of Yankee blood that necessarily followed. The ball at short range, doubtless, frequently executed its mission of death upon two or more of those in its course. We have captured several thousand prisoners—lost but very few on our side. At present our line of battle extends in a sort of zigzag manner the general direction being semicircular, the convexity towards the enemy. From all I can see and learn, our line is about 8 miles.

But the fire has become heavy again and we shall probably have an engagement this evening—May 13th—There being nothing to do to-day but keep yourself dry, await rations and the Yankees; two of the most important subjects of our solicitude, I must conclude this letter.

Yesterday we had a heavy battle raging all day from day break till dark. The enemy fought well—with desperation indeed, but were repulsed at all points, with heavy loss.[10]

With one exception our arms were successful in repelling his attacks.

But for the present I must close. I shall take this up in my next which shall be forthcoming in a few days.

In front of that part of the breast work occupied by Edward Johnson's Div.—there was a heavy body of woods; the morning was rainy and misty, and under this cover the enemy marched a heavy column with which he charged our lines. The men delivered fire, but before they could reload their pieces the enemy was upon them. One Brigade gave away; the Yankees poured through the opening, flanked the portions of the Div. on either side, got entirely into their rear, while they were attempting to hold the works, etc. Of course our men had to surrender. Some few fought their way through and escaped, but Maj. Gen'l Johnson, and a considerable part of his Div., was captured. The enemy did not long hold the breast works and artillery, however, as they were driven out by reinforcements that came up—and all the guns were taken back. From all I can learn the enemy lost at least 15,000 or 20,000 prisoners, and killed & wounded. Our loss would be covered by 3,500 or 4,000. In the previous day's fight, we lost but few; they, as I said before, very heavily.[11]

Today has been raining near all day; no firing of any account. Tomorrow will probably see hot work. Our men are in good spirits, tho' tired. They are pretty well supplied with ammunition and food.

But I will write you of particulars at a future time.

Send shoes when done, to the University.

Write soon and direct to me, 8th Ala. Infty., Wilcox Brigade, A.P. Hill's Corps, A.N.V.

Affectionately yours,
Charles W. Trueheart

Line of battle near Gaines' Mill,
Henrico Co., Va.,
June 6th, [1864]

My dear Minnie

My last letter written home of the 24th May, was to Cally, so this should be to you; and I hope that you will not be slow in dispatching me a lengthy reply. Tell me how much you weigh & the same for Cally & Fanny and your respective ages. Give me the names, ages, etc., in full of all of Sister M[ary]'s & E[lvira]'s children, not that I don't remember their names, I want to have my recollection reassured. What I have passed through, since the war began, has very seriously impaired my memory. Let me see now if I haven't got them all right, Fanny Overton, Lucian Minor, Margaret Bell, Thos. R . . . Edgar, Chas Henry are all Sister Mary's—Peyton, Fanny Goode, Bobby & Nelly are all of Bow's little flock, I believe. At any rate, give me a full list of their names and ages. Don't fail to do this, Minnie. At present our entrenched line of battle extends for some miles or so beyond (from here) Mechanicsville to a mile below the Gaines' Mill farm; our Right flank resting on the Chickahominy River. By the way, this Gaines' Mill and farm is the one formerly owned by Grand Pa Trueheart—pardon bad writing—the Yanks are shelling us, we are all squatting behind the breastworks and every time a shell whizzes close over head, my neighbors, at either elbow give a dodge, and thus jog my hand. Mr. Grant's people have been in the elegant and now classic language of the old ape, "peging away" at our lines in vain, but strenuous efforts to break through

Much Dreaded Place

◡

and consumate his boasted "on to Richmond" project. So far has only resulted in piles of Yankee dead "so that vultures shall be fed on his minions." I send enclosed a beautiful song composed by a Ky lady. Have you all met with it before?

God has been with us and blest our efforts in this campaign in a more marked degree, perhaps, than ever before. For 33 days Grant with heavy forces, well equiped and under the leadership of the best Generals that the Abolition Nation affords, with the best soldiers that he had in his "Victorious Western Army," has thundered against our earthworks & charged us in from 3 to 10 lines deep; but all to no purpose. While our losses have been unprecedentedly small, they have lost men by tens of thousands. In the battles of the Wilderness, and Spotsylvania C.H., his losses in killed, wounded & missing, are estimated at 60,000. Which figures are owned up to by several of the more independent Northern sheets. On our present line and that about Hanover Junction, they lost at least 25,000. Our losses at the first mentioned places did not exceed 10,000. By many was estimated at only 6,000. Down here we are said to have lost from 1,000 to 1500; certainly it does not exceed 2500. The disparity is so great as to be hardly credible. It is nevertheless so.[12] Our cautious, wise & noble Lee has fought his men behind good breastworks; our cannon being posted along the line every 100 or [1]20 yards. The enemy has been charging us in from 2 or 3 to 8 or 10 lines deep. Our men received their fire till they come close up, and then pour into their bosoms a well directed sheet of fire of minnies, grape & canister, which sends the hireling hosts back in dismay & confusion; leaving the ground in front of our works literally blackened, or rather blued, with their mangled corpses. Again & again they rush to the charge, only to have the fate of the lines that preceded them. What a horrible, what a grand picture to contemplate. Occassionally two lines of our invincible fellows are posted behind simple breastworks of rails, or logs & earth, hastily thrown up with their bayonets, tin plates, cups, etc. (but few spades are to be found in our army), with field pieces with double charges of grape & canister posted at intervals, the Yankees trusting in the multitudes of their boasted numbers, move down upon them, 6, 8 or 10 lines deep;—their arms glitter in the light, the "stars and stripes" flutter in the breeze. On they come in beautiful order, line on line. Nothing breaks the dread stillness that reigns, save the puerile charge-cheer, peculiar to the Yankees, consisting of scattering, feeble "hurrahs" or "huzzahs," spiritless and flat. The first line has come within a 100, 60 or even 40 yards—and on they steadily move. One not acquainted with the fighting qualities of the combatants would expect them to carry everything before them. Presently their cheers are drowned by the deafening roar of a score of our cannon. The grape & canister mow horrid lanes in their ranks, and each rifleman brings down his man. Their line falters, halts, & delivers a scattering fire; breaks, and what's left of them, rush back in confusion upon the next line, where some of them rally, while others break through & fly to the rear. Then there goes up from our fellows a wild defiant shout that's heard far & near—such a shout as they only can give. The next line & the next move up, but less resolutely. They march over the prostrate, bleeding, shrieking comrades of the first line; then too, the fire directed at the first line has played sad havoc with them also; the minnies & the grape & the canister ball, that slew its man in the first line, has victimized those in the line that followed close behind. Yes, they come to the charge, but only to share their predecessor's fate. The "hurrahs" of each succeeding line is more feeble than the one that preceded it. At last they're all repulsed. The smoke clears off revealing the ground blackened, or rather blued, with the mangled carcasses of the vile invaders.[13]

From present appearances, Lee intends to let Grant exhaust himself in attacks on our breastworks, when having gotten his men pretty well demoralized, will then assume the offensive, vigorously, and drive him back to his Abolition den.[14] As I told you in mine to Cally I am Asst. Surgeon to the 8th Ala. Reg't. Infantry, Wilcox' old Brigade, A.P. Hill's Corps, A.N.V. I enclose a letter from Henry which reached me last week. All our friends were well when last heard from. Cousin Mary Blackford's health is impaired, I hear, very much by Mr. B[lackford]'s death. I had a letter from Mary L. Minor which I will also send to you.

I beg that you all will continue to write regularly and send first by one mode of conveyance, then by another. H[enry] and myself will do likewise; and by so doing, we shall at least get letters occasionally.

Best love to all at home, & Sister M[ary] and Mr. J[o]seph, Elvira and Mr. H[oward].

Don't fail to write soon and frequently too.

Your affectionate brother,
Chas Trueheart

Address all letters to H[enry] and me, to me Box 381, Richmond.

Much Dreaded Place

∾

93

Defences before Petersburg, Va,
June 27th, 1864—

Dear Father:

Frequent marches and battles have prevented me from writing home since my letter to Fanny of the 11th inst.

Though you have doubtless seen the account of the movements of Lee's army as given in the papers, I will undertake to narrate things as I saw them, or heard them from reliable sources on the ground when they occurred.

On the 5th of March Grant's Army crossed the Rapidan into Orange Co. where Lee attacked him. The country thereabouts is on the edge of the Wilderness section, and is densely wooded and grown up with underbrush, etc., affording no position for artillery.[15] The battle of several day duration fought here, was consequently indecisive, tho' the loss sustained by the enemy was enormous; we taking the initiative only partially and as a general thing fighting behind breastworks.[16] The woods were filled with fallen trees of moderate size, which formed admirable material for the rapid construction of breastworks, and it was surprising to see how rapid the fellows would erect a good protection against minnies with the fallen timbre and dirt thrown up with tin plates, shingles, by hand, etc.; the earth having been first loosened with the bayonett or knives. Our line of battle at some point, would charge the Yankees and drive them back—halt—straighten their lines somewhat, and in ten or 15 minutes time have a little breastwork thrown up, and there awaiting the enemy's advance, till they came close up—say 20 to 30 yards—pour into their dense ranks a destructive fire of minnies, grape & canister. They charged our lines posted behind breastworks, in from 3 to 7 lines deep. Of course we slaughtered them by thousands. Their papers acknowledge a loss of 30,000 to 40,000 killed, wounded, and missing. After several days fighting in this section, both armies moving parallel with one another slowly towards Spottsylvania C.H., they remained drawn up confronting each other at the latter place, and strongly entrenched. Here Grant made desperate efforts again to break through our line; charged our breastwork again and again, sustaining heavy losses, estimated by Northern journals at 20,000 to 24,000. Our losses here were about 5,000 all told. In the Wilderness they were not more than 3,000. This great discrepancy may appear strange, but it is nevertheless, litterally true, and attested to by friend & foe. I should have said in speaking

Rebel Brothers

∼

of the artillery used in the Wilderness, I should have said that tho'
the Yanks used no Artillery, we used some pieces, howitzers, most
effectively. As well as I remember we reached Spotsylvania C.H. on
the 9th of May, Grant left one front under cover of night, and still
moving the left flank made towards Hanover Junction. Lee made a
rapid counter movement, still parallel with Grant and keeping between him and Richmond. This movement began about the 18" or
19" of May. We brought Mr. Grant to a stand again at, or rather
just before, reaching the Junction. Here again some fighting ensued.
Grant left our front again, moving by the left flank; Lee making a
counter movement & keeping between him & Richmond. Thus
both armies brought up in line of battle extending a mile & a half
beyond Mechanicsville in a semi-circle to Gaines' Farm, near where
your Father used to live, I believe. Both armies speedily entrenched
themselves. Grant again made vigorous efforts to break our lines by
his old plan of massing troops and charging our lines with a reckless
disregard of the lives of his hirelings. His dead were piled—literally
piled in front of our works, where they lay and nearly stank us out,
where they failed to fight us. Finding he could accomplish nothing
here, Grant again executed his favorite movement by the left flank,
moving obliquely to & down the James River. This time he sent
forces to re-inforce Butler on the South side; and effected this
movement so quitely that I am of the opinion that by this means,
and the fact that he (Grant) had better facilities for crossing the
river, Lee was rather outdone by the Yankees.[17] Lee had but a poor
chance to watch Grant's movements on the James river flank, as the
latter held both sides the river in rear of his line, and controled the
water for some distance above his gunboats.

It seems that Grant and Butler combined, succeeded in massing
a force on the So. side but more particularly in front of Petersburg.[18]
By this means they drove Beauregard's men from the first line of
trenches on the South side of Petersburg, and at one point got possession of a part of the inner line of works (below on the river on
the Prince George Co. side). They also got to the Richmond & Petersburg R.R. and did it some damage. Lee, however, crossed the
river rapidly by pontoon bridges 7 or 8 miles below on the James (at
Drury's Bluff), and not only drove the enemy back from the R.R.
but came to the rescue of the "Cockade City" in time to lend a hand
in repelling the Yankees. A portion of the fortifications were taken
back, but the enemy still holds a small part of them, which Lee
don't take because the good attained wouldn't justify the loss of

mean revenge, to burn, destroy and desolate every thing within his reach. Tho' it must be confessed that these raiding parties are sent with the ostensible object of cutting our rail road communications, which would be perfectly legitimate. But as I said before, they burn and destroy all kinds of property, insult our women, and kill [unarmed and unoffending citizens]. This raiding party set out some time about the 16" of last month. Striking the Weldon and Petersburg rail road some 7 or 8 miles from this city, they burnt a few stations, and tore up a few miles of the track. They then moved on through Dinwiddie, Nottoway, Pr. Edward, & Charlotte, and returned through Mecklinburg, Lunenburg, Brunswick, Greensville, & Dinwiddie. In their route, they destroyed as much of the South Side (running from Lynchburg to Petersbg), and the Richmond & Danville road, as possible; stole horses, mules, negroes, burnt houses etc., as usual. But they had to do everything hurriedly, as Lee was on their track with his Div. of cavalry. They failed to destroy the High Bridge, and other important structures, they being guarded by Infantry who drove them off.[20] At about the same time, Hunter, who had defeated our forces under Jones in the Valley, captured Staunton, and destroyed the Va. Military Institute, was advancing on Lynchburg. Sheridan (Yankee) in chg. of another cavalry raiding party, was moving on Charlottesville through King & Queen Caroline, Spottsylvania, & Louisa. Grant all the while was thundering away below Richmond and Petersburg. Things began to look rather gloomy. But by the help of God, the valor of our soldiers, and the wisdom of our leaders, they were foiled and severely punished [at every point. Ewell's old Corps, under Maj.] Gen'l Jubal Early was detached from this army, and sent to meet Hunter. He defeated him near Lynchb. and chased his flying army out into Southwestern Va. captured, or caused them to destroy all his wagon trains, artillery, etc.[21] Then leaving a sufficient force to watch and farther chastise his demorolized army, Early started down the Valley, and is now probably crossing into Md., on his way to Penn, McNeill's Rangers accompanying him.[22] Washington is thus threatened, and this part of the country will probably be more or less relieved. Maj. Genl Hampton, with two divisions of cavalry, met Mr. Sheridan's party near Trevilian's Depot; routed him, making large captures, and causing him to retrace his steps in hot haste, and take refuge at Whitehouse on the York river.[23] Grant's immediate army below Petersburg, has not only failed to gain any important advantage in its present position, but has met with sundry serious reverses on its flanks. My

Much Dreaded Place

∼

97

you girls would write that often, what a host of letters would gladden my heart, & Henry's. Perhaps you will argue that even if you wrote that often, we would not get half your letters. Certain it is, the more letters are started to us, the more will reach us. It's not necessary for you all to go to the trouble and expense of sending all your letters by private hand. The Confederate mail is now running between this and the Trans-Miss. country; and in the present more or less completely blockaded state of the Miss. River, and occupation of intervening country by our troops, it doubtless is brought through with considerable regularity and certainty. I would advise that you all avail yourselves of every opportunity for sending letters by private hands gratuitously; send occasionally by the individuals who charge so much per letter. In addition to these letters, dispatch others through C.S. mail, prepaying them with 40 [cent] postage stamps.

The destruction of the railroads leading South, by the recent Yankee raids, have prevented the reception of any mail from that quarter for two weeks, until within the last four or five days. I hope to get several letters from home when the Richmond Army P.O. department where all army mails are sent for distribution shall have been able to assort the accumulated bags of mail matter. I am happy to announce that the Rich. & Danville, R[ichmond] & Petersburg, Petersbg and Lynchburg, and P. & Weldon road, which had been somewhat injured by the raiders, have all been repaired again, and are running as usual; and that too, with troops so disposed as to be pretty certain of deterring the enemy from interrupting them again. The Orange, Alexandria & Lynchbg road is also repaired, and the Central too, or soon will be. So Grant's mighty efforts in the shape of pusilanimous raids, the while his "grand" whipped army, cowered behind their breast works, or vented their spleen in shelling the city, have proved, as all the numerous "on to Richmond" movements, miserable failures. You all have probably heard ere this of Early's expedition into Md., D.C., Pa., etc. After chasing Hunter & Co's army far out into S.W. Va. having several times defeated them, and caused them to destroy most of their artillery, wagons, etc., he moved rapidly back to Staunton then down the Valley into Pa. and Md. He entered Md. about the 6th or 7th of this month. After destroying a considerable amount of the Rail roads, Government property, etc., in & about Washington & Baltimore, making heavy demonstrations against both places, with a view, it is supposed of relieving Richmond & Petersburg, gathering in all the cattle, horses, etc., and everything useful to the C.S. government & army, he came

Much Dreaded Place

99

back into Va.[26] He is reported to bring with him about 3,000 head of beef cattle, 7000 horses & mules, besides furnishing the cavalry, artillery, and other teams in his Corps, with fresh horses.

'Twas expected (by the people at least) that Washington or Baltimore, or even both places, would be captured. The more "blood thirsty" of the C.S. people and news papers were anxiously looking for the system of house burning and devastation of country practiced upon our people by Yankee armies and raiders, being meted out to the "loyal people of Md." in retaliation. But wisely, or not, (I am at a loss to decide) no houses were burnt, except the splendid country mansion, some 5 miles from Balt. belonging to the Abolition Gov. Mr. Bradford of Md. When our men were turning Mrs. B. & family out to set fire to the establishment, she entered strong remonstrances; Thereupon they showed her a written order from Brig. Gen'l Bradley T. Johnson (a Marylander) C.S.A., that the house & everything in it be burnt in retaliation for the burning of Governor Letcher's house, etc, by Hunter & Co. So say the Yankee papers.[27] They further state that the "Rebels treated Mrs. B. and family with marked polit[e]ness," quite an admission to Southern gallantry. Only a few other houses, belonging to obnoxious Lincoln public functionaries, were molested.[28] The invasion of Md. and threatening of Balt. & Washington, while it caused a good many troops to be withdrawn from Grant's Army, failed to relieve Petersburg. But by many it is contended that the move into Md. was undertaken more in hopes of obtaining cattle and horses, than anything else. But I am at a loss to say as to this. Grant's Army still confronts us, tho' its lines are contracted on the right (their left), so that the Weldon and Petersburg R.R. is less exposed to inroads.

Some time has elapsed since any active operations (comparatively speaking) have taken place; not since the 29th last month, when the Div. to which I am attached, now temporarily commanded by Brig. Gen'l Mahone, threw its formidable self in the path of return of the Wilson & Kautz raiders, causing them, (as I recounted in a recent letter) a deal of trouble. I say quiet—comparative quiet— has prevailed, but scarce a minute passes without the sharp crack of the Enfield rifle, or the thunder of artillery rudely breaking in upon the silence. So accustomed to this have we become, that we sleep, eat, and chat, while the missiles of death are whistling past us. Every now and then, some poor fellow gets knocked over,—killed or wounded; his comrades of the Ambulance corps bear him off to the ambulances that stand a few hundred yards in the rear of the breast works, behind some abrupt, steep hill that affords a grateful protection. The Asst. Surg. dresses his wound, and sends him several miles to the rear, to the field Infirmary. Or the fellows dig a hasty grave for the reception of his mangled corpse. They cover him up and some friend carves in uncouth characters his name, Company & Rgmt., on a rough head board to mark his resting place; or his grave remains unmarked, and is soon trodden down by other troops that occupy the ground. But altho' the "shelling" and piquet fire is so continuous, but a small number of men are hurt.

Our piquet line at the part of the line occupied by our Div., is some 800 or 1000 yards in front of the breast works. A truce or rather tacit cessation of fire has prevailed between the opposing piquet lines, which are only from 75 to 150 yards apart, and I go several times daily out to our line to exchange papers with Yanks, hear the news, etc., and to graze my riding horse, the forage rations being so small as not to keep an animal in marching trim.

But I find that I am near the close of this desultory epistle, and I must devote a small space to this, my eighth page, to other than war matters.

My last from Henry was of the 1st July, which I forwarded in one to Father (as well as I remember). He has gone to Md. & Pa. with Early's Corps. I saw Will Overton yesterday—he tells me the late raiders under Sheridan did his neighborhood no harm, being fully occupied by their Rebel friends of Hampton's Cavalry. Uncle Wm. has heard from H[enry] & Mr. Edlow Bacon since their arrival in Md., both were well.

My best love to Father & Mother, Cally & Fanny, Sisters M[ary] & E[lvira], Mr. J[oseph] and Mr. H[oward]. No time to read it over so excuse ommissions, etc.

> *Yr. loving brother,*
> *Charles W. Trueheart*

[Probably July 1864]

. . . farther to the left where, tho' we 'wd have no hard marching, or hard fighting, we should have to keep to the trenches continually till after dark, when one would be continually annoyed by Yankee sharpshooters, mortar shells, etc.

Petersburg is very much, tho' not entirely, desserted by the people. They seem to have become accustomed, if such a thing is possible, to the passage of the noisy, death-dealing, missiles, as they rush through the air above, or crash through the buildings around

Much Dreaded Place

∽

them. Tho' these much dreaded shells are not so very destructive of life and houses, as one unaccustomed to them would be disposed to imagine. The enemy has shelled this place for several weeks, night and day, and I don't think that more than a dozen people (citizens) have been killed or wounded by them. I rode down into that part of the city where most of the shells fall, to see how things were going. I found a number of families still at their homes; particularly the poorer class of the people, free negroes, etc. Twas truly surprising how utterly indifferent the women and children had become to passing shells. As I rode along, a huge one bursted about a hundred yards from two ladies who were crossing the street. I expected to see them faint, scream, run, at least dodge, but no, they only looked at it and went on without even quickening their pace. A Sergeant in my rgmt. has his parents and sisters living in town; he says his sisters (two young ladies) hooted at the idea of being driven from their home by the shells of the vile Yankees. Seem to think it unpatriotic, and beneath a Southern woman to manifest much fear on such an occasion; and it was only after one of the missles had burst in their bed chamber, while they were in the room below, that the family could be persuaded to seek a place of greater safety. Probably, one reason why more of the people don't leave is because they know that they could not find food, etc. elsewhere. Many families are living in tents a few miles out of town; but tents are as hard to get as houses; and certainly very comfortless and inconvenient to ladies & children.

We had expected heavy shelling of the city, and our works—and probably a general assault—but the day passed off in comparative quiet, only occasional shells being thrown into the city. Martial music was more plentiful on both sides than usual, the Yankees indulged in "Yankee Doodle," "Hail Columbia" etc., while our bands played Dixie, etc. The enemy made a grand display of the Stars and Stripes—typical of Federal tyranny and a consolidated government; while we threw to the breezes our little battle flags, many of them riddled by bullets, and soiled and blood stained by a score of battles; and State flag emblematical of State's Rights. No firing was going on in front of our part of the line, and the opposing piquets came fearlessly out of their holes, and sat cross-legged on the ground looking at each other, or engaged in cards etc. cooked their food etc. In the afternoon, a large dog that belonged on the Yankee line, was coaxed into our line by some of the men who attached a canteen to his tail and started him off. The affrighted animal ran for 3/4 of a

Rebel Brothers

mile down between the two lines, producing roars of laughter and shouts of applause.

You ask me to advise you as to what course you ought to pursue towards soldier visitors, who are your inferiors in education & social position.

This involves an important question. A woman's social position & happiness in both single and married life, depends upon the young people she accepts as her associates. I should advise by all means, and *at all hazards*, to permit the attentions of only those who are your equals. Because a man is a soldier is no reason he should be received into the bosom of the family circle "hail fellow well met." Give the soldiers something to eat when you have it to spare, but don't ask them into the parlour to entertain them. If they call & ask for you, exercise a lady's privilege, and beg to be excused. Do this to a fellow a few times, and he will soon see that you want none of his company. Please don't accept as associates, men that H[enry] and myself would feel ashamed to meet on terms of equality. Remember Nanny Edmonds—she married a low-bred fellow—a printer.

Give my best love to all the dear ones at home. Write us frequently. Bear in mind what I say about the soldiers.

Your loving brother,
C. W. Trueheart

Defences around Petersbg.
August 6th, 1864

Dear Henry

My last letter to you was of the 28th ult; on the 3rd inst. I forwarded to you in one envelope, sundry letters from Mother, Cally, and Sister Mary, received on the previous day. These letters were addressed to me, care Wm. M. Blackford, Esq., save one to "Lynchburg." The latter was forwarded to me by Doctor Minor; the others by some means or other reached the University and were forwarded by Uncle John. I can't say where or how they came to be so very, very long en route. Possibly they may have laid at Mrs. Blackford's for some time (i.e. those forwarded by Uncle J.), but I hardly think Mary Isabella would have let them remain there more than a few weeks at most. 'Tis certainly unsatisfactory very, to have our letters thus old when we read them; but better thus, than not at all. For the past four months, (since being assigned to the field) I have instructed them in every letter, (and I have written 14 in that time) not to direct any more letters to Lynchburg, but to send all for you and myself, to my address Box 381, Richmond. The box is rented by myself and my friend Alexander. He forwards to me, wherever I happen to be. When you write to any of them give instructions to have all letters sent to Richmond.

From the tone of the letters, may we not infer that the family are getting on pretty well? In my next, I shall interrogate them particularly as to their welfare. Henry, I'm going to get a transfer to the Texas Brigade; indeed, I sent up an application for it some 8 or 10 days ago; shall probably hear from it tomorrow or next day; tho' I do not much expect to succeed in obtaining it by this effort. Surgeon Powell, Chief Surg. of Hill's Corps, the only one of my superiors, who refused to approve it, at this time, promised to do so at the close of the present campaign, if I still insist upon it. In the mean time, I shall make application directly to Surg. Genl. Moore, with whom I think I can carry my point through the influence of some of my friends. By being in our Texas [Brigade], there are sundry advantages that I shall enjoy in addition to those now mine. Everybody from our state visiting this section, communicates either in person or by letter with the Brigade; so with persons going to Texas, furloughed, detailed or discharged men, and others. The Brigade being very small and all efforts to recruit it, or even to bring back those gone home on furlough, it is not at all improbable that it will be sent to the Trans- Mississippi this winter.[29] Or should the war come to a close during my life time and yours, I would thus stand a better chance than in any other command, to go back to the Lone Star State at an early period. You being an independent, can go as when and where you choose; so we could both get off homeward bound together, or should you be unable to do so, I could easily get a transfer from the Brigade so as to remain in this state with you. The officers (Brig. Surgeon and Reg't. Surg. in Texas) seem very desirous to have me. Tell me in your next what you think of this matter. By the way, when do you propose to turn your face homeward? Or have you laid any plans? When does your Assessor and Collectorship expire? And will you not then be liable to conscription? If so, what will you do? Will you join some command in Virginia, or go to the Trans Miss. country? Can you lawfully remain with McNeill after (in consequence of the expiration of your Ass. & Collectorship) you cease to be an exempt? You know the Act authorizing the organization of partizan troops, specifies that they shall contain and be composed of only such men as are exempt, or at the time of enlistment in such partizan command, residing within the lines of the Enemy, and thus placed beyond the operation of the Confederate Conscription Law.

You beg that I will keep you posted as to military operations in this quarter. The next movement after the repulse following the explosion of the . . . that is the next movement of importance—occurred on the North side the James.[30] On the 13" or 14" ult. the enemy by massing troops, gained a temporary advantage in the shape of the capture of some breast works on our extreme Left; but 'twas only a temporary advantage, for the works were retaken. On the 14" additional troops were sent from Petersburg to the North side, our Brigade among others. We set out at midday Sunday, 14" ult. during a heavy and continued rain, and with only a few minutes notice. After a march of 3 or 4 miles through mud and water, we embarked on the cars—Petersbg. and Rich. R.R. that being the nearest point the trains can come without danger of being knocked to pieces by Yankee shells. I and another Asst. Surg. were assigned to the charge of the Brigade, our horses being sent through by a turnpike. We disembarked at 11" p. m. in two miles of Drury's Bluff. The horses not coming to hand, we set out on foot with the troops. After a tramp of 1 1/2 miles through the mud, my brother Med. concluded he "would have to wait for his horse." Feeling that duty demanded that I should keep up with the Brig., I determined to make the trip on foot. We crossed the James on a pontoon bridge just above Drury's (here is drawn a sketch of the pontoon bridge). There are two pontoons, and one permanent bridge with a draw to it, crossing the river at this point—All beautiful structures. After marching some 10 miles, we halted at 4 a.m., and laid down in wet clothes to catch a little repose. At 6 o'clock we were roused & set out again. Marched 1 1/2 miles and came to the point on the line, that we were to occupy. I have seldom been so much fatigued by a march. Unaccustomed to walking, I had marched in heavy cavalry boots & spurs, with my baggage on my back, through rain, mud & water, and the night quite dark, for a distance of 12 or 15 miles. The men were badly used up by it. Not more than 1/4 or 1/5 kept up; but they were strewn along the road side fast asleep. Several got hurt by being run over by the wagons that followed the troops. I became so sleepy and worn out that I lost my invaluable india rubber blanket, by its slipping from my grasp as I walked along in my sleep. I also lost a spade that I undertook to carry for one of the men who was sick. But 'twas on the 16th that the tug of war came. I had

Much Dreaded Place

~

established my field hospital about 400 yards in the rear the line of works on the Darbytown road. Genl Lee, and two of his staff, were riding up and down the road, or sitting their hors[es] in an expectant attitude. At about 8 or 9 a.m. the ball opened by the enemy's assaulting our position most furiously. The artillery fire was terrific. Genl Lee rode to & fro on the road, sat listening most intently (a dense pine wood concealed the contending troops completely) as tho' to gather information of how the fight was going, from the direction and character of sounds of strife. Shell and minnies frequently struck or passed very near him, and I was very fearful for his safety, But he seemed quite indifferent to the dangers of the hour. For several hours he remained near where my hospital was. At one time the Yankees broke through our line, and captured several hundred yards of the works. 'Twas where Wright's Ga. Brig. was strung out in one rank. The enemy massed in heavy force, under cover of a dense wood, which so concealed their advance as to enable them to come within from 20 to 40 yards ere exposed to our fire. Thus they received only one fire from the Georgians; and ere they could load up again rushed in upon them with impunity. The Brig. gave way in confusion, many being killed or captured. Their young Brigadier Girrardy, only a few days before promoted to that rank from a Captaincy for gallantry, etc., fell a corpse, shot through the head while vainly endeavoring to rally his men.[31] I said the Yankees broke through our line—Yes, and many of the men of the routed Brig. came running past. Genl Lee pressed me into service, and made me do the work of Provost Guard (rear guard) in stopping stragglers, and sending them to their respective comds, dressing the wounded, and attending to the sick. When he halted a fellow, and he plead sick or wounded, and couldn't show blood as evidence of the truth of his assertion, he called on me to examine, etc. To some, those who were going to the rear with an insufficient excuse, he administered a stern rebuke, and sent them to their commands under guard. To the wounded he gave consolation most sweet and soothing. To the troops, fresh or just rallied, he uttered words most cheering. His word seemed to exert a magical influence upon all within hearing. Tho' charged in this trying hour with the direction of the movements of an army—tho' weighed upon by the mighty responsibilities that devolved upon him, with his well ballanced, comprehensive mind; he attended to the smallest matters—was accessible to all—even the lowest private. Now he directed thirsty men with bunches of canteens, where to find water; now he scrutinized a

Rebel Brothers

~

wounded man, and ordered someone to attend to his wants. With heartfelt sympathy, he expressed regrets etc. at the killing or wounding of his officers or men. He addressed them as "my friends." To show how closely he notices what's passing around him.

I will narrate an incident in my next. This must close now to go to the mail.

Your loving brother,
C. W. Trueheart
Asst. Surg.

Defences around Petersburg
Aug 7th, 1864

Dear Henry

Your letter of—(about 29th ult. reached me on the 3rd inst. No letters from home later than those you speak of having already received. I have been in the habit of writing to some member of the family once a week of late, and forwarding all your letters in mine. Aunt Livy and Clara both sent me letters to forward to Mother; they are written in a tone of heartfelt affection for her, besides containing much in regard to persons and things in Va., which will delight the dear old lady's heart greatly. I have written to Mary Overton (Uncle Charles' daughter) with a view to inducing her to write to Mother too. I will enclose Aunt L's accompanying to me, for your perusal. If you deem either or both of them worth the trouble and postage forward them in your next letter home.

I will forward you from time to time, coppies of the Central Presbyterian, which I doubt not will interest, and I hope may serve in some measure at least, to promote that growth in Christian graces and enlightenment in religious truths, which I trust, my dear fellow, you will not fail to strive after continually. Do not let the life of a soldier, with its sore trials and temptations, cause you to lose sight of the great, grand objects of life—this uncertain fleeting life—or to make shipwreck of the faith that is in you. And pray for me (as I do for you) that I may be preserved body and soul, through this fearful war.

I also sent you the Semi-Weekly Enquirer. Let me know if you receive the papers. I think they will prove a pleasant pastime for you.

I have not written to you of late as often as I would have liked to, because I was in doubt as to your getting them. I send this letter to Harrisonburg, and dispatch another containing extracts from this, addressed to you thus;—McNeill's Partizan Rangers, Imboden's

Much Dreaded Place
⁓

Cavalry, Early's (2nd Army) Corps; in hopes that it may reach you sooner than this sent to Harrisonburg.

And first as to that horse. You are mistaken in thinking Petersburg an invested city, or that I have no use for a riding horse. The Yankees do not occupy more than 1/4 or 1/6 of a circle, the center of which is the Cockade City, their line immediately operating before and against it, is probably about 5 to 7 miles; ours, the arc of a smaller circle, say 3 to 5 miles. The Div. to which I belong is on the extreme Right, and is constantly liable to rapid moves to other parts of the Line, as on the 30th ult. (of which I will say something further along) and to be called upon to make hasty and lengthy marches out on the line of the Weldon and Petersburg railroad, to repel the Yankees and guard the road. Then I have to go almost daily, to the Field Hospital, a distance of 1 1/2 or 2 miles. Then too, it is hardly probable that we shall remain in this state of comparative inactivity, for the remainder of this campaign,—certainly not till the close of the war: and even if I did not now need a horse, I certainly should when we come to make an extended march. The duties of an Asst. Surgeon, when his Regiment is on the march, are of such a nature as to make it imperatively necessary that he should be mounted. Indeed it is conceded on all hands here, that he stands more in need of a horse than any officer in the rgmt. Upon him falls in great part, besides attending to the sick, the onus of keeping up the stragglers. His place (and he is expected to keep it) is in rear of rgmt. If a soldier falls to the rear, claiming to be too sick to keep up, he is arrested by the rear guard, and the Asst. Surg. has to stop and make an examination of the case, and decide whether the man is capable of marching with his company: a soldier faints, or is taken sick, etc., the Asst. must stop, examine and administer needful remedies, give the man a pass to "march at his leisure," ride in ambulance, or send him under guard, or otherwise, to his company officer. Not infrequently there being none of the Ambulance corps at hand, he has to get the man water, stop to have him put in the ambulance, etc. All this throws the poor little Asst. far behind his rgmt., and he must if on foot, double quick, to overtake it and be in place to attend to his duties. I stood it on foot till I was so used up that our Brigadier took compassion on me, and allowed me to ride a Government horse, till I could supply myself with one. But apart from all this, my toe nails, by growing into the flesh, have so lamed me up as to make walking utterly out of the question; and I had determined, in the event that I fail to obtain a horse by borrowing, to sell out my

Rebel Brothers

watch, etc. and get one even tho' it be a broken down old hack not worth having.

I couldn't consent to your "giving me a horse" as you so kindly offered to do when I have established to your satisfaction that I really need one; but I should be very glad if you will lend me one of your numerous captures, if you have it to spare. The forage allowed by government, with what I can "pick up" will keep him in good order—certainly during the summer & fall—and if I find that I can't keep him up when I go into winter quarters, I can get Uncle Lanty, Uncle Wm. O., or Cousin Wm. Minor (of Albemarle) to winter him for me. Should he get killed in battle, having been appraised, the value will be paid me by Govt. Now as to getting him down here: you could have him sent to some point near the [Virginia] Central [Rail]Road, and I could get a few days leave and come up after him; or you might take a short leave and come to some point over the mountains, and I come up to meet you. But probably you could devise some plan, better than I could.

As to the boots, Henry, don't put yourself to any special trouble about them. I have one pair that I obtained from one of the men on tolerable terms; giving my shoes and $25.00 boot; [but have them] made if you can on reasonable terms, and without much trouble. Try to get me some pocket handkerchiefs, neckties, shirt collars, shirts, socks, or the like.

Aunt Livy says in her letters "they write me from Prospect Hill that nothing has been heard from Henry for some weeks." She then inquires very particularly for you, and begs I will write and let her know if you are safe, etc. I infer from this that you are dropping off in correspondence with—— I am sorry to see it. If you feel assured that your affections are not misplaced; that the object is worthy of them; you ought certainly to perservere in such case. I say, if the game is worth having, it's worth waiting and working for. Of its worth I am convinced, and I know her well. Woman has no means of testing man's sincerity & constancy, ere she takes him to her embrace, than by keeping him for a time on probation at arms length. Don't be fickle. "Faint heart never won fair lady." Perseverance conquereth all things—yes, even a willful woman. Do try to write more frequently.

Affectionately your brother,
C. W. Trueheart

Haven't time to read this letter over, but pardon all ommisions, and note and send misspelt words. Charles.

Find I burnt Aunt L's letter by mistake.

Much Dreaded Place

⌇

Left of our line,
2 miles below Richmond,
August 16th, 1864.

Dear Thomas M. [Joseph]

On Sunday last at noon, when torrents were falling, two Brigades of our Division (Anderson's) Wilcox' old Brig., and Wright's Ga. Brigade, were dispatched from Petersburg defenses to this part of the Confederate line, the enemy having transferred forces hither as tho' he contemplated attempting something out here.[32] We marched three miles and then took the Rich. & Petersburg railroad. I and another M.D. were ordered to take the cars with the troops taking the whole Brig. We disembarked within 1 1/2 miles of Drewry's Bluff at 9 p. m. and took up our line of march, for this point. After marching a short distance, my brother Med. concluded, that he would wait for his horse, which was being ridden through by one of the men. But I declined waiting for mine, as I did not deem it consistent with orders and duty, and determined to make the march on foot. We marched till 4 o'clock next morning to reach this place. Being unused to marching of late, and encumbered with heavy cavalry boots, I was much used up by the trip through the rain. Became so fatigued and sleepy, that my oilcloth one of the best I ever saw, and to me in the field, an invaluable article [was lost] August 18th—Just here the battle opened suddenly and tremendously upon us. The shell and Minnies came so thick and fast I had to stop writing and look to other more important items in soldier-life's drama.

I lost that oilcloth, it slipped from my grasp as I was walking asleep I suppose. The command was halted at 4 o'clock in the morning, and told to get what sleep they could—wet to the skin I lay down in the rain without covering or anything between me and the ground and slept soundly for 1 or 2 hrs., when we were roused to resume the march to take position on the line; not more than 1/3 or 1/2 the men and officers of the line had been able to keep up and 10 o'clock a.m. found them still stretched along the road for many a mile fast asleep. But why do I talk thus at length of such an every day occurence, of the hard march! 'Tis not because I have not endured my share of them but because I was all unaccustomed to walking on such marches of late and this one made a deep, a painful impression upon me. I was stiff and sore at the time of writting.

I said the battle opened tremendously with shell and Minnies falling thick, Genl R E Lee and Staff were standing on horseback near by.[33] He seemed restless, rode up & down the road, put his hand to his ear frequently to catch the direction, etc. of the sound of strife. He well knew that our force over here on the left was small, that at the part of the line thus suddenly and vigorously assaulted, the troops were strung out in one rank. His fears were not ill founded. The enemy had massed a heavy force under cover of a large body of woods, and near this line, and suddenly hurled them on this weak part of our extended line. After a brief, (and spiritless) resistance Wright's old Brigade gave way and fell back in confusion with considerable loss in killed, wounded and more especially in prisoners. Gallant Brig. Genl Girrady, but a few days before promoted from a Captaincy, was among the lamented dead. He was shot down while trying to rally and lead his men against the foe. These bull dog Alabamians had a large share in driving the exultant Yankees back and retaking the lost works. Not more than 3/4 of an hour did the vile wretches hold them, and deadly enough did pay for that 3/4 of an hour, as the battleground thickly strewn with their dead and wounded, negroes and Yankees lying side by side, told in words traced in blood. Our loss in prisoners was equal to or even surpassed theirs, but theirs in killed and wounded greatly exceeded ours.

Genl Lee busied himself in rallying and reassuring the troops, who had been driven back. To some he used words of gentlest kindness, praising them for what they had accomplished; others he sternly upbraided and ordered them back into the fight. His presence and words seem to exert magical influence on both classes. He addressed them thus, "my friends, rally, and go back and help your fellow soldiers, drive those people back—we must drive them back, and retake those works." To wounded men and officers he was all tenderness and sympathy. For some time I was the only Surgeon thus near the line of battle at this point (on the Darbytown road) and as the wounded arrived and their injuries being cared for the Genl would ride up and inquire for their welfare and ordered me to dress wounds and send off out of danger, in ambulances all, without regard to what particular Brigade, etc. they belonged to. Time and again he called me up to examine men, who were going to the rear under plea of sickness & wounds—or again he would make me do rear guard duty sending me hither and thither to halt and turn back men who were running out of the fight (this was in the beginning of the engagement before the wounded began to come out). One poor fellow was brought out with his leg carried away just below the

Much Dreaded Place

knee by a grape shot; another with one arm taken off near the shoulder. Being much exposed to the fire I did not deem it prudent to keep the lives of these men thus exposed, only to apply dressing, that would be removed on their arrival at the hospital, a mile & a half distant so after administering brandy to one with the lost leg (he was nearer dead then from shot and there was no danger from hemorhage) and taking measures to prevent hemorrhage in the one with the lost arm, I sent them off as speedily as possible to the Hospital. The one with the leg shot off died in 10 minutes after he started, and his corpse was laid on the roadside. The other went on and was doing well when I last heard from him. The Genl met the ambulance and after getting past me turned back and asked me if I had seen "a man with his arm shot off," I told him I had just sent him off to the Hospital, "The wound had no bandage on it, Doctor," rejoined the Genl. I explained the reason to him, he seemed satisfied and rode on. I cite this to show the interest he takes in the wounded of his Army, and how closely he observes what is going on around him.

My latest from Henry, forwarded to Fanny in a recent letter from me tells me that he is well. Mail communication 'twixt this and the lower Valley of Virginia are so infrequent and uncertain, that I seldom hear from the dear fellow nowadays.

Tell Sister M[ary] that her most welcome letter of March 10th, 1864 came to hand safely today, will reply in a few days. Ask her for my sake to abbreviate the name of my namesake by dropping the T. Charles Henry is enough for all purposes, practical and ornamental. Tell her not to fail to do this if she doesn't I shall certainly disinherit the young man. Love to Sister M. [Mary], and your mother. Kiss the children for me, my kindest remembrances to my old, faithful friend Mag.

Affectionately your brother,
C. W. Trueheart

N.B. Address me at Richmond Box 381.

Petersburg, Va.,
August 24", 1864.

Dear Sister Mary

'Twas with no small degree of pleasure I assure you, that I read and re-read your letter of 16" March last, received by me only on the 18" ult. I had really begun to think that you were so absorbed with your husband and children, and your farm, etc., as to be forgetful of the existence of your two brothers; or least too much occupied with other matters, to spare them more than a passing thought. Elvira too, has seemingly at least, quite ignored me, tho' I have written to her several times (as also to you), perhaps she has never received any of my letters. Please give my warmest love to her and Mr. Howard and Peyton and Fanny Goode, the only ones of her little flock old enough to have any recollection of me; 'tis such a long, long time since I left home.

My last letter was to Fanny G. enclosing one from Henry to her. 'Twas written among the dead and wounded on the battlefield of last Sunday's fight, for the possession of the line of the Weldon and Petersburg Railroad and was necessarily brief. I had just gotten through dressing wounds, and had laid down on my blanket to sleep off a bad headache, caused by the fatigue and loss of sleep attending the march of the previous night, and the battle of the day, when a letter from Henry and several from other quarters, were handed me by the Brigade mail rider. I immediately set to work, wrote two pages to Fanny, and enclosed them with that from Henry. I herewith send one to me from the same dear fellow. Read it and send it to Mother & companions. Your letter, which was addressed to me & H[enry] jointly, I forwarded to him on the 19" inst., while I was down below Richmond, just after the battle of the 16" inst.; battle of "White Tavern." We repulsed the enemy on that occasion, and punished him severely.

On Sunday last, we sustained a partial repulse. This mishap befell our ("Mahone's"—"Anderson's old") Division. 'Twas the first time during this campaign. The reverse was due to the fact that we went up expecting to meet a comparatively small force, and at only a short distance from the point in the wood where the charge was begun. After a rapid charge of 600 or 800 yards, we came to the piquet line—a very heavy one—drove them pell-mell from their pits, capturing some 300 prisoners. But instead of the line of battle being near at hand, 'twas found to be some 800 or 900 yards farther along. The men had to pass over a level field exposed to a murderous fire from a large number of the enemy's guns that now mowed them down with grape, cannister, schrapnel shell & solid shot. I have never seen so large a proportion of men killed and wounded by artillery.—I had intended writing you an 8 page letter, old lady, but orders have just come for the rgmt to get under arms immediately, and I must reluctantly close. I herewith send letters for Mother from Aunt Livy. Read and forward to her safely.

Much Dreaded Place

〜

My best love to Thomas M. and the children, as also to Mrs. Joseph Sr. My kind remembrances to Mag. if she is still with you. Present my respects to Mr. Edgar & family, Mrs. Henry, & Wright Andrews, Mr. Hamilton Stewart & family and Miss Mary Scott. In haste I must stop with best wishes for you and yours, spiritually and temporaly.

> *Your loving brother,*
> *C. W. Trueheart*

Address me at Richmond.

Defences around Petersburg,
Aug. 28th, 1864

Dear Henry

Today is Sunday: a lovely Sunday afternoon. Nevertheless I must avail myself of the quiet and repose that is mine today to write to you my dear fellow; for tomorrow—nay tonight we may be called upon to resume the weary march and bloody fray. Your letter of the 22nd inst. written from Rockingham Co.—somewhere in Rockingham Co.—you dont say where—reached me this morning; and afforded me much pleasure. My letters to you for the months of June, July, and August are as follows[:] June 4" 27" July 4" 18" 20" August 7" 19" and this present writing. Those from you:—June 23" of 16" July 4" of 1st 28" of . . . Aug 3rd of . . . Aug 21" of 8" Aug. 27" of 22—Remember old fellow that I am situated like yourself as regards letter writing. My duties as Asst. Surg. occupy some portion of my time. Then I have my horse to attend to; do own cooking, etc. so I have but little time—suittable time—for letter writing. My letters home are as follows: June 5" to Minny . . . " to Fanny[—]28" to Father—July 6" to Mother[—]8" to Cally–15 to Minny, Aug. 5 to Fanny[—]16" to Thomas M.[—]22nd Fanny, 25" Sister M[ary,] 28" Elvira. Received from home—June 21st one enclosure of Apr. 16" from Mother & Cally, July 20" in one envelope Mother to H[enry] & C[harles], Feb. 1", August 18" Sister M[ary] Mch. 16" to H[enry] & C[harles]. Now all these letters have been duly forwarded you. How does my count tally with yours?

Of the "explosion of the mine" by Grant's motley crew, on the 30th ult. you have doubtless ere this become fully posted. I have never any where seen such a slaughter as there was enacted. Negroes and Yankees those vile deceivers and ruiners, lay so thick that one could have walked over several acres of ground stepping from one corpse or wounded wretch to another. And in many places you couldn't walk without stepping on their carcasses lying one two or even three deep. Here and there (comparatively speaking) lay some luckless Confederate, a bloody offering on the bosom of Mother Earth—the altar of his country.

The Crater is something which my pen would fail me to describe. Imagine if you can, an immense chasm 80 x 140 feet wide, and 40 feet deep:—in the bottom and on all sides round you see giant clods of earth, from the size of a bushel measure to that of an ox cart, fragments of timbre from the structures of the bombproofs breastworks, etc., pieces of gun, carriages, Small arms, etc., and more horrible still legs, arms, heads, mangled and blackened by the powder strewn in wild confusion by the explosive force. And strewn over all this are the dead and wounded, of either side that fell in the obstinate struggle that ensued after the explosion. Sticking out of the ground here and there, are the bodies of the poor fellows, so suddenly launched into Eternity by the explosion. Some of these men were thrown to a distance of 75 yards. One of the cannon was thrown 35 yards from its place towards the enemy. The negroes who were wounded and lay there for 36 hours before they were attended to, bore their sufferings much better than the Yankees. Scarce a groan escaped them;—or nothing more occasionally one of them would ask in a most abjectly submissive tone, "Master, please give me a little water; I am nigh dead for want of it," etc. I noticed that [a] number of the poor fellows spent much of their time upon their knees, engaged in prayer apparently. Almost all of them stated that they had been forced to take up arms; that they had been most cruelly treated, and worked hard by the Yankees. Those of them who were slaves—(and such came principally from Md. and Va.)—begged that they might be turned over to their old masters. Some of them, goaded on by the white Yankees that stood at their backs, fought with an obstinacy that was really surprising; and held their ground till our fellows came to close quarters and knocked them in the head with muskets, or bayonetted them. One black fellow stood up boldly at a distance of 30 paces, and had a regular duel with the Sergeant Major of our reg't; a fearless, highspirited young Southern blood, armed only with a pocket 6 shooter. He fired at the negro five or six times; the negro the mean while loading and shooting at him as fast as he could. At last he plugged the Sgt. in the forehead. Fortunately his head was as thick as his heart was brave, and the ball glanced upwards inflicting not even a fracture of the skull. The negro is said to have been shot by [one] of our men on the spot. An

Much Dreaded Place

~

officer in our Brigade, having captured a negro in the trenches, told him to turn and fire upon the retreating Yankees; which he did very rapidly, going through the manuel of arms from beginning to end, and down to the minutest detail. The officer made him fire at them thus six or seven times, and then started him to the rear.[34]

The battle occurred on Saturday, 30" ult. The weather was intensely hot and sultry. The putrifying bodies lay there till the following Monday evening. The stench was horrible beyond description. A flag of truce was sent in Sunday afternoon by Burnside, asking leave to bury his dead. 'Twas refused by Gen'l Lee because it did not come from the Commandg. Gen'l Grant. On Monday a truce was agreed upon; and the captured negroes in our hands were made under guard to convey the bodies that were near our works, to neutral ground. Then the Yankees took and buried them. As to Confederate and Yankee losses on the occasion, I presume you are fully posted. They acknowledge a loss of 5,000 killed, wounded and captured; besides which they lost a number of colors, small arms, etc. We lost nothing of the kind. Our total loss by the explosion & fight, in killed wounded and captured did not exceed 1100.[35]

On that field I witnessed some sad scenes. In passing over the battlefield a few minutes after the enemy had been driven back I saw a boy bending over the dead body of a Confederate, taking the contents of his pocket, and as I very naturally supposed, ro[b]bing the dead. I ordered him in harsh terms to stop it at once. The fellow turned his face towards me revealing a countenance, the very picture of distress, and with tears streaming down his sunburnt face, and a voice tremulous with emotion, he said "This, Sir, is my brother and I wish to save the valuables about his person.["] Shocking as it may seem to you, Henry, many—no I won't say many— some of our men are getting heartless & thievish that they plunder all the corpses, without regard to whether they are Confederates or Yankees. At another place I saw an old grayheaded man bending and weeping over the mangled corpse of his son, a lad of 16 or 17. But ere I forget it, I must tell you how a cur dog distinguished himself. He had taken up with the Genl & Staff, and the Brigade generally, and went with them in the charge. When they raised a yell, as they neared the crater, the dog, either braving, or in blissful ignorance of the danger ran along before the rapidly advancing line, and dashed over into the crater barking most fiercely. But he soon came out with a "flea in his ear" and ran off yelping and limping. But I must postpone till my next, telling you more on this subject.

Rebel Brothers

I shall, ere this reaches you, probably be transferred to the 5" Texas, Gregg's Brig. but continue [to] write to me as heretofore for "there's many a slip 'twixt the cup and the lip."

Affectionately your brother,
C. W. Trueheart

Haven't time to read this over, so pardon faults and don't fail to send a list.

Defences around Petersburg,
August 28", 1864.

My dear Elvira

Many months have elapsed since anything more than "love" has passed betwixt us by mail; but never the less, you and yours my dear Sister, are very dear to me; And though I haven't written, you have been daily the subject of my thoughts and prayers. And the first wish of my heart is to come home and be with, and see you all once more.

I visited the Texas Brigade of this army the other day; and finding the officers of that Brigade enjoy much better advantages for communicating with their homes than I do, situated as I now am, in an Alabama Brigade, I at once determined to apply for a transfer to the 5th Texas Regiment. I shall probably get it in a few days, certainly at the close of the present campaign. When this transfer is accomplished, I hope to be able to communicate with youall more frequently and certainly, than for some months past. I trust too, that other advantages will accrue; the Brig. being much reduced in numbers, and it having been demonstrated that recruits or even men sent home on furlough cant be gotten back to this far distant region of the war, it is not improbable that it may be sent to the Trans-Mississippi Army. And so I shall stand a chance for getting home. Henry too, being a non-enlisted freefighter, who goes when and where he choses, can immediately follow in my footsteps. Accompanying this letter I send you the latest received from him. Read it, and pass it, as well as mine, around. I forward all of H[enry]'s to you all. I hope you and Sister M[ary] will try to cause the children to remember and love me. Do write to me or Henry, at least occasionally, and let us know how you and yours are doing in these hard trying times. Where is Brother Bob, and what is he doing? Give me the ages, etc. of the children, from Peyton down to little Nellie; as indeed for any others that have recently arrived. Tell Sister M[ary] that I insist upon it she must drop the "Trueheart" in the cognomen of my little namesake. It's simply ridiculous; the name is enough to

Much Dreaded Place

weigh the poor little fellow down to obscurity. It's well enough for Joneses Smiths etc., to stick three initials before the Surname, but with an outoftheway, F.F.V., name such as Trueheart or Joseph, one Christian name—or two at most, is enough. I have half a mind to drop the William in mine.

Grant's "sieg[e]" of Petersburg, still drags its tedious, bloody length, towards an apparently indefinitely distant termination. He has tried direct assaults sundry times, only to meet with repulse, with heavy loss, and without gaining the smallest advantage. The only permanent success that has crowned his strenuous, butcherly efforts, was what he gained by stealing a night march on Lee after the sundry repulses at Cold Harbour, below Richmond. By hurling his "veterans" against a small force, principally undrilled militia, he did succeed in wresting from us, a part—a small part—of one defensive line of works on the right bank of the river, below the city, wh. enabled him to bring his heavy batteries near enough to indulge in the savage pasttime of shelling without notice, a city filled with old men, women and children. Unfortunately, the position thus captured and misused, was too strong to be retaken by us, without too great an expenditure of precious Southern blood & life. And our noble Lee is ever careful of that. He [Grant] has tried flank movements to our Right (on Weldon Railroad), and on our left (at Deep bottom below Richmond). He has tried raids by cavalry, on the most extensive scale, to cut our rail road communication and thus starve Rich., and Lee's army into surrender. Having failed utterly above ground, he tried it under the ground, but all his grand plans "that were to astonish the world & the rest of mankind,["] came to nought. And today with "the finest army in the world" greatly reduced by the casualties of battle, and the diseases of the tadpole section his men are located in, he can so far from not urging successful offensive operations, barely hold his own.

But I must close Elvira. I shall write to Bro. Bob ere long.

Please don't fail to send an early reply to this letter. Best love to Mr. Howard, and kiss the children for me; and don't let them forget me.

Present my kindest regards to the Rev. Mr McNair, Miss McClellan & Mrs. Reading, Miss Mary Scott, and all inquiring friends.

Love to all at home and at Tom Josephs.

Your affectionate brother,
Charles W. Trueheart.

Address me at Richmond, Box 381. Excuse all epistolary sins of omission and commission in this letter. I haven't time to read it

Rebel Brothers

~

118

8" Reg't Ala. Infantry Wilcox'
old Brig. Anderson's Div.
A. P. Hill's Corps, A.N.V.
Defences around Petersburg,
September 7th, 1864.

Dear Father

Altho' both Henry and I have been wishing for, and by all rules entitled to replies to our various letters, not the first line or even message, has either of us received at your hand. I do beg my dear Sir that you will write to us occasionally at least; and not thus ignore our very existence. 'Twould afford me (apart from other things) much pleasure to have your views upon the civil, political & military aspects of affairs; to know how you are doing in your business, etc. Do write to one or both of us immediately on receipt of this letter.

Grant and his mixed crew of negroes, Germans, French, Irish, English, Spaniards, etc. etc., is still bombing away at Petersburg; no nearer taking it than he was when he first squatted down to the hopeless task before the city. He now calls most lustily for additional re-inforcements, to the "moderate" tune of "100,000 men"—only 100,000 men, to complete the job of taking Richmond, and crushing the "Rebellion." His line now extends from Deep bottom, 12 or 15 miles below Richmond, on the North side the James, to the Weldon Railroad., a distance of 20 miles. He is very strongly and extensively fortified; and has a large amount of artillery, light and heavy, in position, bearing on our works, and some of it on the city. But at every point we are ready for him; and all his efforts by direct assault and flank movement above ground and under ground, have so far, by the blessing of God, the valor of our troops and ability of our leaders, proved utterly futile. The character of the position he occupies, with his gunboats and shipping, and base of supplies close at hand, and the great strength of his works, make it probable that he will be allowed to maintain his position as long as he wishes, and peg away, thus exhausting his strength and that too with very little cost to us.[36] In every attempt Grant has made against us, he has come off badly worsted.

Sheridan, the Yankee Maj. Genl, now in command in the Valley—the lower Valley of Va.—has met with as little, or even less success; for he has not only sustained defeat in every engagement, but been unable to hold his ground against Early, who has pressed him back to Harper's Ferry.

Much Dreaded Place

〜

Genl Hood for some cause or other is forced still farther back into the heart of Ga., whether from lack of men or ability as a leader, is in these parts, a muted point—the latter I think. But reverses seems to have caused only a temporary depression with people here.

Henry is in fine health and spirits; still with McNeill's Partizan Rangers, operating in the lower Valley and Western Va. I expect him over here to see me, as soon as cold weather puts a stop to active operations with his command. I am at present on duty with an Ala. rgmt. but am expecting a transfer to the 5th Texas, of this Army, Longstreet's Corps. My chief reason for wishing the transfer, is the greater facilities I shall have for communicating with my Tex. home. Then too it is not improbable that that Brig. may be transferred to the Trans Miss. this winter, and then I can get home.

Give my love to them all at home, and at Mr. Howard's and Tom Joseph's.

Your attached son,
C. W. Trueheart.

Please mail the enclosed letters.

Defences around Petersburg
Sept. 14th, 1864

Mr. Robt H. Howard
Galveston, Texas.
My dear Sir

The great anxiety that I have for a long time felt, to hear directly from you as to the wellfare of yourself and family, prompts me, after long continued good intentions, marred by a shameful procrastination, to overcome the aversion I have for writing and endite to you this in hopes of eliciting a speedy and lengthy reply. And in writing, I beg that you will not confine yourself to news items, but rather speak at length and without fear of wearying me by a narration of home circle minutia,—the doings and sayings of the children, etc. Tell me too, their respective ages, appearance and dispositions. You remember, I have not seen the dear little things for upwards of four years. One of the most pleasing anticipations that I entertain, looking towards a return home, is being thrown with yours and Tom. Joseph's children; and having them as an object of interest, and of attachment. I am devotedly fond of children; and as I seem doomed by an indefinite continuance of this antimatrimonial War, and a combination of hindrances over which I have no control—such as never being able to bring myself to love or address any women, but those

Rebel Brothers

predestined to tell me nay—I shall have to divide among your children and Tom's those paternal yearnings and the affection, which nature has implanted in my bosom, in so decided a degree. But lest you should be disposed to think me the sentimental individual that I was four years ago, I turn to themes more becoming my years, and gray hairs;—of which latter my head is full. Gray with Wisdom, not years (?) Yes, it is a lamentable glaring fact, that I have grown as gray as a badger. Five months ago, when I came to the field, there were only a few stray white hairs to be seen; but the terrible and continuous hardships to which I have been exposed during this campaign, have pulled me down decidedly. Speaking of getting a wife; Mary Launcelot, Uncle John Minor's daughter, tells me that she wants me to make the acquaintance of a much admired and esteemed friend of her's, Miss Street; who by the way is, if I mistake not, an acquaintance of yours. Can't you tell me of some charms she possesses of character, person or purse, which will serve as an incentive towards taking Mary L[auncelot]'s advice? It's the youngest Miss S[treet]. I dont remember her name.

Grant is still indulging in what he and the Yankee nation are pleased to style investing and "besieging Petersburg & (Richmond indirectly"). The only step which he has recently taken of a nature threatening to put this little city in a state of sieg[e], is making a lodgement on the Petersburg & Weldon Railroad[.] This same Weldon road has already cost him some 15,000 men, 30 pieces of artillery, thousands of stands small arms, and a number of Colors. But we must not thus underrate our adversary. This last effort has been partially successful; for he still hold[s] 3 or 4 miles of the road, & thus prevents our using it for the transportation of military stores, a serious loss to our people.

I have, in late letters to different individuals of our tribe, spoken of the recent engagements occurring in Virginia. And the newspapers have doubtless appraised you all of all of them long ere my letters reach you. Artillery duels, shelling the city and piquet fire with small arms are going on at all hours of the twenty four. Shells screaming or bursting over head; minnies whistling through the air, [k]nocking up the dirt or lodging in the trees near by, and a constant bang of musketry and boom of artillery is the music that we have to sleep, eat, and fight to. Of course everybody is tired of this state of things; and the men and officers often wish that a grand battle—a grand finale to the campaign might come off and put an end to this killing by piecemeal—this whipping the Yankees by detail. I say

Much Dreaded Place

121

whipping, for Lee's men dont entertain the idea of defeat being possible. From present appearances we shall winter here. The enemy have built a rail road from City Point, their base of supplies, to the rear of their line of work for this place. This enables them to transport their supplies through the marshy section that intervenes between the points. It also, unfortunately for us, enables them to make sudden and rapid concentrations of troops on any part of their line. Deserters state that its their intention to connect this with the Weldon road. It is also stated that Grant has impressed all Saw mills below here, with a view of sawing up lumber for building winter quarters. We too are making movements that look towards procuring supplies of wood etc. A short rail road leading to a heavy body of timber north of this place, had been surveyed, and it is said that its construction is being pushed forward. A small canal, suitable for batteaux, running along the bank of the Appomattox, will be another means for bringing us a supply of wood etc. Many seem to dread the idea of wintering here in such close proximity to the enemy; say that the enemy will shell us at pleasure and make it impossible to occupy winter huts with any safety. But I have no fears on that score; the Yankees too must have and occupy huts to protect them and this thing of shelling, is a game that two can play at. I am not sufficiently posted, to say what effect the occupation of the Weldon road by the enemy will have upon our prospects for supplies from Wilmington by the blockade vessels, and from the states South, of this I hear no fears expressed by officers, and those informed on such subjects, as to our ability to procure and transport supplies, for this army. The impression here is that a heavy fight will shortly occur on the Weldon road, or rather, between that road and the South Side, for the possession of the latter. I care not how soon it occurs; we are ready for such an event now. The enemy will have to be thrashed severely to bring them down from the high horse they have mounted in consequence of taking Atlanta.[37] And the sooner its done, the better for us, and the Peace party North. The health of the army is surprisingly good. Nothing save a few cases of intermittent fever, bowel complaint, jaundice, etc. Our supply of medicine is tolerably good, tho' of late they have become more scanty, than ever, heretofore, within my observation. By substituting indigenous remedies, however, we manage to get along tolerable well.[38]

But I am drawing to the close of my last page, and must therefore close this desultory communication. Pardon the scattering style of composition. It has been written under many hinderances, a crowd

Rebel Brothers

◈

around me talking all the time, and part of the time, shells flying over head or striking near by. We have almost become used to such dangerous visitors—intruders, but in spite of me, they will cause my ideas to form and come forth by jerks, and interruptedly. Give my best love to Elvira, and kiss my little nephews and nieces for me, my kindest regards to your brother John.

Yours very truly,
C. W. Trueheart.

Tell Cally her letter of the 29" of July has just come to hand. Address me Asst. Surg. 8" Regt, Ala Infty, Wilcox old Brig. Anderson's Div., A.P. Hill's Corps, A.N.V. Tho' you had probably better direct to Richmond Box 381 simply; then if we have moved, it can be forwarded to me.

Yrs,
Chas.

Defences around Petersburg
September 19th, 1864.

Dear Henry

Your letter of the 7" inst. is the latest received. It reached me on the 14", and I replied to it at some length the same day, promising to write again in a few days telling of an incident connected with Gen'l. Lee, and forwarding a letter from Caroline, received on the 12" inst. I hope in this that the sundry letters forwarded to you on the 3rd inst, from Mother and Cally with a P.S. from Sister Mary have reached you. I cant account for the small number of letters that reach us. Henry L. Allen of bookstore notoriety in Galveston, who is a member of the Washington Artillery stationed near here gets letters quite frequently and that too of late dates. By the way, he has improved considerably with years and knocking about in the World. He spends some part of each day with me; seems to have contracted a decided fondness for me; and is really sometimes annoying by the frequency and prolonged character of his visits and his extreme boyishness. He is a good natured, cheerful, kindhearted fellow; and I am pleased with him;—that is when he dont come too often. But I must tell you of Gen'l Lee.

'Twas at the battle of White Tavern, near Deep Bottom, on the 16" of August. Two poor fellows, one with a leg, the other an arm torn off by a cannon ball, had been sent to my hospital. The fire being heavy and the position an exposed one (only some 400 or 500 yds in rear our works) I dispatched the wounded to the rear, with as

Much Dreaded Place
◡
123

little delay as possible. The one with the arm off was doing well; walked about in the most unconcerned manner looking at and inquiring after the welfare of wounded comrades. The other poor fellow was near dead, from the shock sustained. The Field Infirmary was only 1 1/2 miles farther to the rear, where they could be cared for by the Surgeons, so the first case I hurried off with only a bandage bound round the arm above to control bleeding and with out putting anything around the ragged stump. The other man was pulseless and I did not think could live many minutes, so after administering several doses of brandy while I was dressing other wounds, I started him off in ambulance without putting any dressing to the stump. This man died ere he had gone 1/2 a mile. Presently Genl Lee came down the road, having met the ambulances, one of which contained this man. Having gotten past me he turned back and calling to me said, "Doctor, did you see two men, one with an arm, the other with a leg shot off?" I replied, "Yes, Sir; I have just started them off to the Field Infirmary in an ambulance. He rejoined, "I didn't see any ligature (meaning, I suppose, tourniquet) on his leg." "No, General, none was necessary in that case," I replied. Now what a striking spectacle; the Genl, our chief taking note of every thing going on around him, even to the dressing of a wound.

Since my last to you, I have been applied to to take the post of Asst. Surg. in the rgmt of Sappers and Miners officered by the Engineers. Thus situated I should be less exposed to bullets, be enabled to associate with educated men;—live more comfortably, and have the advantages of access to medical books, etc., and the intercourse of a well-informed M.D. a friend & classmate of mine at the University, who is Surgeon of it. I postponed a reply till I have settled this matter of a transfer to the Texas Brigade. Advise me as to your views in your next.

Hampton, with 5 Brigades of Cavalry, made a raid to Grant's rear a few days since, capturing way in rear of his army, 300 prisoners, 2486 head of splendid beef cattle, 10 wagons, 50 mules, and some small arms, camp equipage, etc.[39]

Try to write more frequently than heretofore. And tell me what are your plans for spending you[r] furlough this winter.

Your attached brother,
C. W. Trueheart.

To—H. M. Trueheart, Valley of Virginia. I saw the beeves, they equal Texas 6 year old cattle. Many of them were branded, and had extensive horns as tho' they might really have been raised in Texas.

Rebel Brothers

Defences around Petersburg
October 1st, 1864.

Dear Mother

The mail of the 29th ult. brought me a welcome letter from Cally to Henry, containing a P.S. from you and her, to me. My last letter home was to Cally; written on the 22nd and of some length too. In future, I shall write to each of our tribe *about* once a year;—that is I shall while absent write one letter a month addressing them to each of you in succession, beginning with Father and so down to Fanny G. In addition to this monthly letter, I shall send one in return for each one addressed to me individually. Those to Henry and me conjointly I shall leave for him to answer; indeed *I* had rather youall wd not thus address letters; let them be to me or him alone. All letters from home are read by and doubtless intended for us both anyway; but let the responsibility of answering the inquiries, etc., rest upon one—not both of us. I wish you all would observe this hereafter.

I shall only be able to write a short letter this time, Mother; it's almost dark, and we are now in the midst of a stupendous struggle with the foe. Last Friday, the ball opened by the enemy's massing troops on our flanks. Every day since then they have been fighting and manoeuvrering at different points along the line. So far, thanks be to God and bravery of our troops and skill of our leaders; the vile foe has gained little or nothing; and while we have sustained a loss of not over 1500 all told, his has been 6,000 to 10,000. But the main fight has not yet come off, and I can communicate little or nothing of military interest; as my Brigade has not been engaged, being with others, assigned to the work of holding the works along the Centre of the line.

[Jubal A.] Early, in the Valley, has now checked the enemy, and is driving them down towards Winchester again. In consequence of the retrograde movements of the Army of the Valley I have not been able to hear from Henry lately, his partizan band being probably in the Yankee's rear, and continually on the go.

I enclose in this, a letter from Mary L[auncelot]. and Uncle John M[inor]., the latest intelligence from our Albemarle friends being therein contained. Your love to Cousin Bettie Hill and other friends has been daily forwarded by me to its destination.

Henry Minor, of whom I have spoken in former letters, is now off on a sick furlough, visiting Uncle John[,] Cousin Mary Blackford, and Uncle Lanty.

Much Dreaded Place

∾

125

I learn that poor Nagle reached Va. only [to] find his affiance dead. Of the particulars I know nothing. I am delighted to find that so many of my letters and Henry's reach you all. Continue to write regularly and frequently. We will do likewise. I believe I have averaged one weekly for the past three months. Say to any of Henry L. Allen's or Jeremy Price's friends *that you are in reach of, that* they are both in fine health.

Fanny C. Minor (now Mrs. Berkley) is now the mother of a fine boy called Lanty. She is one of my decided favorites;—warm hearted, affectionate and sincere, tho' a person of strong prejudices. You would delight in her.

> *Best love to all,*
> *Your loving Son,*
> *C. W. T.*

Defences around Petersburg,
October 9th, 1864.

My dear Cally

Today is Sunday; and as duty will not admit of my going to preaching in the city, (there is none out here, there being too much danger from the enemy's artillery fire) and I am without reading matter, I shall, notwithstanding that it is Sunday, devote an hour to writing to you.

I shall not undertake to communicate army news; but refer you to the enclosed clippings from the Richmond newspapers, as my Brigade did not directly participate in any of the recent engagements, and you can there get a tolerably full account of the fights— at least all that I know about them.

Lee's Army has now been in and about these trenches for over three months. This mode of fighting was novel to this Army; it is more wearing out—in mind and patience certainly, than the open field campaign. Then we fought a battle, the dead were buried, the wounded sent to the rear, and we generally enjoyed a period of comparative quiet, and absence from the presence of the hated Yankees. Now the Stars and Stripes flaunt in our faces, only a few hundred yards distant (indeed, in some places their lines are only 75 or 100 yards apart). The bang of musketry and roar of artillery is heard almost continuously day and night; the shells howling over head, bursting or striking in the earthworks nearby, while the Minnies whiz through the air at every turn. Some poor fellow of our Brigade of 600 is almost daily borne to the rear, killed or wounded.[40] Some days, when the skirmishing is brisker than usual, as many as 6 or 8 are placed hors de combat. I have thus far been most singularly, and I hope mercifully spared, without even so much as a scratch.[41]

A considerable time has elapsed since I heard from Henry. Nor can I gather from the newspapers or otherwise, as to the where-abouts of McNeill's command. I suppose however, that the little band of Rangers are somewhere in the enemy's rear; and hence cut off from communication with this section. I have not yet forwarded your letter of the 8" Aug. containing a few lines from Mother & you to me, less they should fail to reach him; but sent him a synopsis of contents, and will forward them as soon as I learn definitely as to his whereabouts. I subscribed to the Central Presbyterian and Rich-mond Enquirer, to send to him, but unfortunately the Presbyterian seldom comes to hand, strange to say, tho' the Semi-Weekly En-quirer comes almost invariably. I think he must enjoy them very much, cut off as he is from reading matter and news of all kinds. As for myself, I get the Richmond dailies by 8 or 9 a. m. every day. You all must make yourselves easy about H[enry] & me. It's a small mat-ter if we are exposed to hardships; we are both in splendid health, and shall be perfectly satisfied if we can only feel assured that our loved ones at home have the comforts of life. What we ask of you is to write to us *frequently;* and *not* to fail to pray for us, that we may be preserved body and soul, and that what ever befalls our bodies,— tho' it may never be our happy lot to see you all again in this world that we may in that to come

Love to all

Yr loving brother,
Charles W.

Defences around Petersburg
October 17th, 1864

My dear fellow

Your letter of the 10" inst. came to hand today, relieving my mind of a weight of anxiety, any thing but pleasant to be burdened with.—Why I have not heard a word from you since the reception of your letter of the 7" of September—nearly six weeks. And the only allusion made to your Command, at least in any of the newspa-pers that I have been able to lay hands on, was an item contained in one of Sheridan's dispatches to Sec Staunton [Stanton], to the effect that the noted Guerrilla chief, McNeil[l], was mortally wounded and a prisoner.[42] This in connection with the reports that our cavalry had suffered severely and the fact that they had had frequent engagements with, and sustained sundry defeats at the hands of the numerous and well appointed Yankee cavalry; together with your unprecedentedly long silence,—and that too when I felt that you must know that I would be anxious—very anxious to hear if you had come through safe, forced me—almost, forced me—to the conclusion that some mishap had befallen you. That perhaps you were captured, wounded or killed. You must see that I had just cause for my forebodings of ill? Some days since I addressed a letter to your Capt. and was intending to spend the very time spent in writing this, in writing to some of my friends in the Army of the Valley, on the same subject or rather to get them to make inquiries for me—as to you or at least as to the whereabouts and condition of your company.

You speak of having received my letters of Sept. 14" & 19", and Aug. 6" & 28". What can become of others sent. Let me give you a list—a leaf from my memorandum book—Written to Henry Aug. 7" (probably alluded to by you as of the 6" Aug.) & Aug. 19"—Aug. 28"—and Sept 3rd, Sept. 7" Sept 14th—Sept 19", and Sept. 30th". [T]hen too I have sent you sundry newspapers, Semi-weekly Enquirers, Presbyterians, etc. Yours of the 7th ultimo, until this today was the latest from you.

In mine of the 7" Sept., having just received sundry letters from home, and being unwilling to risk the precious documents again to the (unsafe) keeping of the mails, I gave you a synopsis of the contents, and postponed forwarding them till I should hear from you again, and know definitely of your whereabouts, etc. You will be able to get some of the letters alluded to as having miscarried by sending to Hdquarters of Early's Army; as after our people fell back this side of Harrisonburg[,] I addressed them to you thus:—Private [H. M. T.] McNeil[l]'s Partizan Rangers—Cavalry, Army of the Valley. Enclosed in this I send you the letters from home alluded to. Also an envelope and sheet of paper, which may find you in need of such articles. In future I will do likewise when ever I write; i.e. if I can obtain the paper, etc., which are sometimes not to be had out here in the Army.

I was much interested in your account of the condition of things in the Valley, and the doings of McNeil[l]'s little band. I regret that you do not speak more particularly, and at length on such subjects in your letters to me. Please do so in the future. But why can you not forward all letters home through me? I kept pretty well posted as to the arrival and departure of persons from the TransMiss. country and besides my having the pleasure of reading your letters, they would really go to their destination with greater speed and certainty. The 40 [cents] postage on those you have recently dispatched by the C.S. mail, was all required by that mode of conveyance.

In regard to my transfer to the Texas Brigade, I am sorry to say it is—at least until after this campaign—impracticable. But of this I will tell you in my next. I am much hurried tonight; am writing by candle light, being kept too busy during the day in the superintendence of the construction of bombproof room for reception of wounded in this cold weather. But of this too I will tell you in my next.

On last Thursday, Grant made determined and heavy assaults upon our works below Richmond; two in the morning, and one—a prolonged & vigorous one in the afternoon; in all of which his troops were repulsed with heavy slaughter. The greatest vigor is now displayed in sending men to the FRONT from all quarters. As a sample, our Brigade has run up from 800 to over 1,000 in the past two weeks, and men are still coming in. The troops are in splendid health & fine spirits. By today's mail I send a couple of Enquirers.

Pardon all errors of commission & omission; I haven't time to read over; my light is near gone.

> Your brother,
> C. W. T.

Defences around Petersburg
Tuesday Nov. 8", 1864.

Dear Minny:

The year 1864 is near its close, and you have neither written me a word or so much, as sent a kindly message through the letters of other members of the family. The last letter from you, written sometime in Sept. or October *1863*, reached me on the 13th November of that year. You may have written others that failed to reach me. I hope such is the case; I should be sorry indeed to think, that you had been thus forgetful, or even nelectful of me. Never a day passes—nay, many times a day do I think of you and long to see you. Your letter of the— ... , 1863, that reached me on the 13th. Nov. was duly answered, and ever since I have been expecting to get letters from you. I have written three letters to you during this year, viz; on Jan. 4" June 5" and July 15th.

Much Dreaded Place

∼

My last letter home was to Cally on the 28" Ult. Since that writing;—(indeed it was sent from the vicinity of the battlefield) another of Grant's movements on our flanks—on the Weldon R.R. and the North side the James have been made and repulsed with considerable slaughter of his minions, and but small loss to us. Today is the day for the presidential election in Yankeedom. As far as the real good of the North is concerned, I hardly know which would be preferable, Lincoln or McClell[an]. I suspect tho' it's six of one and half a dozen of the other. I, and a majority of those around me, think that it will be best for the interest of the South that the former be elected. I should like to see him elected by a majority of the Electoral College, and defeated, by a popular majority, as I think this would be very apt to cause an armed and perhaps serious collision between the contending parties; thus weakening the North for agressive operations against us. But so far as we are directly to be worsted or benefited by the election of one or the other, I can't see that it makes one grain of difference. If any, it is in favor of Lincoln, as "Little Mac" might offer plausible, but to us, if accepted, ruinous peace measures, that would make the pusilanimous and weak-kneed among us, desert our Cause, and thus divide, and weaken us for resistance.

Piquet fire all the time with occasional shelling continues along the line as usual. I may say that hardly a minute in the twenty four hours elapses without my hearing the crack of a musket frequently the whiz of a Minnie. Of course I am heartily tired of this state of things but all this and much more, and worse, is, as nothing to the grand all important object for which we are fighting and enduring these grievous things.

When I last heard from Henry, he was well. I am daily looking for letters from the dear fellow. How happy we shall be, when we both get back and can all be together again. But it may be, that this cannot be our happiness in this world. Let each one of us, Minnie, strive so to live that we shall be certain to meet in that World beyond these fleeting years. Read your Bible and try (praying for the assistance of the Holy Spirit) to live up to its teachings. And don't forget too to pray for me and Henry. We both stand greatly in need exposed as we are to "foes without and foes within" for the prayers of our friends. Best love to all.

Your affectionate brother,
Chas. W. Trueheart

Camp Sanders near Petersbg,
November 17th, 1864

Dear Henry
   Yesterday's mail brought me your letter of the 8th inst.
   Boots, or shoes—particularly a pr. of nice Sunday's—a wool hat,
gloves of any kind but more particularly a pr. of buckskin gauntlets.
Pocket handkerchiefs—silk or linen (would like to have part of one
kind and part of the other and as many as a 1/2 doz.). Neckties—
linen for shirt collars, etc. Flannel undershirts, knit or sewed as suits
you best. Calf skin for footing one or two pr. boots—Cloth gray or
other color, for making a cape—and some red flannel or other
woolen stuff for lining it. (I am without a Greatcoat, and want it
as a substitute therefor). Any one or more or all the above articles
will be acceptable to me; provided you can get them on good terms
and can bring or send them across the mountains to me. If they
dont come too dear, I can reimburse you when we next meet.
Do you think you can manage to capture me a Yankee horse,
saddle and bridle to take care of for you till you stand in need
of him?
   Since my last letter to you our Division has been moved some
three or four miles to the Right of the position we have occupied
for some months past at Battery 30" abreast of the City, from the
Appomattox river, to a position in the woods some 3/4 of a mile or
more to the rear of the trenches where we are busy building winter
quarters. The Breastworks are now held by a strong piquet line and
artillery. I was sorry to have to leave my bomb-proof winter quarters
for myself and horse even tho' we were under a constant fire of small
arms and Artillery. But on account of the men, and for other reasons,
I am pleased with the move. From all I can see and learn, the whole
Army is preparing winter quarters, either in the rear, or in the
trenches. At the same time they are held in constant readiness for
active operations; and if we may judge by the tone of the Yankee
Press, and the recent order from their Secty of War [Stanton], order-
ing "all men able for duty, absent on furlough, to report to their
commands immediately," we may look for another grand attack on
the Richmond lines ere long.
   Henry, I really do not think that you ought to remain in McNeill's
command any longer. There are many reasons against your doing
so; and in favor of your joining some body of troops in the regular

service. Let me enumerate a few that suggest themselves to me just now. As the war is now carried on, you are liable to be hung or shot if you fall into the hands of the enemy. Under the circumstances your continuance with the Guerillas will cause me and your friends in Va. to say nothing of those that love you at home, a deal of anxiety, even tho' you pass through the war unscathed, and should you be wounded or captured, (as you may any day) and thus fall into the hands of the enemy, who would certainly hang or shoot you. The grief of those who cherish and love you would be infinitely more poignant than had you fallen in the fray of battle. Should you be killed, rather than fall into the hands of the enemy, we could not recover your body; in all probability t'would remain uninterred and the food for animals. The Partizan Bands have (and I suspect justly) fallen into disrepute with the better class of people; have the character, for being composed of reckless, lawless fellows, who do our own people, in the sections where they operate almost as much harm, as they do the Yankees and even worse than they (the people) receive at the hands of the enemy. Be this opinion well founded or not, it is extensively entertained, as is man invariably judged of by the company he keeps and a gentleman who care to "avoid even the appearance of evil." Not being possessed of that cunning, through knowledge of the country, and helterskelter dash which would fit you for a Partizan leader, you can hardly expect promotion by election at the hands of your present comrades, whom I suspect value a man more on account of these qualifications, and the amount of whiskey he drinks and treats them to, the number of black guard stories he tells, the extent of license to rob, plunder, murder, rape and do as they please; that he allows; than for the possession of those truly manly Christian virtues which I conceive my Brother to possess;—those qualities which were he in the regular service secure his promotion by appointment or election. But again; situated as you now are, we are almost as much separated as tho' you were in Texas; and we could hardly come one to the other in case of sickness wounding or death of either[.] I should be happier and feel better satisfied (as would Mother and the rest at home) were we closer to each other.

Now my advice is that you get a furlough sometime shortly and come over this side the mountains and effect a transfer, to one of the Va. regts., either under [Brig. Gen. Thomas] Rosser or better still with Lee's army proper under [Maj. Gen. Wade] Hampton,—[of South Carolina], But I will write on this topic at some future day.

There are no 2 [cent] Stamps to be had. I would advise you to send your Yankee papers by the letter mail. The paper mail is most unreliable. I send you some 20 [cent] Stamps (they cost me only 10 [cents] apiece) to use for that purpose, 30 or 40 [cents] will pay for the largest newspapers.

I see that Lt. Col. Marshall of the 7th Va. Cavalry was killed in one of the late cavalry fights in the Valley. Shall I make inquiries among my Cavalry friends for a good company for you to get a transfer to? My winter quarters will be done in a few days. The Adjt. is my only tent and messmate. A bed and extra ration will be in readiness for you and I doubt not, that apart from seeing & being with me, you can spend some days both profitably and agreeably in seeing sights in the Grand Army of "Northern Va."

Aff. yours,
C. W. T.

Camp Eng. Troops A.N.V. near
Petersburg, Va,[43]
Dec 29", [1864]

Dear Henry

I find my new post of duty a decided improvement on the infantry, in point of social advantages, comforts etc., but I miss the stirring excitement of life in the fighting department no little.

You will find no difficulty in finding me, when you come over on furlough. The detachment with which I am on duty is stationed in sight of Dunlap's where you disembark from the cars, or which you will pass in traveling the Rich. and Petersbg. turnpike on horseback. We are at work on the extension of the Rich. and Petersburg R.R., about 3/4 of a mile from the Depot (Dunlap's). I can give you a soldier's fare; meat & bread the main stay extras, such as sorghum, potatoes, turnips, etc. occasionally.

By tomorrow mornings mail I forward your Richmond papers, which will give you all the news afloat. I also send you enclosed herewith, letters from Father, Mother and Cally, they came to hand yesterday by the C.S. express mail.

'Twas Uncle Lanty who begged you would write to him and when over the mountains on furlough not to fail to pay him a visit. All at Uncle John's were well when last heard from.

Much Dreaded Place
∼

I told you in my last that I would be glad if you would bring me a horse, saddle and bridle if you can, without too great a sacrifice to yourself.

Your aff brother,
C. W. Trueheart.
Asst. Surg. Eng. Troops,
A.N.V. Care Col. Talcott

To: H. M. Trueheart, Esq.

Camp near Petersburg, Virginia
December 31st, 1864.

Dear Father:

Your letter of the 23rd October 1864 reached me on the 28th inst.; affording me as I know it will, Henry, much pleasure. Its arrival was delayed by having to be remailed from Richmond to the 8th Alabama Infantry; and as I had just been transferred to the 1st Reg't Engineer Troops, the letter had again to be remailed to me here, and probably reached Richmond about the 15th or 20th. My last home was on the 7th inst. to you. On the 20th, I forwarded to Cally and . . . I sent letters from Henry with a P. S. from myself . . . not written as frequent as formerly owing to marches, etc. While with the 8th Alabama. . . . coming to the Engineer troops. You all can now rest easy, as to my safety. The implements of this command are . . . pick, spade, etc. I am well pleased with the change, tho' miss no little, the excitement, etc., of the fighting Department. The advantages gained by coming to this Reg't are such as I would not suffer to influence me were I a combattant;—freedom from the dangers of battle, etc., and comparative comfort and exemption from hardships,—such as exposure to all sorts of weather, and heavy marches. Yes, and another and potent advantage is, that here I have as much work as I can stand up to, the Reg't. being full, and I am thrown with men of education and refinement; in addition, to the white soldiers connected with these troops, a large number of negroes are employed as. . . . This affords me a fine field for practice. I fully concur with your views as to the war. I am now despondent as to the final result of the struggle, 'tis only a question of time and depends upon the manner in which our rulers wield their resources of the country, which if properly used are ample for every emergency. Certainly we have never as yet met with crushing disaster, Sherman's march through the heart of our country, destroying as he went; the defeat and failure of Hood's army in Tennessee; the capture of Savannah by Sherman ... the latest ... in fact not a very serious loss to us otherwise, than morally.

The issue now is clearly drawn; with us the alternative is victory, or subjugation, followed by the most degrading and galling yoke of bondage; that ever any people were called upon to bear. Everybody that I have been thrown with of late is in favor of R. E. Lee's being made Generalissimo with a carte blanche and guarantee that Mr. Davis nor ... else shall interfere with him in the management of the armies of the Confederacy. This would be very popular with the army. Many too, are in favor of arming from 200,000 to 500,000 negroes. I can but question the expediency of such a move. Of the propriety I have no doubt. A friend of General Lee, was heard to say a few days ago, that the General was in favor of its being done immediately. The Richmond journals assent the same to him.

The Army is in a prostrate condition. Tho' much exposed, the health of the men continues very good. Officers and men are awaiting with intense interest the action of Congress in regard to the Army reorganization and consolidation. As a general thing ... would be a popular—no, not a popular thing—but all see the necessity of something of the kind so clearly, that men and officers would be willing to sacrifice personal interests and prejudices for the general good. Many of the regiments are merely skeletons in point of numbers, etc. There is in some a large excess of officers, while in others, there are not enough to give each company an officer (commissioned). Our officers that are thrown out by it, will probably be allowed to direct their branch of service and company; so it would not go very hard with them.

In future, letters for Henry and me had better be sent to University of Va., care of Uncle John; address them all to me, then I can read and forward to Henry. Best love to Mother and the girls, Elvira and Sister Mary, Mr. Howard and Tom Joseph. I hope it will not be long ere you treat us to another letter. Henry will probably be with me in a few days.

Your affectionate son,
C. W. Trueheart

Much Dreaded Place

CHAPTER 5

⁓

"That All Important Arm of the Service,"
1865

Camp, detachment Eng.
Troops, A.N.V. near
Petersburg, Virginia,
January 20, 1865

My dear fellow [Henry]

Yesterday, Lt. Col. Blackford sent for me to come over to see him on "special business" which proved to be connected with yourself. Both he and Col. Talcott want to get you as a Lieutenant in their Engineer Regiment.[1] Will you accept it? Take the advice of your brother, and what would be that of all your friends who have your best interest at heart, and say you will accept. Col. B[lackford] says that officers are *much needed* in this branch of the service; that with your business habits practical good sense, and readiness at calculations, etc., and even limited acquaintance with land surveying, and the use of the compass, you would be an acquisition to the Engineer Corps; and that with the practical lesson before you daily, and books on the subject, (which are furnished by the Government) you would soon become an efficient Engineer, and earn promotion. Your associations here with [educated] men as compose our officers would be first rate and very improving. Your occupation would be equally so . . . both well calculated for fitting you for the duties of life after the war. The advantages for religious advancement too, would be greatly better than in your present position. You are needed in this department; you can do the country more efficient service here as a Lieut. than as a private in the Partizans. Then too, we shall be together, and in case of mishap to either, the other could have the satisfaction of ministering to him. In the event of our services being demanded at any time by the condition of the country, you would be on hand at the theatre of war, par excellence. You could retain one of your horses with a view to being in readiness, as also your arms, etc. You could keep him at some point in the country convenient for any emergency; or one of our field officers, who are all entitled to two horses would be glad to keep him and draw forage for him and let you ride him occasionally to boot. There is no doubt as to your getting the commision. Texas is behind hand in her quota of officers in this Corps. If you will accept;—send me letters to your acquaintances in the Texas Delegation to Congress, or other influential Texans immediately. I and Col. Blackford can manage the rest and send you an order from the Secty of War to report to Col. Talcott, etc. etc.

At the request of Col. Talcott, I have just completed a lengthy report, in the shape of suggestions as to the measures to be adopted in the construction, etc. of quarters, Rations—Police—Sick—discipline, etc. with the negro hands to be attached to the Corps of Engineer troops. If it meets with the Colonel's approbation it is to be forwarded to Brig. Gen'l. Stevens, Chief Engineer of the Army of Northern Virginia.

I have written to Uncle William in regard to wintering my horse for me, etc.

Dispatch a reply to this letter immediately on its reception.

> *Your attached brother,*
> *C. W. Trueheart*

Winter-quarters,
Army Northern Va.
near Petersburg.
January 26th 1865.

My dear Fannie

Your letter of the 20th Nov. 1864, with a P.S. from ever faithful Cally, addressed to me Box 381, Richmond, was forwarded by my kind young friend, Mr. Alexander, and reached my hands on the 22nd inst. I was much gratified at its reception. It was the first from you since one received by me last April. I shall enclose it to Henry today. He too, will be delighted to receive it. Why dont you write more frequently? Besides the deal of pleasure it will afford H[enry] and myself, it will be very improving to you. Being a good letter writer *is* a rare accomplishment with both ladies and gentlemen. To acquire it, you only require a little pains and practice;—and then what a source of pleasure you would have at your command[,] pleasure to absent friends, and pleasure to yourself, for being able to write agreeably to others, and with ease to ones self is a most delightful pastime. The occurrance of the war and your limited opportunities at school, has doubtless seriously interfered with your's and Minnys' educations. But by application to reading, writing letters etc, you make up for all lost time. Determine at once my dear girl to make continuous efforts for improving yourself. Employ all your spare time in reading, carefully and thoroughly, history, well selected novels, poetry, etc., and write regularly and lengthily to your brother Henry, myself and others. If you wish to be the pride of your friends, and brothers; a useful. . . . Your last letter was a very good one in most respects. But how much better it would have been had you been in the habit of writing two or three letters a month to Henry and me, and as many to other persons. I should think it would be an admirable plan for you and Minnie to spend a part of each day in regular studies,—arithmetic, history, geography, etc. This would be much better than for you to spend your time in visiting, and frolicing about, with the scatterbrained, ignorant girls that abound since the war interrupted the schools, etc. You could recite to Mother or to Cally.

Henry paid me a visit of four or five days last week, which was a delightful treat to me, I assure you; and he seemed to enjoy himself no little. We spent a whole day in riding around the Lines looking at the extensive and truly wonderful works for defence both on our side and the enemy's. Henry brought me as a present, a riding horse saddle and bridle, gray woolen cloth for an entire suit, a fine wool hat and 1/2 doz handkerchiefs; now was not that a present worth having? And it all came in most opportunely for me. I had just been thrown afoot by having to turn into Govt a captured horse that I had been riding all summer, and as my duties require me to move about a good deal I had found it no easy matter to get along without a horse. The Government supply of clothing for officers not being forthcoming, and my salary too small to admit of my purchasing a suit at $1500.00 (Fifteen hundred dollars), I had grown sadly threadbare. Henry seems to make warm friends wherever he goes. You

Rebel Brothers

all need have no uneasiness on *my* account as far as the dangers of battle are concerned; since my transfer from the 8th Regt Ala. infantry, with which I had been from May [1864] to the middle of December [1864] . . . to these Engineer troops . . . am not at all exposed to fire. Nor is there much probability of being again while I stay with this Regiment. Henry is in the fighting department, and hence your tender solicitudes are henceforth [to] be for him alone. I have just written to Henry to know if he would accept a Lieutenancy in this Regiment, which is offered to him. I am anxious for him to do so, as he has been in the fighting department for a long time and his services are needed in this Regiment; he can do much better service as an officer than as a private. We shall then be together, and in case our services are needed at any time in the fighting department, we shall be on hand at the seat of war, and can go in together. I fear that he will not accede to it, tho' he has such a keen sense of honor, and patriotism as to the duties of able-bodied men, etc.

Give my love to Father, Mother, Cally & Minny, Sisters Mary and Elvira, and Mr. H[oward] and Mr. J[oseph]. In future, address letters to me, care of Jno. B. Minor.

Your loving brother,
Charles W. Trueheart

Camp, detachment Eng.
Troops, A.N.V.
January 29th, 1865

Dear Henry

On the 20th inst. I wrote you as to the acceptance of a Lieutenancy in this Eng. regt., to which I am anxiously looking for a (favorable) reply. On the 26th, I forwarded you letters from Cally, and Fanny G., of the 20th Nov. ult. Today I send enclosed, a letter from Mother to you, and one from Mother to me. Also a letter from my messmate Lt. Gordon, which please mail for him within the enemy's lines so it will go through to its destination.

The heavy rains that have fallen since you were here, have damaged the military works about here considerably. The pontoon bridge across the James at Chaffin's farm was carried away by the freshet in that river. That large dam, the pond of which formed part of our Line in front of Battery 45 gave way, precipitating the vast collection of water above on to the country below. Trees were torn up by the roots and in the passage to the Appomattox, it swept away the aqueduct to the canal and that portion of the South-side R.R.

Arm of the Service
∼

that lay across its track. So powerful was the force of the water that it swept a number of blocks of stone, from the aqueduct clear across the swollen Appomattox landing them on the opposite shore—a distance of several hundred yards. Those who saw the flood as it rushed down the river say the wall (Red sealike) was several ft. high. One of the pontoons below was somewhat injured by it. Three of the men of the Regt who happened to be out in a boat on the river at the time, were drowned. Report persists in saying that Mr. Stephens of Ga., Senator Hunter of Va., and Judge Campbell, Asst. Sect. of War have been sent as Commissioners to Washington.[2] I can't vouch for the truth of it. My hands are so benumbed with cold I can hardly write.

Yours in haste,
Charles W. Trueheart.

To H. M. Trueheart

Camp Detachment Eng Troops,
A.N.V. near Petersburg,
February 13th 1865.

My dear fellow [Henry]

Your letter of the 26th ult. reached me some days ago I began a reply to it on the 10th inst., but was called off to see a sick man, and one thing and another has prevented me from resuming. While on many accounts I regret your refusal to accept the proferred Lieutenancy in this Regiment, I can but feel an admiration, for the sentiments that dictate it, and a pride in my brother, who is governed by such unselfish and patriotic motives.

The weather here is intensely cold. On dipping my pen just now, in dating this, it encountered a mass of black ice, which I was at some trouble to liquify, ere I could proceed further with tracing my ideas for your benefit. Since yesterday morning, I have suffered more with cold than at any time during this winter. The frigid breath of the North Pole regions has been rushing and howling over this level country in a perfect gale, since night before last. Our Texas "northers" are nothing to compare with it. The wooliest of garments fail to prevent its keen searching air from penetrating to the skin, and making poor soldiers shiver. Yesterday I went to church, but my teeth chattered so I could not sing or enjoy the sermon. After service, I went round to the house of a friend, by invitation of several days previously, and partook of a first rate dinner; turkey, corned beef, etc. Met my "intimate friend"—Harry Lownes Allan; who

seemed most delighted to see me and greeted me most patroniz-
ingly, as "Charlie, my boy." "Why how are you, Charlie, my boy?"
It's a pity the boy doesn't know how to deport himself as becomes
his years, etc. Nothing of interest, military or otherwise, has tran-
spired worth writing, farther than what the Examiners sent you, contain. You say "don't send me papers unless they contain something
of special interest." To me, all of the numbers—of the Examiner,
particularly—seem so interesting, that I send them along. When
you write me that the papers to which you subscribe reach you with
regularity, I will resort to the plan of cutting out only the articles of
special interest, and such as you would fail to see in that wishy-
washy "Sentinel" and enclosing them in my letters. But unless you
write with greater frequency I shall not promise to be as punctual
and frequent as even heretofore, much less "weakly." I shall have
my hands full for the future, as we are receiving daily acquisitions
to the force working on the R.R. Did I tell you that my position here
was to be still further enhanced, in my estimation, by the transfer to
the regt of an esteemed friend and former tent, and mess-mate,
while in the old Rockbridge Artillery?[3]

No letters from Texas, the University, or other points of interest
to you, have come to hand since my last writing.

In regard to the Lieutenancy, I believe it is still open. Should you
change your mind, as I hope you may, I'm going to Richmond the
last of this month, and by invoking the aid of Senator Oldham, with
whom I am acquainted, together with the application and endorse-
ment of Cols. Talcott and Blackford, there would be no doubt of
Gen Stevens giving you the appointment, or rather, so recommend-
ing Col. T's application that you may be certain of getting it. You
will then be on hand here with me for any emergency of the war,
and at any time you get sick of your commiss[ion], you can resign,
and go into the fighting department, par excellence—*the Army* of
Northern Va. This Regt is not as bomb-proof as you seem to imagine. They are armed and drilled for the deadly fray, and when ever
a battle of any magnitude comes off, they take position in the Front
with the Troops of the Line. The Regt. is largely made up of picked
men, skilled mechanics, etc., selected from the bulk of the army,
and thus thrown together to heighten their efficiency in that all
important "arm of the service," the Engineer Corps. They are exempted from piquet, guard duty, etc., that they may construct defensive works. They are held as a reserve corps, and take their place
in the battle whenever they are required, as was the case in several

Arm of the Service

instances during last year's campaign. The officers thrown out by "consolidation" would not suit this position. It requires men of good sense, intelligence, industry, reliability, enterprise, etc. As I said before in case you do not like the service or the exigencies of the service demands on you, in the cavalry, artillery or elsewhere, you will be on hand ready for any emergency, and if my services are not clearly needed in this physicing department, we can go in together. You can retain horse, arms, and accoutrements as suggested in my letter of the 20th ult., resign with honor to yourself, and go into the cavalry again.

Your attached brother,
Chas. W. Trueheart.

Detachment Engineer
Troops, A.N.V. near
Petersburg, Va.,
February 16th, 1865.

My dear Cally

The meanspirited despondency that I am sorry to say took possession of some people in this and some of the states South for a time, is giving place to renewed confidence, and a sublime and stern resolve to conquer an honorable peace or die in the attempt. Lincoln's peace proposition as communicated to Mssrs. Hunter, Stephens and Campbell, seem to have had the effect of arousing everybody, to a just appreciation, of what awaits the people of the South should they, through voluntary submission, or by force of arms, submit to Yankee rule. Accompanying this I send an account of proceedings in Richmond just after the return to that city, of "the Peace Commissioners."[4] I also send the latest letter, that I have received from Henry.

The only military movement that has taken place in this vicinity recently was that against our Right,—week before last. The enemy was repulsed at all points, tho' he made desperate and repeated efforts against our line of works. He failed to get either Boydton plank road, or the South Side R.R. or even to get in a position, where he could deter us from using them, by his artillery. He only *extended* (not advanced) his lines farther to the Right (his left); which was not a matter of much moment to us.[5]

The weather this winter, and particularly for the past few weeks, has been very cold. No snow or but very little, has fallen. Our kith and kin are well as far as heard from. Yesterday I rcvd. a letter from

Miss Sally Huskins, saying she was at Chester (between here & Richmond), and asking how to get letters to Texas.

Best love to all. In future direct all letters, for H. or me, to Uncle Jno.'s care.

Your affectionate brother,
Charles W. Trueheart.

Miss Cally Hill

Detachment Eng. Troops,
A.N.Va., near Petersburg, March 11th, 1865.

Dear Henry

Tho' interruption of communicating, caused by the operations of the enemy's raiding parties on the Central road between here, and Staunton, has deterred me from writing, since mine of the 1st inst. I do not know certainly that this will reach you, but make the effort notwithstanding.

No letters from home since Mother's of 1st. Dec. '64 to you. So far we know little or nothing of the particulars of the Sheridan raid.[6] The Richmond papers and others, have been admirably discret and reticent in not publishing, to the Yankees the much coveted information in regard to this and the movements in S.C. Yesterday's papers brought a telegram, from Genl Bragg, which with other items of interest, I clip out and enclose. I have not been able to learn any thing definitely as to how the University and Albemarle people fared at the hands of the Yankee raiders. It is pretty certain tho' that they did not burn any of the houses. From all accounts I do not think they extended their operations as far as Uncle Wm's. As you may well imagine I have been on thorns about my horse. I have made sundry efforts to obtain a short leave to go up after him but having a good number of patients I couldn't get away. The spirit of the army has improved considerably to what it was when you were down here. Quite a number of deserters, etc., have come back to their commands under Genl Lee's amnesty proclamation.[7] In the 10th Ala., 42 men diserted at one time some 6 weeks ago. Of that number 36 have returned. Other reg'ts. of the Brig. are getting back men too. If men will come out only tolerably well, I believe we can whip the Yankees into making peace with us, before another year rolls round. But I believe, (as I have always done), that our Independence is only a question of time the length of its continuance, depending upon the way we do our duty. From what I have seen and heard the spirit of our people everywhere is assuming a healthier

Arm of the Service

tone. I will send extracts from papers, when any thing of special interest appears in them. Some of the members of our Texas Delegation start for the Trans-Miss. this week. I shall write by them and forward your last. I have sent in my resignation, as Asst. Surg. and am going into artillery. The service has twice as many medical officers as needed. I don't choose to belong to a class of drones; and more particularly, when the country needs every man at the front.[8]

> *Your affectionate brother,*
> *C. W. Trueheart*

Detach. Eng. Troops,
A.N.V., Extn. R&P R.R.
March 27th, 1865.

Dear Henry:

Your letter of 24th Feb. came to hand today, seems to have been mailed March 17th at Dayton. It must have come by way of Lexington and Lynchburg, as the Sheridan raid broke up the central railroad. You ask what was thought of McNeill's capture of Kelley and Crook, by this army,—General Lee spoke of it in very complimentary style and 'twas everywhere pronounced one of the most daring exploits of the war.[9] I will forward your article to "The News." As soon as I can get off, I want to go up to Louisa after my horse. Uncle Wm. called to see me a short time since, when on a visit to Bill. The enemy have not molested him. He inquired particularly after you. Enclosed I send some newspaper clippings, and some P.O. stamps.

All were well at the University at last accounts. Nothing from Texas since Mother's of 1 Dec. ult. which you speak of having received. Have neither time nor paper for more. Do try to write more frequently. Your last was read with much interest by a number of persons.

> *Yours,*
> *Charles*

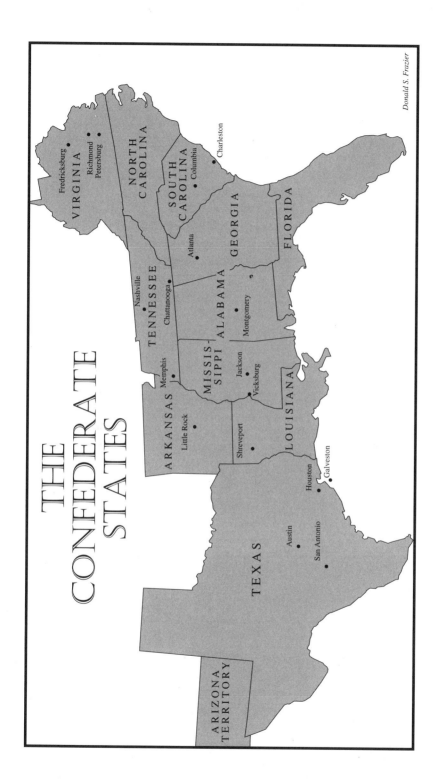

THE CONFEDERATE STATES

Donald S. Frazier

VIRGINIA
Fredricksburg
Richmond
Petersburg

NORTH CAROLINA

SOUTH CAROLINA
Columbia
Charleston

GEORGIA
Atlanta

FLORIDA

TENNESSEE
Nashville
Chattanooga

ALABAMA
Montgomery

MISSISSIPPI
Jackson
Vicksburg
Memphis

LOUISIANA
Shreveport

ARKANSAS
Little Rock

TEXAS
Austin
San Antonio
Houston
Galveston

ARIZONA TERRITORY

145

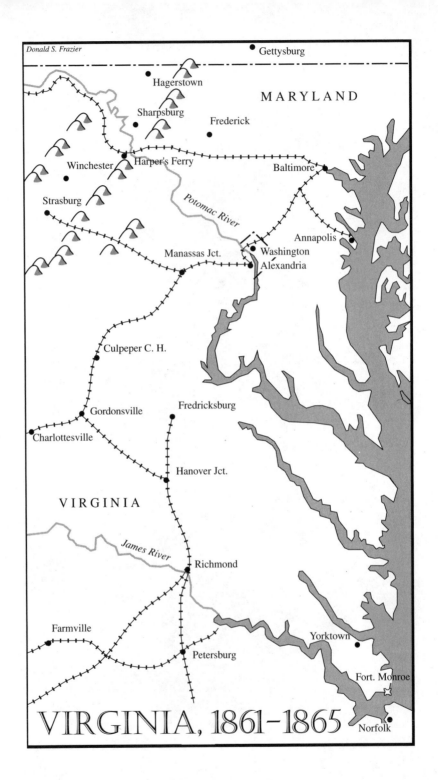

Donald S. Frazier

Gettysburg

Hagerstown

MARYLAND

Sharpsburg

Frederick

Winchester   Harper's Ferry

Baltimore

Strasburg

Potomac River

Annapolis

Manassas Jct.   Washington
Alexandria

Culpeper C. H.

Fredricksburg

Gordonsville

Charlottesville

Hanover Jct.

VIRGINIA

James River

Richmond

Farmville

Yorktown

Petersburg

Fort Monroe

VIRGINIA, 1861–1865   Norfolk

146

SHENANDOAH
VALLEY

Romney

Allegheny Mountains

Romney

Sharpsburg
Shepardstown

B & O Railroad

Potomac

Harper's Ferry

Shenandoah River

Winchester

Kernstown

Snicker's
Gap

Bull Run Mountains

Ashby's
Gap

Strasburg

Front
Royal

Manassas Gap Railroad

Mount
Jackson

Blue Ridge Mountains

Rappahannock R.

Orange and Alexandria Railroad

New
Market

Massanutten

North Fork

South Fork

Luray

Thornton's
Gap

Culpeper

Harrisonburg

Conrad's
Store

Swift
Run
Gap

Cross Keys

Rapidan R.

Port
Republic

Brown's
Gap

Gordonsville

Staunton

Mechum's River Station

Charlottesville

Virginia Central Railroad

Donald S. Frazier

147

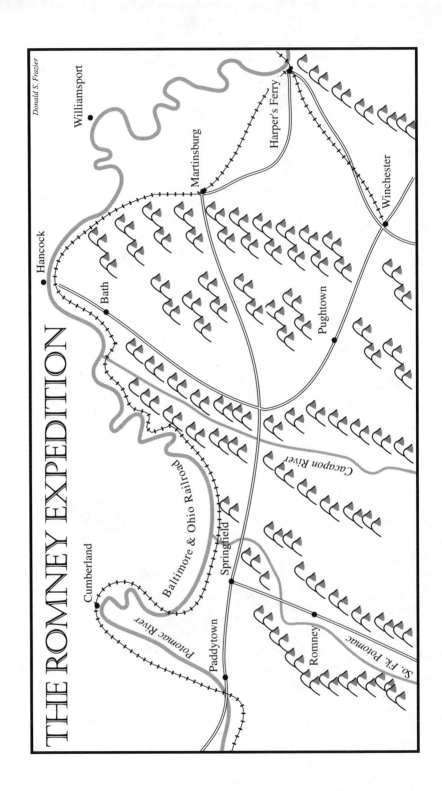

THE ROMNEY EXPEDITION

Donald S. Frazier

Williamsport

Martinsburg

Harper's Ferry

Winchester

Hancock

Bath

Pughtown

Baltimore & Ohio Railroad

Cacapon River

Cumberland

Springfield

Potomac River

Paddytown

Romney

So. Fk. Potomac

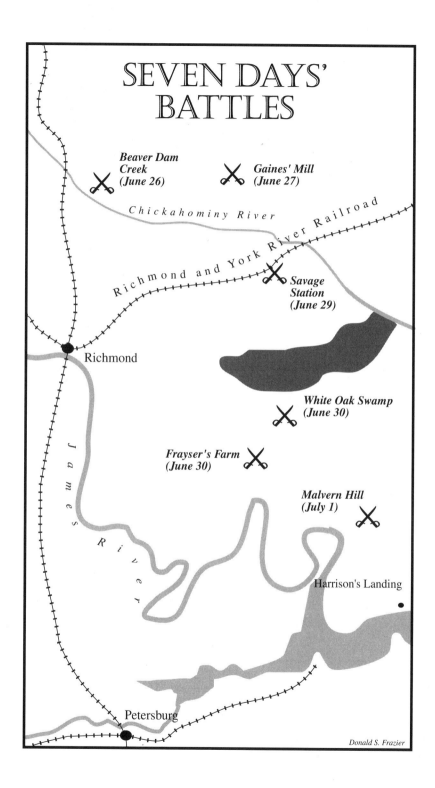

SEVEN DAYS' BATTLES

Beaver Dam Creek *(June 26)*

Gaines' Mill *(June 27)*

Chickahominy River

Richmond and York River Railroad

Savage Station *(June 29)*

Richmond

White Oak Swamp *(June 30)*

James River

Frayser's Farm *(June 30)*

Malvern Hill *(July 1)*

Harrison's Landing

Petersburg

Donald S. Frazier

149

BOOK II

Selected Letters of Henry Martyn Trueheart, 1862–65

~

CHAPTER 6

"Prepare Quietly to Evacuate the Place,"
1862

Galveston,
May 17",/62.

Dear Cally

I snatch a moment to enclose you all an Extra [Galveston newspaper, apparently] and to write a few lines. An Extra issued yesterday also, but has been mislaid. It contained little of interest, except
a report that the French Minister's visit to Richmond was to offer a
mediation & Northern accts which indicate that they feared "something more than simple *mediation.*" Northern accounts of Battle of
Shiloh show it to have been a most disasterous affair.[1] Today at an
early hour the people were all thrown in to a high state of excitement by the appearance of the "Sam Houston" approaching the entrance with a flag of truce. The steamer was immediately got under
way & went out to meet her—whereupon a Fed. Lieut. communicated with Col. Manly who went out on the steamer & said that he
had a sealed package which he was instructed to deliver, in person
to Gen Hebert. Col. Manly declined letting him come up to the city
but offered to convey the same, and after some parley and hesita-
tion, & conversation he sent the document in by Col. Manly. It has
since been transmitted to Hebert by telegraph—but as yet we are
in total ignorance of its purport. It may transpire tomorrow & if so &
in time for the boat, will send you its contents.

The Federal remarked that "we were now all quiet but that in two or three days we might be cutting each other's throats." Col. Manly replied "that it might be so and that if called upon to do so, we had the metal in our hearts and the steel in our hands to meet the issue." The Fed. replied 'That we had given them good evidence on that point".

A majority seem to fear that the document may be a demand for the surrender of the town—as another steamer was seen hovering off the coast this morning.

Col. M[anly] says that "It is nothing very serious & need not cause much excitement[.]" Of course there are a thousand & one rumors and versions of the affair in circulation—All that I have told come to me from the lips of those who went out or those who had just heard it from their lips.[2]

The big battle had not been fought—but had begun at Corinth, as you will see in the Extra. The Fed vessels being within 15 miles of Richmond is probably true as West Point is much farther than that from Rich.—But I'll add a line in the morning.

                    Sunday morning.
I have written to Tho M & have not time for more—Love to Sister M. & Mrs. J. & Tommy & all the children.

                    Ever your aff. Bro.
                    (Henry).

Galveston,
Sunday morning 8 1/2 clock
a.m. May 18"/62
Thos M. Joseph Double Bayou

Dear Tom,

Our surmises relative to the contents of yesterday's dispatches have proved true. Mr. H. Stuart informs me that the purport of the dispatch is "That in a few days the Federal Fleet will be here to attack the place & the Comm. of the Santee desiring to prevent the useless effusion of human blood demands its immediate surrender. Expecting a reply today" (Sunday)[.][3]

The Genl has sent Col. Cooke orders to prepare quietly to evacuate the place until further orders from him.[4] I presume it will not of course be surrendered to the Santee—but there may be other vessels to assist. Everybody is asking where you are—You ought to be here & I get Capt Chubb to carry this to "Chambersia" & send over

Henry Martyn Trueheart in later life. (Courtesy family of the late Elva Trueheart Brown)

to you by special messenger. I don't know what Mother is going to do—She insists on remaining at home.

I think she had better go to Clear Creek—what does Sister Mary think?[5]

John Westerlage just informs me that [Refford] is also absent. Of course I shall leave the place when the Fed's come in. I am confident we could not agree. Of course Fanny & Cally must not think of coming down here until further news from us. It may be a ruse of the Com'd of the Santee to get possession of the city without adequate force—but then it *may not* be. But I just learned that the Extra will be out in time to send up—Kiss my sweet little Fanny for me & tell her I would write but I have no time.

I just learned that there is some *stirring* news in the Extra today. No time for more.

Yours truly,
H. M. T.

Houston, Dec 23rd, 1862[6]

Dear Sister Mary

I had accepted the terms of explanation required by you through Cally i e—to make the same in person on Xmas day at your house & for the purpose had obtained a furlough for seven days. Mother had written me that Father was going over to D.[ouble] B.[ayou] with Capt. Kipp on Monday—I reached home Sunday night to accompany the party but F[ather], very unlike him had left *before* his time—The result was that I am completely deprived of the pleasure of the visit to which I had so fondly looked forward. I shall be able to remain at home long enough however to meet Cally if she gets back by Friday or Saturday—unless an attack is made at Va Pt to which the authorities are looking forward today, having recd some intelligence on that point.[7]

Bow & family were well some ten days ago when I saw them. Mr. H. had very painful risings on both hands. Have been over since then but at night as guide to the waggon train engaged in hauling coal & iron from Close's foundry & had no time for visiting. Two additional co's have been thrown entirely across to the Gulf west of McKinney's Bayou so as to completely cut off communication with town. Mr. Doebuer & B. were well & sent much love to you all. Mr. H[oward] has provisions for several months—tho' there is already much suffering among the poor. Permission for the people of Galveston to leave has again been granted on yesterday—though I doubt if many more will leave—Banks & Hamilton have arrived in New Orleans.

I am sorry that I missed seeing Mr. J. when last up here. I am not surprised at his opinion that it is much more convenient for us to visit him, than "vice versa."

Mother & Minny & Fanny are well—She has determined to sell M. & A. & Wm. & John—and I suppose if she has made up her mind to sell the boys—it's no use to endeavor to change it.[8]

We recd another letter from Chas this morning dated Winchester, Nov 21st. He is well, & communicates nothing of particular interest—

He reports himself scarce of money & I send by Jim Nagle $100 to relieve his necessities—also a $10.00 in a letter which may reach him somewhat sooner. Cally will of course have left before this reaches you. Love to Mrs. Joseph and all the children. Tom in particular—tell him I tried to come to see him & Eddy, but the boat left me—Also to Mr. Joseph—tell him he is always prompt in his appointments—for instance his meeting me at Va Pt in 2 weeks.

But I must stop & attend to some business. Shall be glad to hear from you and Thos M.

Your aff Bro
H. M. Trueheart

Evacuate the Place
∾

◯

CHAPTER 7

"A Texan and Possessing 'Winning Ways,'"
1863

Office Prov. Marshal
Galveston,
Jan 22nd 1863.

Dear Sister Mary

Your interesting and agreeable surprise of the 27th ultimo (concluded on the 5th inst) has been recd and I can assure you, afforded
me much pleasure. What on earth stirred you up to write to me and
then so long a letter too? Surely you are determined on a reform and
I as the recipient and beneficiary, have good reason to congratulate
you. You desire that I will give you some account—"spirited account" of the fight [battle of Galveston, January 1, 1863]. Now I
don't promise to do that—but will give you a lame acct. of things as
I saw them.

Well, to begin at the beginning—Capt. Adkins[,] Jeff League,
myself & two other men were sent over on the day preceding to
ascertain the exact position of all the vessels and make a general
[reconaissance], which we performed satisfactorily to the Genl returning about 3 o'clk p. m. of the 31st[1]—We saw a plenty of Abs.
[absentees?] at the Western Cotton Presses & they scattered about
considerably, as we galloped two or three blocks to the South of
them & while we went to the East part of town threw out a line of

Pickets as far South as Ballinger's, & had 100 men sent out to extend all across to the Gulf & cut us off—but we galloped right through their line not knowing what they had done but keeping a sharp lookout, guns in hand and ready for action—They were not sufficiently numerous at any one place to stop us & so did not fire or show themselves.[2] We returned & the Capt & myself made the report to the Genl in person and at Col. Cooke's request, I assisted in making a plan of the city & wharves & principal houses etc.[3] Our little Co[mpany] was drawn up in front of Hqrs and about one half was detailed–2 & 3 at a time—as guides etc., to several of the Genl's staff and to Maj Von Harten etc and the remainder acted as body guard to the Genl.[4] Jeff League & I were detailed to report to Major Cave one of the Genl's vol. aides for Hospital duty. I was much chagrined when I heard the call & the order to report to Dr. . . pples—especially after our Capt had been called upon for two "active and intelligent men who knew every house in every portion of town" however we made the best of it, but I felt very badly when I saw numbers of litters for bearing the dead & wounded off the field—come by, and supposed we would have to pick them up but Maj C[ave]—soon took us [to] one side & showed us that we were assigned to very *important* duty—one portion of which was to enter town in advance of the troops & notify Father Chambodout of the attack and offer the Genl's ambulances and our services in removing the nuns to a place of safety—They declined going—preferring to face the danger and minister to the wants of the wounded & dying. We took some five ambulances loaded with ladies however out to Tom Power's place and then returned to Headqtrs (General Nichols') to await the Genl's orders. The troops and the long train of artillery looked grand drawing its slow length along through the darkness for with the ambulances & wagons and caissons, etc., it made a magnificent show—When the Genl reached Guy Bryan's he halted the train & troops and issued his orders—I being near him all the time.

By the time we had moved the ladies and returned to town, the fight had been progressing some half hour.

From that time we were used to carry dispatches etc to various parts of town. The shells frequently falling & bursting near us. The Batteries were stationed at various points along the Strand from the most Western to the most Easterly wharf, and when they all opened, and the Federals replied, there was an awful roar.[5]

"Winning Ways"

~

Was interrupted here by a Summons to Headquarters & resume again.

The fight lasted from 2 1/2 to 3 hours.[6] The gunboats which were to advance at a preconcerted signal had failed to arrive at the time expected and as day had dawned affording the Feds an opportunity of getting the exact position of our Batteries—the storm of grape, and canister and shell & shot was more than mortal man could stand.[7] To fight Gunboats carrying the heaviest metal with light field Artillery was a severe test for raw troops—Veterans *might* have stood it for a short time. But for a raw recruit to see a green bucket-full of grape thrown at him for a single dose was trying to the nerves—very.

At this awfully trying moment some of the men left their guns and broke for the beach enquiring with an anxious look for the way to Va. Point. Cavalry was sent out by Maj Watkins, of the Genl's Staff—with instructions to gather up all the stragglers, and bring them to Headqtrs, and to bayonet without ceremony any who hesitated to obey the order. Genl Scurry rallied the reserve of infantry and without guns or weapons of any kind led them down at a full run in face of the Enemy's fire to rescue the guns which had been deserted—In several instances, all the men left their guns except two or three and they continued to fight them desperately—In another instance all left but one & he was found loading and firing manfully. At this moment every man's countenance looked as long as a hoe handle—Genl M. [Magruder] had sent a courier to Fort Point directing the guns there to be withdrawn by way of the beach, as speedily as possible and planted a battery at Eagle Grove.[8] They had become so imbedded in the sand however that they could not be moved and were spiked. The Gunboats had hove in sight too early in the night and had moved off again—nothing could be heard of them. The Genl had not reached the scene of action as soon as expected & hence the Boats might conclude that the expedition had failed, or been postponed.

All at once a cry arose, "Here come the Gunboats under full head way making right for the [Harriet] Lane"—and then such deep & meaning thunder as followed—it fairly shook the earth. A few minutes more and a courier came to Hdqtrs at full speed & with drawn sword—& handsomely dressed—with such color and animation in his countenance as only that moment could inspire, reported that "the Horse Marines had boarded and carried the Harriet Lane, and that all was right." He was Captain John Payne one of the Bayou

Rebel Brothers

∼

City's officers. The Genl seized his hand in both of his and pressed it extolling their bravery, etc. A few moments more, and the 42" Mass[achusetts] Regt on Kuhn's Wharf had surrendered at discretion and were marched past Hqtrs. Our men were disposed to hiss them and it might have grown to something worse, had it not been checked by Maj Watkins. The steamer Neptune had made the first onset on the Lane but striking her fwd of the wheel had not been able to throw her grappling iron aboard and just had time to get to the edge of the channel before she sank from the fire of the Lane and the force of the collision. The Bayou City then put at her & struck her in the wheel & stuck fast when she was immediately boarded & carried the boarders cutting away the netting before being able to jump aboard.

As soon as the Owasco saw the condition of the [Harriet] Lane she came straight down—right in front of all our guns and steamed down so close to the Lane and the Bayou City that you might have thrown a biscuit aboard and poured in a broadside of 11 inch guns—her decks were crowded with men when the 300 Horse Marines on the Lane & the two gun boats responded with a deadly fire of musketry & shotguns—the crowd of men on the Owasco's decks seemed to melt like snow under a summer's sun—She could not stand but the one volley and retired immediately raising the white flag, as did all the vessels in the Harbor. General M[agruder] then gave them 3 hours to make an unconditional surrender—And before the time was out they all commenced moving off very slowly at first until they passed our batteries and then ran as fast as possible. The General would not believe for a moment that they would dare so to pollute a flag of truce, & consequently did not give the order to fire until late—We then turned loose on them and gave them fits as they ran they not firing a gun till they got round the point when they stopped & fired 2 shots to protect their hindmost vessel.

A most touching incident occurred on the Lane. Maj. Lea happened to be here as bearer of dispatches from Richmond Va. and reached the scene in time to clasp his son in his arms ere he died & receive from his dying hand his sword and epaulets.[9] The crew of the Lane fought well and gallantly—The officers stood to their posts—The Capt (Wainwright), 1st & 2nd Lieuts all fell at their posts. The Capt was called on to surrender—but replied "Never" & was immediately shot through the head.

One of the Horse Marines jumped aboard the Lane & seized a Yank by the throat and demanded a surrender. The Yank begged the Marine "to look him in the face—he looked—and beheld his own *brother.*

Maj Lea read the Episcopal burial service at his son's grave and which was a most touching scene. He said that his "son was a brave man and died doing his duty" and begged "that people would tread lightly over his grave."

The Yank officers denounced the movement of their vessels leaving the Harbor and all in command of them for not coming to the assistance of the Lane.

They all regret the continuance of the war and were very much surprised at their treatment expecting to be butchered at once. The fact is they don't deserve any better fate.

A day or two after a transport arrived off the Bar having on board Col. Davis (brother of W. S. Davis) & two hundred & fifty men, nearly all refugees from Texas. She supposed that all was right, & sent Nicaragua Smith & six men in for a pilot—he went aboard the Lane & did not discover the real state of the case till he stood on the deck.

He was condemned & shot a day or two afterwards.[10] Capt. John Payne was then sent out in the Pilot boat to pilot the st[eamer] in—but after he got on board and our pilot boat had left—the st[eamer] got under way & left for N[ew] O[rleans] in a hurry—Payne was probably known to many on board and suspicion aroused in that way. One st[eamer] was sunk & the other fast in the H. Lane, or we could have captured her— . . . tried to sail one of the captured boats out and board her—but no wind. Well I've spun you quite a long yarn—so good bye—kiss Tom and Ed.[11]

We have just heard of Maj. Watkin's success at Sabine.

> *Your loving bro*
> *H. M. Trueheart*

Office Provo. Marshal,
Galveston Jan'y 26th 1863.

Dear Cally

Your letter from Houston has been recd, and I am uncertain whether or not it has been replied to—I know that I took up a pen a few days ago to do so—but something may have prevented it. I therefore drop you a line or two now. It is raining and almost cold enough to sleet—The state of the weather however prevented a bombardment today. The Brooklyn followed by all the smaller fry—came round in front of South Battery and drew up in line of battle—

Rebel Brothers

⁓

but just then there came out a heavy blow from N[orth] & N[orth-west] and the air so thickened up with rain & mist that they all hastened back to their anchorage and are now rolling & pitching at the discretion of the elements. I went out yesterday under the flag of Truce and had a fine view of the splendid Sloop of War "Brooklyn" and the remainder of the Yankee vessels—also the fine English Corvette "Rinaldo" of historic fame—She having had the honor of bearing Mssrs. Mason & Slidell to England.

Though her guns look like pop guns or play things when compared to those of the "Brooklyn." Our vessel, the "Royal Yacht," was boarded by a Yankee Lieut some two miles from the ship and we then took him in tow & sailed up to within 400 yards & anchored. I did not go on board as no officer is permitted to do so unless mentioned in the cartelle. I got some of the fine Yankee & English Segars though and enjoyed them hugely. We saw a boat from the deservedly ill-fated Steamer "Hatteras" and got some of the particulars of the engagement. The "Hatteras" left this bar yesterday evening two weeks ago, and when about opposite to Col. Hall's met just after dark the "290" & hailing her the "290" replied "Her B[ritish] M[ajesty's] Steamer Spitfire." The Yankee rejoined "all right, I'll board you" by this time the Yank had lowered a boat with 10 men & an officer and started & the "290" had come up very close & ranging a little ahead so as to have a full broadside on the Yank but she could only bring a portion of her guns to bear on the "290" At this propitious moment Semmes let fly his broadside—the Hatteras replied as best she could—but soon went to the bottom—The boat's crew which had been lowered put off to the fleet at our bar. The Brooklyn went down *next morning* and picked up several boats—but could see only portions of the mast and pieces of wreck. The Alabama—alias "290"—probably picked up many of the survivors—though nothing is known of the matter.[12]

Mr. Howard has just recd a letter from Elvira tonight in which she says that Mother is desirous to come down and remain a few days—Tell her it can't be possibly done—that everything is too uncertain at this time for her even to think of it—Let her go to Houston, or any where else—but not here.

If she thinks that a little trip would do her good advise her to go to see Cousin Lucy Byars for a week—'twould not cost much and she might arrange with Cousin Wm to come down & take the negroes up. There is no probability of Mr. J[oseph]'s coming up—says he can't do anything—& there is no possibility of my being able to

come so long as we hold Galveston—Love to Fanny & Mother Elvira & Minny, and kiss the children. Tell Fanny Goode that her little
hair brush is safe. Write soon.

H. M. T.

Galveston
Jan'y 30th 1863.

Dear Sister Mary

Mr. Joseph has just shown me a letter recently received in which
you take occasion to pitch into me for not having written to you. But
really if you had seen the constant manner in which I was employed
for the first ten days after the Battle you would fully exonerate me
from all blame. Since getting into this office I have had a little more
time and much more paper ink etc, and within the past week—it
may have been longer—have written you a letter of 6 pages (this
size).

Why Cally has not written I can't tell, unless it be that for the
past two weeks she has been at Houston on a visit and is so carried
away with the stir and bustle there that she has forgotten—or may
be could not get paper for it is 10 or 20 [cents] a sheet there. I went
out to the Fed fleet under the flag of truce a day or two since & saw
some live Yanks as well as the famous English Corvette "Rinaldo."
We learned definitely that it was the C.S. War Steamer "290" that
sank the U.S.S. Hatteras off the coast on the 11th inst. She came
up close enough to speak & replied to the Yankee Capt's demands
that "She was H[er] B[ritish] M[ajesty's] S[hip] Spitfire" the Yank
replied, "All Right, I'll board you" & lowered & manned a boat
accordingly—when the "290" which had passed a little ahead &
occupying a favorable position—poured a deadly broad side into the
Hatteras. She soon going down—fight lasting some 1/2 or 3/4 of an
hour. The boat which had been lowered escaped to the fleet some
25 miles distant. The Brooklyn went to the scene of action next
morning but found only fragments of the wreck. Nothing as to loss
of life etc is known—Captain Semmes can no doubt tell all about
the whole affair.[13] But I must tell you of family affairs. I have advised
Mother to go to Columbus herself, and get Dr. Byars to come over
and carry up the negroes as neither Father nor M[other] will, and
I can't.

I hear that she is troubled with a bad cough again and thought
that a short visit—say 1 week, to Cousin Lucy would probably be
of benefit. I advise by all means not to sell the two boys but if she

Rebel Brothers

~

insists she had better do it as failing to do what she believes to be right would probably be as tormenting to her and injurious to health as if really annoyed by the negroes in person.

Father has received an appointment as asst. Engineer at $130 per month and is now I suppose at work in making a topographical survey for the Govt. Fanny is also at Houston on a visit, & has been for some ten days. Mr. Howard could not stand the possibility of remaining here under the rule of the Yanks again and so sent his family off to Clear Creek where they are staying at our house for the present. I have given him the position of Assistant at $83.33 per month, which will be better than nothing to do.

We heard from Charles a few days since, he was still at Lynchburg Act Asst. Surgeon under Cousin John Minor (your old flame). He writes no war news now—having gotten entirely out of the ring. He speaks of our relatives as being generally well—and of Uncle Lanty as a dear kind fellow.

I don't know what Mr. J[oseph] does with himself. He certainly does not come down my way often. He is generally rubbing his beard when I see him—he may be ... I took breakfast with him this morning. I am boarding at the quarters of my old co., at Brock's stable—being very comfortably fixed up—and well fed—It is true that we only have corn meal for bread—and most excellent beef—usually having a magnificent loin roast for dinner—with nice vegetable soup—the vegetables we buy of course our selves. A recent letter from Va. says; Fred Harris, Dr. Julian Kean & Frank Johnson have all passed away & that Jimmy Winston was killed at the 2nd battle [of] Manassas. Martha Winston was about to marry a Mr. Payne much younger than she.

Well that is all the news that I can trump up now and you must not fail to write me in return or our correspondence may suddenly cease. We had a small bombardment yesterday. Some 48 shells thrown into town, but we opened on the Brooklyn with a little Parrott Gun from the beach, and made her turn tail the first shot. It is thought that several of our shots struck the enemy.

Mr. Joseph was not killed and says he needs no urging from anybody to keep himself out of danger but is always inclined to *run* when called for—and may run even sooner. Love to old "Tommy" and tell him he's got to call me *"Capt Trueheart"* now, and touch his hat for a salute every time he passes me or I'll put him in the Guard House.

> Good by,
> H. M. T.

"Winning Ways"

~

Dear Sister Mary:

An opportunity offers to send '[mail] up this morning and I drop you a line—I leave here tomorrow—a couple of days at Clear Cr[eek] and then off—Have been delayed some time by being summoned as a witness in court.

Nothing of int. here except that the Feds pitched into us last evening with a few shells—no damage done. Our guns opened with two shots at them this morning just to show that we had not evacuated—but at very long range—Some 75 or 100 guns fired yesterday—probably cleaning out their guns—Kiss Tom & Edgar for me and love to the other children—& Mrs. J[oseph]. Will reply to your letters always—May write first and let you know where I am. Cally came down yesterday with Father—returns tomorrow with me.

Your Loving Brother—
H. M. T.

Galveston
June 16/63

Shreveport, La.
June 27th 1863

Dearest Mother

I arrived here yesterday afternoon (Friday) after a wearisome trip mostly day and night.[14] We had the most delightful rain every day commencing Monday the 22nd and continuing to this point. As far as Rusk, in Cherokee Co. the crops are almost entirely grain and very fine; from the latter point to Shreveport they have suffered to some extent for rain—but are still in a condition to be very much benefited by the rains. Every thing wears the appearance of plenty.

My arrival was welcomed by the news of Lee's advance into Maryland the capture of 6,000 or 7,000 men of . . . assisted by Longstreet . . . fight at Vicksburg & Port Hudson all of which is very gratifying. Enclosed I send you an Extra containing an account of same.

This is quite a large town scattered about the hills, immediately on the bank of the river & extending back a mile or more. Have met various acquaintances here—Among them Maj. G. M. Bryan[,] A. A. Genl to Lt. Genl E. Kirby Smith[,] who has treated me with much consideration. He took me to the Navy yard this morning to see the Rebel Monster—somewhat after the model of the 1st Virginia though much improved—It would be utterly impossible to form any correct idea of her strength and immense powers of resistance without seeing & having same explained—which was done

Rebel Brothers

by the polite & accomodating contractor—showing me into every portion of the Monster & explaining as he went along. I predict that she will carry a wide row when she gets out if well officered and mounted. Her speed will be better than any "Iron Clad" afloat— Has already made the trial trip—though still lacks time for thorough completion—Have seen Genl Smith. He is a quiet, fine looking gentlemanly man—was at the table twice with him before I knew it—wears citizen dress and behaves like any other gentleman.[15]

Saw two one-armed soldiers just across the Miss—who got in half an hour ago—They say that heavy firing continues—on day before yesterday was heard & supposed to be at Vicksburg—that Genl Johnston had already moved forward with a fine army and I reckon the thing is "out" before now—If not, I shall be ready to participate in about 4 days more.[16]

Shall go from here to Monroe, La. & cross at Natchez. No chance of crossing at Vicksburg. Send this down to Messrs. Joseph & Howard when you read it—Address me, as before advised, at Jackson, Miss—till further.

Very warm here.—Best love to Fanny Cally & Minny Bow & Sister M. [Mary] & Father—Tell me if Father has concluded his business with Eng Dept.

Ever yours,
H. M. T.

Monroe, La.
June 31st[?], 1863—

Dear Tom

Since writing yesterday I have obtained some interesting news from V[icksburg]. Have just met a very intelligent Capt of 27[th] La. Vols direct from Jackson Miss and not long from Vicksburg— He tells me that on last Sat. week Pemberton notified Johns[t]on that his supplies were nearly out and that unless immediately rein- forced he should be compelled to surrender[.] The courier of course fell into the enemy's hands as was intended and in four hours after- wards Burnside, who is now there led the assault[17]—The enemy approached with a shout & getting within 30 yards of the entrench- ments Pemberton mowed them down like wheat–10000 would cover the loss of that day.

He tells me that P[emberton] had only about 15,000 men at first & that our total losses are 6,000—leaving 11,000—The Yanks are dying by thousands—Johnston's army amts to about 30,000—

"Winning Ways"

~

The Capt thinks from the indications that Johnston will make no attack inside of a month—that they are being killed off faster than in any other possible way—Couriers go and come from V[icksburg] to Johnston's Army continually[18]—He also informs me that he saw some two hundred and fifty wagons already laden with stores & provisions which Breckinridge with 10,000 men is to cut his way into V[icksburg]—

I saw this evening, some 6[oo] or 700 men arrive out of the swamps opposite V[icksburg]—the dirtiest and most delapidated set of poor fellows you can conceive of—they were the broken down and sick of the command—Some had no shoes and were ragged and dirty—not being permitted to carry clothes with them.

Fighting is now going on in the swamp between the enemy and Walker's [Texas] Div.

The raiding party captured several hacks full of our officers back of Natchez but were in such a hurry that they released them just telling them to consider themselves paroled. I shall be on the alert in going through there.

Your . . .
H. M. T.

Lynchburg Va.
July 21" 63.

Dear Cally

In accordance with programme it is your turn next having written to T. M. J. from Mobile, to Fanny from Natchez—to R. H. H. from Monroe & to Mother from Shreveport. I almost fear that this writing is useless as there is no private hand by which to send it & the mails are uncertain—very. Arrived here day before yesterday & took Charles entirely by surprise—[found] him well and looking much as usual [and very comfortably] situated. Dr. M[inor]'s Hospital [cleared of patients] at this time but daily expecting [a resupply] of the Gettysburg wounded. [I regret to see] reported in the "Richmond Enquirer," as among the killed at Gettysburg [three old acquaintances] all reported as belonging to Company L, 1st Texas Regt viz. J. W. Southwick[,] J. D. Waters, Theo. Melhousen the latter being the little boy that used to live with us named *Theodore*.[19] Would send the paper if there was any chance [of its getting] through. I leave here tomorrow [for the front] Lee's Army—Will write to Charles frequently and he will communicate with you when opportunity offers. It will be best for you to address all letters to

Rebel Brothers

care of Chas. at Lynchburg & he will forward to me. Recollect that the more frequently you write the more you increase the probabilities of my hearing from you—all will certainly not miscarry—Send to Cushing of the [Houston] Telegraph who can always forward by someone. Although the Yankees may hold the Miss they can[not] prevent the continual crossing of the River to save their lives. Have been treated very kindly by several of our relatives here, and more like a *child* by Cousin Mary B[lackford] than anything else. Tells me that if I am [sick or wounded] she wants me [to come straight] to her house and that I shall [lack nothing]—Charles has had many offers [of kindness] from & seems to be warmly attached to [Cousin] Chas. Moseby & family. Expect [to call to see] him this evening. [Our friends in Virginia] and . . . generally well. [People all over the] country are of course [depressed at the] fortunes of war which have been going [against] us for several weeks past—but [nobody is] cast down. Confidence in the [ultimate result] is still unshaken. I notice Capt. [D. U. Barziza] reported among the missing at Gettysburg.[20] Love to Mother Fanny & all at our house and Bow's & Sister M's. Tell Mr. Joseph that I collected for Mr. Southwick at Mobile by request $138.40 and that he will oblige by handing said amount to Mr. S. & charging to me.

Yours lovingly,
H. M. T.

P.S. Tell me whether Father has collected the amt due by Govt— knowing that the matter is settled will relieve me very much. [Also say] how Mr. Joseph is getting [on in the A[ssessor] and C[ollector] affairs.]

Near Rixiville on Hazel
River, Culpepper Co., Va.
September 8th, 1863.[21]

Dear Bow:

I write again altho' I have not received a word from home or Charles, or anybody else, and am just in the service a month. Charles has not written a word to me since I left him some forty days since. I shall continue to write as you all may not have an opportunity, and some of the various letters may find their way to Texas. You can't imagine the anxiety that I feel to hear from home. Use every exertion to send me some intelligence, and don't forget to tell me how my office business is getting along. Urge Tom Joseph to write me. Since crossing the Mississippi I have written to T. M. J.

"Winning Ways"
∽
169

July 13th, Cally 20th, to Minny 9th of August, and to Fanny from Natchez—

Now to tell you about what I am doing—My regiment has been on active picket duty ever since I have been in it.[22] It is composed of men from the Valley of Virginia, and Western Virginia—and stands very high on account of the services rendered. [Turner] Ashby's old company is "A" of the regiment, he having commanded this regiment up to the time of his death. The Brigade to which our regiment belongs is now commanded by Brig. Gen'l William E. Jones of Virginia, and formerly of the old Army.[23] He stands very high as an able and efficient officer. I have not slept in a house for 30 days past and was never in better health. When it rains we lie on 3 rails some pine brush, and really I sleep delightfully—occasionally having to get up and make a fire—an oilcloth thrown over keeps us dry or nearly so. We are on duty every other day, alternately, as Pickets and reserve to Pickets. In the latter position we are not permitted to unsaddle, but may tie to a tree—in the former, we are on our horses all night, but in the daytime can graze with the bridle in hand. Our pickets and those of the enemy, stand from 200 to 500 yards apart, and about 150 or 200 yards apart along the line. Our boys occasionally crawl into the enemy's lines, and secrete themselves in the bushes, come out the next night bringing a horse or two each. A party went in a day or two ago and captured 16 fine horses, killing 2 or 3 Yanks, wounding a number, and capturing 1. We had 2 men wounded but brought them out. I have not been over the lines yet as my company's turn has not come. I have been over and talked with one Yank picket and tried to trade knives and hats with him but he was too green. They frequently come up and wave paper at us, and on our making signs that we will not shoot they come half way and we meet and have a talk, always shaking hands on meeting and parting, and rarely ever giving them anything in return, except maybe a little piece of tobacco. Some 4 or 5 of our boys have actually traded horses with the pickets theirs being government, and ours private horses—we giving a mean old poor horse for a fine fat one— the Yanks saying that all he wanted was a Rebel horse. We then frequently exchanged buttons, or any other little thing we happen to have, just as a memento.

As we were coming off twenty four hour duty last night, a courier galloped up and handed a dispatch to our Colonel, and in a few minutes we were on the march to a point 7 or 8 miles distant, with the strictest injunction as to silence, and readiness at a moment's warning, to go into action. We lay in the grass with bridles in hand, and the old hillside fairly trembling with the tramp of Cavalry around us. This morning we beheld the hills and valleys alive with Cavalry drawn up in line of battle, and found that three Brigades were on the ground, and in a short distance within the enemy's lines. At daylight we fell back—none of us knowing what we went for except to fight, or what was the cause of the move. One thing is very certain that some moves are being made which will give us work to do in a very few days. All are anxious for it to come off, and the feeling of confidence which pervades all branches of the Army is the sure prelude to victory. Already the tide of war has been changed in our favor by General Price on White River, Ark., and General Sam Jones in Western Virginia near the White Sulphur Springs.[24] Our rations are very much improved in the last week in quantity and quality—beef and light bread for two days, and bacon and crackers for the third. Up to within ten days past our horses have subsisted almost entirely on grass, but are now getting regular rations of corn, and mine is improving rapidly, and has proven to be a very fine riding animal, jumping ditches and clearing fences like a deer. She cost me saddle, etc, about $550.00. Shall sell her after the first fight when I expect to capture a finer one from the ever well supplied Yanks. All our fellows supply themselves with all they want from the Yanks–9 out of every 10 ride the McClellan saddle, which is a very good one much resembling the Texas tree.

You must not expect me to tell you everything about our relatives here as I don't know any more except that they were all well a month ago. Oh, tell Mr. Howard to give me the whereabouts of that pretty cousin of his—I don't recollect her name, or County, the one that he recommended so highly. I shall probably get a furlough sometime this winter and would like to visit about some—when all the army movements cease. I am sitting under a pine tree on the side of a hill, and writing on the brim of my cap. Have drawn some clothes from the Q.M. and can get plenty more. In my short experience have learned to wash my clothes and catch lice very expertly. . . . It is utterly impossible to keep entirely clear of them, camping on the sandy ground with thousands of other men. Love to all at home, and sister M. (she is last but not least). Will write to her next.

H. M. T.

"Winning Ways"

⁓

Near Rapidan Station,
September 16th, 1863.[25]

Dear Sister Mary:

At last your turn has come, and it affords me much pleasure to think that I am in converse with my dear sister. Some how or other you seem farther off than any one else; perhaps occasioned by the experienced difficulty in making the trip to Double Bayou. I am lying out in a field grazing my horse—enemy about three miles to our front. We are between Rapidan River and Robertson River; I've at last had two days experience in fighting; our Regiment was aroused on the morning of the 12th at about 3 o'clock, in the midst of a pouring rain, by the report of an advance of the enemy on our extreme left. One Brigade of strong Cavalry and our Regiment advanced to meet them. After advancing several miles we found that this was only a feint, and that they were advancing rapidly along the turn of the O. & Alex. R.R., being our center, towards Culpepper C.H., and had gotten two miles to our rear. Their line extended about four miles, advancing steadily and very rapidly with Cavalry, Infantry and Artillery. We have one or two Brigades of Cavalry, and five or six pieces of Horse Artillery only, and fought them till dark making a stand on one hill after another, and holding on till forced back by superior numbers, and flank movements. My squadron composed of two companies acted as sharpshooters on foot; our horses to the rear, a half or three quarters of a mile, one man leading three horses. After the first stand, having held the position till the enemy got into our flank and rear on the right, we had to fall back down a steep hill for more than a mile under an awful fire of Artillery, and sharpshooter's rifles—the silent little sharpshooter's bullets cutting down a poor fellow here and there, and the shell grape, canister and shrapnel crashing, and slashing above and around us, and in our midst most fearfully, one man second from me was shot through the head and fell into the arms of one riding next to him; but believing that he could not live, and pressed by the enemy, he dropped the poor fellow in the bushes, maybe never to be found until his bones shall have been left bare by birds of prey.

At another standpoint on this side of the Culpepper C.H., our sharpshooters were pressed hard and my squad was ordered up a steep hill at a double quick to support them, we going through an open field and the Yanks protected in a skirt of woods extending for about 300 or 400 yards. Our Lieut. Vandiver asked permission of the

Major commanding to charge them, and also get a position in the woods; and being granted, he rushed forward waving his cap and calling on Company F to follow him, and in we went with a yell that made the woods ring again.[26] It required a great effort, but I was determined to make my first charge in good style, and followed close to the Lieut, cheering and hollering as loud as I could after the long run up the hill, and across the field. We drove the enemy back to the center of the woods, we occupying the edge; and then such hot work I never saw, and the boys of the company said that they never were in a worse place. We continued the fight here for about a half an hour—our Artillery a half mile to our rear throwing the shell a little over our head, and bursting among the enemy a little beyond us; and the enemy's guns occupying a position a little on our right flank, and pouring into us a perfect stream of shells and grape; and such cutting down of tree tops, and slashing among the bushes, I have conceived of but never before saw. The sharp sound of the small arms, the zip-zip of the passing balls, the thug-thug of those that hit, mingled with the roar of the bursting shells, and the crashing of the grape, was truly terrific—all of this fighting occurred with the enemy at 80 to 100 yards distant, depending on the position they occupied in the woods. When we had been here about a half an hour, the Yanks rammed a battery of guns up to within 75 yards of us, and were unlimbering their pieces, when we poured such a volley into them, that they had to fall back behind the hill. On our left, however, the sharpshooters had worked round under cover of the wood, until they were considerably in our rear, and we received orders to fall back, which we did most willingly; the enemy's sharp-shooters outnumbering us two or three to one.

While loading my gun I saw a fellow six or eight feet from me throw up his hands and utter a heart-rending cry, and running over to where I was, threw himself down. I noticed the blood spouting from his heart in a great stream and running all over the man next to me, who I suppose may have been an acquaintance. We both ceased firing for a minute to contemplate the scene, and the last I remember was hearing the death rattle in his throat. We both re-mained there some time afterwards, but were so engaged in watch-ing, and shooting the enemy that I do not remember to have noticed the poor fellow's body, or to have thought of him afterwards, until we had taken a new position. Our noble Lieut. was also shot here, and close by me, but he was gotten out and is now doing well. I shot away all my caps and all cartridges except two at this stand point, and when I reached my horse, was completely exhausted; my tongue as dry and hard as a hammer and feeling as if swollen, and refusing to remain in my mouth. Such was my first day's fight, extending over about eight miles, and fell back six or seven more after night. Out of forty men, our company lost ten captured, two wounded, and one missing, and a number of horses killed and wounded.[27]

On the 14th, our Regiment crossed the Rapidan and lay in reserve supporting the Artillery, which was roaring all day. On the 15th, we re-crossed the river, and sharp-shot with the enemy all day. Here I got a good position behind a fence, and could take my time in loading and shooting. I like this much better, but here I had several narrow escapes. My horse was struck once but not hurt, by a spent ball. I was not on her at the time. I got some elegant shots, and made my man change positions, but can't say that I hit any. Stuart lost two or three pieces of Artillery, and quite a number of men in the retreat, and accomplished all that Lee wished probably, to check the advance. The Yanks are now trying to cross the Rapidan, which is our line. Our little squad of Cavalry had held tens of thousands of the enemy in check for more than a month at Pearl River.

My best love to all of yours, and at home. Do write to me. May a merciful God preserve us all to meet again on earth, and hereafter, to rest in Heaven,

Yours,
H. M. T.
September 19th, 1863.

Since writing the foregoing, I have been in the saddle night and day for about thirty six hours—started on a raid I think, but for some cause returned. Rained in torrents for eight or ten hours, raising the streams. We reached Madison C.H. yesterday—will probably return to Rapidan today. We went within six miles of Culpepper C.H., where there are the largest portion of the Yankee troops,—report says three Corps.

Charles, your two papers came to hand. You had better continue to send them, as I do not get papers with any regularity—particularly if you see anything of interest.

An amusing incident occurred on our falling back from Culpepper on the 13th. An old Yankee Bugler came galloping along past the 15th Virginia Regiment, his hat hanging down on his back, and hollering "Come on, boys, come on boys," supposing that he was with his Regiment. Rain was pouring down at the time, and our men were covered with their oil-clothes. He could hardly believe he was mistaken till he was disarmed.

Madison County, between
Rapidan & Robertson
Rivers, [September 16, 1863] S.T.W.

Dear Chs.

Your letter dated the 9th inst. came to hand today 16th Sept and afforded me much pleasure. I could in no way account for your death like silence. I am glad that it is explained and hope that you will call regularly at the P.O. and also write to me frequently always forwarding everything from home. You must also forward all my letters to Texas—those to yourself as well as to other persons.

Capt. D[.] C. Cady used to be concerned in a drug store nearly opposite Dennis Neil's, Tremont St. and was afterwards about the Federal Court a great deal[,] acting as Deputy Marshal under Cleveland & Ben McCullough. He is a little short heavy set fellow and very obliging—I know him well. He came to Va. as a private in the "Lone Stars" under Capt. McKeen.[28] I am sorry to hear of your difficulties in going before the Board. Hon. Peter W. Gray was our last Rep. and has most probably been re-elected. He is a friend of ours and will, I am confident do all that he can. Col. Wilcox from the West I do not know. Genl John A. Wharton has probably been elected to Congress from his Dist. You may rely on him. I am not acqt. with Wigfall, but I expect he knows our family and connections.[29] I would have you remain where you are even if you fail to get a comm. if you can do it but if unable to remain where you can[,] perfect yourself in your profession. I should like much for you to join the cavalry if you could procure a horse to start on. We have been having some lively work for the last three days—some account of which I will give in a letter addressed to Sister Mary—You must not wait to write to me until I write to you individually as each of my letters will be sent to you to read and then forward—Can't you write me once a week regularly? And I will write as often to you or some of the family. I think you are mistaken about Mrs. Genl [Kirby] Smith being at Lynchburg—as I understood and *knew* her to be at Shreveport, La., when I passed through. But leave no plan untried to communicate regularly with home—as it is absolutely necessary for me to know how my business there is progressing. I think there will be no difficulty in arranging the matter thru Cady.

"Winning Ways"

You can use the $10 I left you to pay the necessary postage and do not forward me the newspapers as I requested—as I can get them long enough to read, from some one in camp—If you see anything interesting from home, (Texas), you may cut out and send to me.

I have not met a soul that I ever knew or heard of before, except, I believe, Richard Davis, Chaplain to the 6th Va. Cav. The gentleman who is Col. of the Reg'm't., is a fr[iend] of & very highly thought of—by Uncle Jno. He is not in command now, not having recovered from a recent wound.[30] It is under the command of Lt. Col. Marshall, a most exemplary Christian, and as brave as a lion. Even the boys who don't like him admit that he never flinches when danger comes and that he goes much farther than they like to follow. He has had two horses shot under him in the last three days.[31] Our Maj is a German, but a good humored pleasant little fellow and equally cool and collected as Marshall. My Capt is Issac Kuykendall of Maryland—a handsome, gentlemanly fellow 25 years old and extremely pleasant to get along with—a little too much so if anything– 1st Lt. is Thornton Parker and 2nd Lt Chas Vandiver—both from the Valley.[32] He led us in a charge on Sunday upon a lot of Sharp shooters—with cap in hand & 10 or 15 paces a head talking to us and encouraging us all the time. He was shot thru the leg on that day, and is now at Charlottesville.

[Unsigned]

University of Virginia
September 28, 1863

Dear Father:

The first line received from home since my departure came to hand on the 24th inst., being a short note from T. M. J., dated the 22nd Aug, and you may well rest assured offered me very great pleasure. It found me flat on my back at Uncle John Minor's, suffering somewhat from a sabre wound just inside and above the knee of the right leg—penetrating to the depth of—and ranging up–2 or 3 inches inflicted I am sorry to say, by my own sabre, which two days before I had ground up as sharp as a knife, with which to slay some luckless Yankee, as of course the cavalry sometimes have to fight them hand to hand.

On the 21st a little before sundown and just as we had unsaddled the bugle sounded to "saddle up" and five minutes afterwards "to mount" and my Regt together with the 11th were on our

Rebel Brothers

∾

way to meet a large force crossing Robinson river at Madison C.H. & at about 8 o'clk the 11th began to meet the advance of the enemy 1 1/2 miles this side of Madison and to skirmish pretty continuously until about 11 o'clk that night, we losing two fine soldiers killed, & 5 or 6 wounded—We then put out pickets & falling back a mile, lay on our arms till daylight, when our Regt was ordered to the front. During the night, a very large cavalry force had come to our support & about 8 o'clk Stuart made a reconnaisance in person & finding that the enemy in force cavalry—infty & artillery were advancing along the pike towards the crossing of the Rapidan at Liberty Mills leading thence to Gordonsville or Charlottesville—the pike at this point being some 2 or 3 miles out west—he lead his whole force in that direction and fought them with his cavalry and horse artillery falling back gradually—all day—inflicting considerable loss on the enemy, & losing himself several hundred killed captured and wounded & capturing about 100 of the enemy. He finally prevented their crossing at Liberty Mills. On the road where they had first shown a disposition to advance—leading to Orange C.H. he left a squadron only of about 50 men, I being one—I was soon put on picket with 6 others—My position was in a very narrow lane on one flank of the picket line & 200 yards in advance of all the rest—they standing near the entrance to said lane. I had not been on post half an hour before the Yanks made a rapid advance, driving our pickets past the mouth of the lane and completely cutting me off—and forcing me to jump the fence and retreat through a corn field—my horse taking me through in gallant style & jumping fences and ditches like a deer. We were under comd of one of Stuart's staff officers and would occasionally check the enemy a little with our sharp shooters—After falling back thus a mile or two—the enemy pressing us hard, and endeavoring to flank us, we were ordered to let down the lane fences on either side, and also a cross fence so as to enable our men to deploy on either side and give the enemy a check.[33] In obeying the order I jumped from my horse leaving her tied in the lane and sprang over the lane fence to let down the cross fence—the impulse of my motion in going over & the striking of the scabbard against the top rail—threw my sabre out, and I came with my whole force against its point. I did not feel the wound but thinking that some splinter had stuck in my pants and entangled my leg, I seized it and endeavored to wrench it out of the way and only then discovered that it had penetrated my leg. I drew it out of my leg and with it a stream of blood gushed down into my

graduate at the Richmond Medical School ere he can be—altho some of his medical friends well qualified to judge pronounce him well fitted for a coms as Asst. Surg now.

Rather unexpectedly to me[,] Aunt Livy Minor with Clara, Lila & Farrell arrived yesterday to stay two or three days. She gave me a most warm reception for Mother's sake and I was much pleased by her sweetness of manner, etc. Uncle Jno's house is perfectly full of Refugees wounded etc. I am the 3rd nephew who has been nursed tenderly and kindly—besides others of Aunt Fanny's relatives and how many strangers I don't know. About the 16th inst. I wrote sister Mary a long letter giving some acct. of the two days fighting and my participation in it—I hope that she may receive and be sure *to reserve* as I should like to refer to it as memo. Letter writing in the army is attended with many inconveniences & drawbacks—being very tiresome to write on your cap brim or an old greasy canteen, or lie flat on the ground and rest the paper on your oil cloth.

I am in fine health—fatter than ever in my life before—and anxious to get back to my Regt in time for the general engagement expected soon. My Capt and me had just arranged to go over into the enemy's camp at night with a small party to capture some fine horses—which is occasionally done with success, and very much to the annoyance of the Yanks. On one occasion they enquired of our men if they had seen any stray horses over our way and on that very night our men had been over and taken three superb horses from their owners while they slept, and the Sect'y of War actually permitted our boys to keep them as private property—I suppose to encourage our supplying ourselves in this way.

There are many conflicting reports relative to the movements of [Maj. Gen. George G.] Meade and Lee & as to the probabilities of a general engagement[,] some asserting that Meade is sending reinforcements to Rosecran [Maj. Gen. William Rosecrans], and others that he is receiving reinforcements.[35]

I think that Meade will be induced to attack Lee under the impression that he has been very materially weakened by the absence of Longstreet's Corps in Tenn. and the rumors that we are still reinforcing from Lee's Army—and from all that I can hear Lee has no objections to his taking, and acting upon this view of the case.[36]

Meade's is believed to be weaker than even the Army of the Potomac was before when advancing to Richmond besides having in his army a large no. of conscripts.

"Winning Ways"

~

However and whenever Meade comes, we—Army & people—feel confident that he comes only to meet a *sure* defeat.

How the news from Bragg's army announcing the victory of Chickamauga thrilled every heart with joy—and many were the silent tears that flowed, and many the grateful thanks offered up to an Almighty God therefore. It was a victory at the right place and at the right time; and altho' another must be *fought* and *won* to secure the full fruits of the first, still it was a cheering success. I regret that Bragg should have used such strong language in his dispatch.

The *"enemy routed"* and a *"complete victory"* conveys a very great deal of meaning and can seldom be used truthfully. Lee never uses such language.[37]

I was truly delighted to see by the Yankee papers—(the only acct yet rec'd) that Genl Magruder and the Texans had again met the enemy so successfully and thwarted his oft repeated attempts of invasion—at Sabine—and then they seemed to be so taken by surprise in the extent of our resistance.—and to capture the gun boats "Clifton" and "Sachem" was admirable—they of right *belong to us*—for we whipped them fairly at Galveston and would have taken possession had not the sneaking rascals *run out under a white flag*. The Yanks admitted that the fire of our batteries was *awfully accurate* and that there was not a man on the afterpart of the Clifton who escaped being killed or wounded. I could see "the two Rebel gun boats" in my mind's eye as they came steaming down the channel and made the attack on the "Sachem," according to Yankee accounts.[38]

A report of a recent victory by Dick Taylor at Napoleon (?) represented to have *been very disasterous*, has also reached us through New Orleans papers.

I am glad to hear from T. M. J. that he is getting on so well with office affairs—He will have to continue to manage them for me as there is no probability of early return as I can render as efficient service here as elsewhere. Hope that he may have no difficulty in being permitted to continue in the performance of the duties since the *call to 45*—even tho' he should cease to be Mayor.[39] In case it becomes necessary, you must call on Mr. Cole who promised me that my interests as A & C should not suffer while I was absent in the Army—so far as he could control them of course. Tell Mr. Howard to send me word where his relatives live & what their names are, etc. as I may have a chance to visit them this winter after the campaign is over. Mention the marriageable daughters of course!

Rebel Brothers

My sweet little Fanny will be next on my letter list—Has she taken good care of Billy? Echo answers—*Yes*—for his master's sake. Unfortunately all of my letters to you all for the first six weeks after entering the army—being sent through Chas—at Ly[nchburg]—were put into an old box that had long since been given up by him & he got them all at once and forwarded to you thru Capt. Cady of Rich, Genl Agt of Texas Brig. He has now gone to Tenn, and I hardly know how to send this unless thro Genl Maury at Mobile.

My warmest love to all Cally, Fanny, Minny, & Mother, Sister Mary & Bow & their respective Husbands and children.

Will probably be well *enough to return* to duty in 10 or 12 days. Continue to direct to care of Chas at Lynchb'g, & he can send to me in Company F, 7th Regt Va Cavly, Jones' Brigade, Army of Northern Virginia.

Your aff son,
H. M. T.

University of Va.
October 14/63.

My Sweet little Sister [Fanny]

Your turn for a letter has again come round—It has been a long time truly—but there are so many for me to write to at home that a letter to any particular one is necessarily of rare occurrence. Yesterday I returned from Harrisonburg in the Valley where I had been with Edlow Bacon to see if I could get into the famous "McNeill's Rangers"—Mr. B. lending me a horse to ride—but starting the day after my first getting out of bed and before my leg had fully healed the wound has reopened and has been quite painful, laying me up for several days and altho' I am walking about now—it is still running a little—but am nearly relieved of the pain. I have joined this commd as it affords me an opportunity of supplying myself with horses & clothing—his company being entitled to all that they capture.

It was with much regret I left the officers & men of the 7th Cavalry.

McN[eill] is very active & his comd performs some gallant feats—with 27 men he recently attacked a train of 27 wagons–6 horses each—& captured the whole, together with the drivers & a guard of seventy men.[40]

"Winning Ways"

More recently still with about 100 men he attacked at night one of the two parties of Federals who were moving to surprise him—both parties of superior force to his—and charging into & trampling down their tents while they were asleep—captured some 147 of them together with their wagons, tents, etc. etc. & altho' attacked by the other party succeeded in bringing off prisoners and property, except some 15 or 20 horses killed in the attack—only having 2 or 3 men wounded—so you see I've got into active service *in fact*. We operate in the Valley & in the rear of the enemy almost entirely. There are several commands of this character who are harrassing the enemy to death. Genl Lee's army made a forward movement on the 9th and at last acct's are pressing Meade closely and capturing prisoners, etc. A general cavalry engagement took place on the 12th in which we drove the enemy several miles capturing some 600 prisoners—loss on both sides considerable. There is no doubt but that Lee is also making a flank movement with the intention of getting a fight out of Meade—but fears are entertained that it has failed in consequence of Meade's running so fast that we can barely keep up with him, much less flank him—However we don't *know* anything about these matters till they actually transpire. At last accts M[eade] had crossed the Rappahanock, not even having time to burn the bridge.

President Davis is now at Chattanooga[41]—Hope that his presence may be of advantage—People are almost breathless in anticipation of the results of that campaign—By the blessing of God we occupy a favorable position and have reason to hope for a crowning success there. The Va. papers are teeming (with one or two exceptions) with the brillancy of the Sabine Pass affair. "The Examiner" is disposed to make game of the whole affair.

I notice Tom Ochiltree's arrival at Mobile & suppose he may be at Richmond soon and hope to send this letter across the Miss. by him. Cousin Mary Kemper has just forwarded me a long letter to enclose to Mother which I do herewith—you all must not attach much importance to her insinuations against the cavalry—It is common for those who have none of their immediate family in that branch to abuse it. And there is considerable ill feeling between the cavalry & infantry—and all sorts of hard jokes & reports in circulation. The infty pretends that they have a standing reward of $300— for a *dead* cavalryman & even go so far as to express the greatest wonder to a poor wounded cavalry man passing by that he ever went close enough to be hit.

Rebel Brothers

Additional accts are just come from the front—There has been a good deal more cavalry fighting & skirmishing—driving the enemy & capturing some 400 more prisoners.

Meade not yet crossed the Rap[pahanock] and Lee pressing a part of his forces so as to get to the rear of Meade.[42]

I regret that this little wound should have laid me up at this time as I should much like to be in the advance. Gen'l Imboden's, & McNeill's forces moved rapidly down the Valley on the 9th so as to press on the flank.[43]

I go down to Dr. Pendleton's tomorrow to get some additional clothing & 2nd day afterwards to Uncle Wm Overton's to get my horse and by the 18th or 19th hope to be well enough to start for my company.

The Valley is a lovely country and the people kind and attentive to soldiers. Stayed all night with a gentleman living close to & in full view of the battlefield of Port Republic, and on next day found that there was a party of ladies & several gentlemen going to explore Weyer's Cave (3 miles distant) and mine host having a beautiful daughter without an escort—I *offered* and was *accepted* & had a most pleasant day of it—but altho' so agreeable to me, it proved very detrimental to my leg which together with my pleasant quarters & company detained me for two days longer. The old gentleman & me—not to mention anybody else—got very intimate. He giving me a regular introduction to his daughter & nieces *after we returned* from the cave. He would not hear of taking any pay for me or my horse—saying "that he had been more than repaid by my agreeable company, etc.," and inviting me to call again. I wrote to Father on the 30th ultimo. sending through Major Burnet, D. H. Maury's Chf. of Ord thinking he might fwd from Mobile. On the 24" of Sept recd a letter fr T. M. J. dated 22nd Aug. & on yesterday one from A. T. T. dated 18" July—the only two that have come to hand so far—but don't be discouraged—the oftener you write—the more of a chance of my getting some of them.

Prest. Davis has ordered all the Consuls of the Eng Govt to cease to act & to leave the Conf. States. Am sorry to hear that you & Cally have been having chills—Hope you are well now. Tell T. M. J. to let me hear how my office matters closed up—Continue to direct to care Chs at Lynchburg—who will fwd to me. My warmest love and kisses to all—big and little—male and female.

Your own loving,
Henry

"Winning Ways"

∾

183

Near Dayton, Rockingham
County, Dec 5th 1863.

Dear Chas

Yours of the 17th & 27th ult. respectively are at hand. The latter enclosing a sheet of paper—most acceptable—and upon which I pen your reply.

I think the last time I wrote you was on the 23rd ult. enclosing a letter to T. M. J. & which you will enjoy admirable facilities for transmitting to Texas since you are stationed at Richmond. You ought to visit the principal hotels regularly—say every afternoon or evening & examine the Register so as to see any persons from Texas who may visit Richmond—In this way you can frequently hear from home & how things are getting on in our state & much more satisfactorily too than the newspaper accts and can also have the very best opportunity of sending letters home and then you will often meet men immediately from Galveston and Houston. By the by—have you seen the bearer of the colors taken at Sabine—I see by the papers that Magruder selected a private from the Company to be the bearer—one who had distinguished himself—it may be that he is an acquaintance of ours as that Company was partly made up from Galveston County. You have not sent me any "Texas" extracts yet—do so—cut out everything relative to TransMississippi affairs. Your suggestion relative to "lettering your letters" so as to enable me to know if I get them all is good—but to no., will be better and I will adopt the same plan keeping dates and nos. in a little Memo book, and to put the plan into operation at once, this will be No. 9 for me, and your last—say No. 12 for you. I have not been getting one every week so far. And another thing always acknowledge the rect of all letters recd since your last writing—either by date or number and then we can always understand each other.

I had heard the report you allude to relative to our relation Mrs. . . . but was not inclined to believe or circulate and concluded that if there was unfortunately any truth in it—it would be fastened upon her too soon anyway.

You ask when I am coming over to the East of the Ridge. I had intended to do so Xmas if we were not in the enemy's line and still think it likely that I shall do so. There is every reason to believe that we shall start on a raid now in 4 or 5 days. I hope that we may be abundantly successful as my finances are getting extremely low—Do you reckon Uncle John can without inconvenience [loan]

Rebel Brothers

~

184

me some money if I should have to borrow? The ladies of the Valley I find as kind to me as can be—One with whom I have become acquainted has made me two nice wh[ite] cotton hdkfs.—(I having none) and knit me an elegant pr of gloves—another presented me with a nice towel for camp use—another furnished me with several pr of warm woolen socks, which are very scarce & worth $5 per pair—and another let me have an excellent pair of jeans pants ready made for ten dollars when they would have brought $50 in the market—so much for being a Texan and possessing "winning ways." Other kind ladies and young and pretty too—have sewed up holes and mended places in my clothing, that I never dreamed of being in unrepair—so close a look out do they keep on my welfare.

Others express sorrow at the moving of my deposit of clothes from their houses lest I may not come back anymore, etc.—So you see I am well taken care of.

By the by don't part with my vest with the staff buttons on it but assure me occasionally that you still have it on hand for me, and the neckties too. Have you any room to accomodate me if I should come to see you? And will you be able to keep up your bill of fare given in your last—without going beyond your income?

I should advise you to have a few select acquaintances among the number the Misses Street. Did you know that they were friends of Mary Launcelot, and that she sometimes stays with them?

Be careful also to have no more *fruitless love* affairs. My affections are still unengaged, wandering about and seeking whom they may devour—for I feel the need of someone to love away so far from home. I find that I am daily becoming more and more hard to please—standard continually advancing. Mr. B. & myself have an invitation to spend Xmas at Uncle Wm O[verton]'s, and are looking forward with pleasure to doing so. Do you often write home? And do you enclose my letters to you—thence? It would be well. I shall write to them when I return from next raid. In meantime give my warmest love to one and all of them. I think of them continuously & remember them twice daily in my prayers to God.

Pray that I may daily grow in grace and favor with God and be ever ready to meet the final summons which may come without a moment's warning, at all times, but now even more than ever. I find Mr. Bacon a very pleasant companion.[44] Do write me regularly.

Your loving brother,
H. M. T.

"Winning Ways"

~

~

CHAPTER 8

"The Wild and Ever Changeful Life,"
1864

Richmond, Va.
Febr 6th 1864

Dear Tom [Joseph]

Yours of Novr 3rd accompanied by eight more from other members of the family—the latest of 5th Nov & balance ranging back for about a month—have all been received and did indeed do my heart good—being the only word from home since 22nd Aug. Your letter was particularly satisfactory as it related to my office affairs and you have no idea how much accounts cheer me up and steady my aim on our vandal enemies. Charles received, read, and then forwarded the letters to me. I was at the time on a raid over in the Yankee lines of 22 days duration—barefooted—or nearly so— through a spell of cold weather such as has not been equaled since 1832 and in which many Yankees and Confeds too were frozen— The Yankees even drawing in their pickets after several were frozen to death—nor had I any great coat—but thanks to God I came out all right except one toe & my heels slightly frosted—but I have given you all a full account of the whole trip in a letter of Jany 25th (?) to Mother, Cally & Fanny of six pages, the lines doubly written which makes it equal to twelve pages.[1] I hope they may get it and think it probable, as it was forwarded by Mr. Barziza—the one next above "Ultimus."

I am now on a week's visit to Richmond, thinking that I had might as well visit about and enjoy myself while my horses are recruiting & which will take them at least a month.

Indeed large numbers of men are being furloughed now from Lee's army and one whole division of Stuart's Cavalry is disbanded and permitted to go home—provided they don't go more than two days march from the place of rendevous, and it is thought that thus giving the men a chance to go home will have a good effect in the prevention of desertion which was becoming very common.[2] It is believed by those in a position to know, that we shall have in the spring a more efficient army than ever before—and no doubt we shall need it. Every thing is being husbanded now for the Spring & Summer campaigns and the armies are consequently on very short rations. In one instance Lee's army did not draw but a 1/4 of a lb. of meat for five days—but they are now getting a 1/4 of lb. per day and alternating between wheat & corn bread & sometimes too a little real coffee and sugar—It is gratifying to see how cheerfully they bear it too rarely complaining—but laughing and joking over it all and wondering how *much less* a man [can] learn to live on and may be winding up by asserting that this *eating* is all a *habit* anyway & can soon be overcome—and to show that the fellows are really in earnest each day brings from the Va & Tenn armies accts of the reenlistment to a man of whole Regts, Brig's, and even Divisions—for the war. With such a spirit the Yankees will fight us in vain. On the contrary they have failed to buy soldiers at $1,000 per head and have ordered a draft.

Chas. is pleasantly situated here and seems to be making good progress—He feels no misgivings relative to graduation—does not have much to eat but still looks well—bill of fare—breakfast, bl[ac]k or Brier root tea—one small piece beef liver & bread; Dinner—one small piece meat—can easily take it into your mouth at once—a *few* pease or turnips or cabbage & bread. Supper (not considered necessary to the well being anyway) small piece of corn or wheat bread and water. I tell him I can't sympathize with him so long as he looks so well. Where I operate in the enemie's lines we have lived on the fat of the land as evinced by my weight 190 lbs— We are glad to see that the Yanks have not accomplished anything except the occupation of some few points on the coast and hope and believe that they will not be able to do much more—They can't possibly *invade* Texas successfully. If there is a prospect of its being done or of her needing men next summer, I shall return—if not shall enter for the war here. Should be glad for you to give me your views. Nothing but a war is before us now and it may be a long one and I have no idea of filling any position except that of a private in the field. Of course shall expect you to wind up my affairs for me. Am out of money & will have to borrow—If you can see any safe chance send me some—if not invest any on hand in bonds or something else. Don't send unless can do so safely. Love to all at home and at your house—and Mr. Howard's.

Yours aff,

H. M. T.

This goes by a Mr. Adams of Harrisonburg or Houston.

Rockingham County Virginia
April 8th AD. 1864.

Dear Charles

Your (always) welcome letter of the 6th inst came to hand day before yesterday. I am delighted at your having seen our old friend and neighbor, M. L. Parry from Texas. An incident of that sort always makes one feel so much nearer home than would the reception of a letter. You dont say whether the letter you forwarded by him was mine of the 11th Mar from this Co[unty] or that of 22nd Mar from Hardy. Try to write more like a business man—come to the point and make comprehensible that which you attempt to communicate. If I'm guilty of the same fault which I think is quite likely, complain of it and I'll endeavor to correct it. But I am sorry to have taken you to task thus finding fault instead of awarding to you the praise so justly your due in having passed your examinations creditably and at last placed yourself respectably in your profession. I suppose I must assume the ground that Mother used to do when she would take me out to switch me—"this gives me more pain that it does *you*, my dear boy, but I do it entirely for your good." Of course you'll believe me more implicitly than I then did her too!

I reached here several days ago—the 8th—from Pendleton Co[unty], coming over in charge of some prisoners and our command being now inactive on account of the Capt's sickness. I shall remain here till he recovers which may be ten or twelve days. He had intermittent fever at Harrisonburg, where he had been summoned to attend a court martial—charged with snapping his shot gun at a man and then breaking it over his head for disobedience—while close to the enemy. We hope he will be able to get off without being broke. It seems to be generally understood that his command together with Mosby's will be excepted by the Secretary of War from the effects of the recent law of Congress disbanding the partizan commands, but we yet know nothing definite. In the event of its disbandment, I think I shall return to the old 7th Regt Rosser's Brigade.[3] I have written to the shoemaker to ascertain if your shoes are ready & if so will go over to Magaheysville after them and forward in accordance to your latest instructions. At present all former instructions relative to the matter stand annulled. I await the next set and the shoes.

I hope you may be able to get an agreeable location when assigned to duty. If not in the field Charlottesville or Lynchburg would suit you admirably. By the by when you go to Amherst give my special love to Uncle Lanty and all of his family. I wrote him when last East of the Ridge regretting my inability to call to see him. Also love to Cousins Mary . . . & Mary Blackford. Do write me frequently while enjoying yourself among our friends. Cousin Polly writes me that they are expecting a visit from you soon at their house. A pleasant time to you. How pleasant it would be if I could join you in your round of visits. A letter from Mary Launcelot a few days since brings me the sad intelligence of dear Cousin Betty Pendleton's death, as also Uncle John's youngest daughter—Bessie. Have written to Dr. P. and shall write to Mary L. in a day or two. It would gratify Dr. P. to receive a letter from you, I have no doubt. The envelopes stamps & paper couldn't have been exchanged for anything more acceptable.

> Your loving bro,
> Henry M.

The latest style of spelling does not recognize "centered" as correct—all else correct.

Rockingham Co, Va
April 14th, A.D. 1864

Dear Cally

A package per express containing a letter from Mother of 28th of Jan'y[,] one from Fanny of 24th Jan'y, and one from Elvira of Nov 1st/63 has arrived. Now I only presume that El's came in the same package from the fact that Chas—who opens & reads all my letters—enclosed to me under same cover with those of 24th & 28th of Jan'y. Tho' it seems very strange—Nor can I tell Bow if the Cravat she so thoughtfully started, ever reached its destination, as Chas does not say. The last letters recd prior to those were A. T. T., 5 &

Wild and Changeful Life

7th Jan'y & Cally's 7th Jan'y. Mother's last does not mention the date of my last—'Twould be a great satisfaction if you all would mention by date the receipt of the last letter always. It is poor encouragement to write when one does not know whether his letters are ever received. Jan'y 23rd I wrote a long letter—*double lines*—equal to twelve pages addressed to Mother, Cally & Fanny. Feb'y 6th to T. M. J. from Richmond. M[ar]ch 4th to Fanny from Wm Overton's—together with five letters to Chas—all of which he is requested to forward to Texas as affording you the same information as if addressed to you all. Now you can tell which you've rcved & which not. Hope from the advantages we have in forwarding directly from Richmond that no letters have gone much more certainly to their destination than yours have done.

I have just returned to this Co[unty] in charge of some prisoners from Pendleton & Hardy Co[unties], in "New Va" where our comd has been for the last six weeks, more on acct of the corn & hay afforded by that country than [anything] else. Having only made one capture of seven Yanks & 15 horses & saddles etc. . . . the likes. Since we drove the Yanks from Petersburg, Hardy Co[unty] we have almost ruined our field of operations. The enemy has had two regt's, cav'ly & infantry in search of us continually for the last month endeavoring to catch kill or drive us out of that region, but so far unsuccessfully. Their force being so large—our company rarely has a chance of striking them a blow. We ellude them when too strong for us by a constant watchfulness for which our old Capt is famed. We camp about in the hollows & gorges of the mountains—never staying in one place more than 20 or 24 hours—moving late in the afternoon & going to some citizen's corn crib & hay stacks & part of us with large bags of corn & the balance of us almost obscured by enormous bundles of hay—tied up in halters & girths & strung out in single file—We select a new camp, never going into it before dark, unless the Yanks are known to be near & watching us when we go into camp before night, build up large fires and afterwards leave them, selecting a new camp. The day time is spent where we passed the preceding night the pickets occupying some commanding hill overlooking the roads & country all around with spy glass in hand. At other times our comd is concealed along the road where the enemy is expected and when the opportune moment arrives, a wild yell and a charge—the charges preceded by a *discharge*, is the only warning the poor Yanks have . . . . No wonder they dread McNeill's men. The command has become noted for its . . . gallant & often wonderful captures and encounters. He has operated principally on their wagon trains & many is the wagon destroyed, or brought off, together with hundreds and hundreds [of] horses.

One of the Richmond papers reports recently that McNeill's comd has turned over to the prisons at Richmond, in the 18 months of its organization, eleven hundred Yankee prisoners. The number of killed & wounded of course we can't know—but many is the Yank who has bit the dust or groaned in agony with the wounds inflicted by this comd.

Our old Capt is sick at present and we are lying inactive, recruiting our horses—till he recovers.

Horse feed has become a scarce article in Va. Imboden's cavalry having nothing but wheat straw *now*, and for the past month with corn once or twice a week. We stayed with the Yanks in *New* Va., & share their corn & hay—much against their will.[4] The citizens are delighted to have us there & glad for us to feed their forage. They furnish us with rations too in abundance. So that you need not think of me as one of the poor soldiers who is starving for his country's cause. There is no question about Lee's army having been on very short rations during the winter, but it was to save . . . more for the spring campaign. . . . they would have hard fighting . . . marching to do & would require . . . And you could not help being touched at the cheerfulness with which the men would put up with 1/4 of a lb meat & equally small proportion of bread per day—or as on several occasions where they got no meat for four or five days together— living on a little *cold water corn bread*. Their noble Genl [Lee] is equally self sacrificing—A splendid house bo[ught] for him by the city of Rich[mond] he declined to receive, while his soldier's families need help.

Or when the people of Rich[mond] were run mad on the subject of parties & balls etc. he was invited to a superb & costly dinner— while there on business—his reply was he 'could not think of feasting when his soldiers were suffering for necessaries.'[5] Can any sane man reasonably expect to whip such an army—led by such a General? A long list of would-be heroes have tried it and failed and so will Mr. Grant, the last of the list. Ask T. M. J. to send me a list of all my land—out and in Counties—as well as all those in which I am interested—Say copy *verbatim* from my property book—*Be sure & soon*. Will write him soon relative to my course and affairs—

Wild and Changeful Life

$\sim$

Also to Bow. Love to *all* no room to name. You'll all be delighted as I am with Charles' success.

Your loving Bro,
Henry.

Rockingham Co. Va.
May 21/64

Dear Charles:

Yours of Ap[ril] 30th enclosing letters from Mother, Cally, & Fanny yours of 3rd inst written from Amherst & yours of 11th & 12th written from the field near Spottsylvania C H have all been received—the latter yesterday. I regret that I have been so situated as to prevent my writing later than the 26th ult. (I think). I had hoped that you might get an assignment to duty at Lynchburg to another hospital, but was not at all surprised to see your last dated in the field. Young able bodied men like you & me (not so very young either) ought to bear the burdens of the service and indeed you seem to bear some of them without much suffering, from the careless manner in which you allude to the dirt being thrown upon you while in the act of writing, etc. I have not become quite so indifferent to visitors of that sort yet tho' still I have never found myself dodging them but I certainly have uneasy forebodings while in their immediate vicinity. On the 27th ult. Mr. Bacon & myself started for Hardy Co[unty] to rejoin our company and the evening after our arrival were selected as two of 59 picked men & who were well mounted, for an expedition to the Balt & O R.R. I shall not give you a detailed account as you have no doubt seen it in the Richmond papers. Suffice it to say that it sorely tried man & beast and in its conception & successful execution it is pronounced by Gen'l. Imboden & regarded by the people here as ranking high among the many daring & brilliant achievements called forth by the times & circumstances surrounding us. We traveled day & night for three days & three whole nights in succession with only 4 or 5 hours rest during the time—Went into Maryland, captured two heavily laden freight & one passenger train—the former loaded with Govt stores & the latter with produce–104 officers and privates, all fully armed & equipped demanded and recd the surrender of the town of Piedmont Va with its garrison of 10 men & a Sergeant strongly posted in a brick house—burned seven R.R. locomotives & machine establishments said to be the most extensive and valuable on the Balt. & O. RR[,] together with 85 RR cars 9 engines large quantities of oil turpentine & paint etc and finally to prevent a force from coming up the road from New Creek Station we sent six other engines down the road under full head of steam & going at a fearful rate of speed without any one to control them. As our lead locomotive rounded a turn & passed out of sight we heard a down train give a signal whistle but our old locomotive disregarded all signals & dashed on regardless of consequences. We also brought out 40 odd horses from a govt stable at Piedmont & taken from a renegade Va'n who had gone voluntarily with the Yankee army, & had given up many a hard fight. Private property was carefully respected. The Yankees value the RR machine manufactories, etc at a million of dollars. We reached Moorefield much exhausted—having successfully eluded cavalry and infty sent to cut us off & before we were half rested were surrounded by 400 cavly and 200 infty. We received one charge from 250 of the cavalry wounding 5 Yanks & capturing 1 fine horse and losing one indifft horse & two men captured—We then took to the woods & mountains hovering around the cavalry night & day to attack them to advantage. They became alarmed and left suddenly one night in the direction of Winchester but meeting with a rgmt of Imboden's command, they were attacked and pursued for twelve miles, losing some 5 or 6 killed their wagon train, twelve wagons & one ambulance, sixteen prisoners & a large number of horses.

We started thirteen hours afterwards & only missed intercepting their disorganized masses at Romney by one hour selecting ten of the best mounted men Lt. Dolan pursued them a distance of nine miles to Springfield at half speed & charging into them killed one Yankee & wounded another & recaptured our two men with three other prisoners that the Yankees had taken—also eight Yanks and ten or twelve horses.

The Yanks were completely demoralized and lost more than half of their horses. Their men leaving them and taking to the woods & mountains for safety.[6] We then heard the rear of Breckenridge's Artillery and endeavored to reach this Valley in time to get into Seigel's [Sigel's] rear and take his wagon train but on reaching Mt. Jackson—Shenandoah Co. found that he had already been soundly thrashed and retreated precipitately whence he came. I hear that he goes thus whipped to reinforce Genl. Grant.[7] Really the Lord of Hosts seems to be with us in every engagement in every portion of the country. The Trans-Mississippi news secured is particularly cheering.

I omitted to mention that just as we had done our work and were ascending the mountain and only seven or eight hundred yards from Piedmont a section of Artillery sent up from Cumberland together with infty opened on us and shelled most furiously for two miles while we were ascending a steep grade. We lost three or four horses killed & wounded and a man badly wounded who was coming out with us and to whom we had loaned a horse. He was shot behind me & a horse wounded next in front of me.[8] My bay mare is regarded as one of the finest and fastest in the command and of course I had the honor of being one of the party of ten who pursued the Yanks to Springfield and recaptured our men. I am sorry I am not in a condition to present you with a horse. Our captured stock is completely used up by being ridden by men that had broken down horses etc

Our command moved again today—Reached here day before yesterday.

I wont send a list of misspelt words now as you have no means of correcting them while in the Field. I shall be more than ever anxious to hear from you now—do write as often as possible. What shall I do with my letters for people at home since you are in the field? Advise me. I wont write till I hear from you. Will write to you again soon. Don't send me any more paper and stamps—I can get them.

Your loving bro,
Henry

Rockingham Co. Va
June 16th 1864.

Dear Chas:

Yours of May 19th from line of battle near Spotsylvania C. H. is the last that has come to hand. May 21st is the date of my last to you. Immediately afterwards my company moved, and we have been incessantly in the saddle ever since—sometimes day and night, and rarely ever getting a full night's sleep. We have been on the flank or in the rear of Hunter's army from Mt. Jackson to Staunton, picking up those who dared to leave their commands to forage through the country, thereby saving hundreds of farms from pillage and destruction.[9] While the enemy lay at New Market we made an entire circuit of his army ascertaining his force's from those of the citizens who had counted them and charging his rear & annoying him as much as possible. We wounded & killed several, capturing some prisoners and a few horses. When they lay at Harrisonburg we were also with them—rarely more than a mile or mile and a half

Rebel Brothers

distant, watching every movement by day, & firing on charging & killing their pickets at night. Imboden had fallen back on the Staunton pike to a strong position just beyond the North fork of the Shenandoah near Mt. Crawford and with all the fords above & for some miles below blockaded all the fords above & for some miles below awaited the coming of the enemy—Instead of following the pike however, they took the Port Republic road which road and ford were not blockaded or even picketted. As soon as the head of their column took this route we dispatched several couriers to Imboden stating the fact and an hour later sent him another dispatch stating that the whole force cavalry & infty together with their train of 200 wagons had gone towards Port Republic—leaving our Regt of cavalry to make a feint towards the Mt. Crawford bridge. All of the dispatches reached him, but yet three hours later after skirmishing with the Yankee rear wounding one & capturing one—we marched up the pike to Mt. C[rawford] and found Genl Jones who had just taken command still occupying his strong position on the pike awaiting the Yanks, who were then at P. Republic, crossing the river without opposition. After finding that we had come up the pike all the way from Harrisonburg and that the Yanks had most perversely determined to go around instead of over his strong position's he put his forces in motion and the next day—Sunday—fought the enemy between Middle & South rivers near a little place called Piedmont [not to be confused with Piedmont, West Virginia, mentioned earlier] about nine or ten miles from Staunton. The general position was the best in that region of country but the men were considerably broken down in the forced march to reach it & then the breast works on our extreme left were—I thought, unfortunately located. It was here that our men, after fighting gallantly & successfully repulsing the enemy from about 8 o'clk to 12 M. finally gave way under a terrible artillery fire enfilading our breastworks & scattering fence rails through the air like straws on a windy day. One or two Regts gave way here after they had repulsed the most desperate infantry charge for the third time and unfortunately at the very time when the Yanks believed themselves whipped & had already put their train in motion to the rear. We were not in the fight but occupied a position where we could see it—had reported to Genl Jones & waited orders.[10] A half hour before our left gave way, he had dispatched us "to go to the rear and attack their train—that all was well in front & that he could manage them there["]—but by the time the courier reached us it was *all wrong* instead of "all well" & we

"Swamps" & finally prevented by falling in with a no. of Yanks who had to be disposed of. On the 18" fell in with 100 "Swamps," killed 8 & by some *accident* took 3 prisoners, also burned two wagons & took 19 horses losing our gallant Lt. Dolan mortally wounded & another seriously. On 19th went after his body and finding that the Swamps were in waiting for us attacked them, killing all we could lay hands on—three.[13] On Sunday the 26th, when near the Balt. & O.R.R. fell in with a detachment of upwards of 100 men, 6th (West) Va. & surprising them took 58 prisoners–104 horses saddles bridles etc—killed 3 & wounded two that we know of[14]—Just reached this place last night to turn after the Yanks & leave this morning with Early bound I hope for Penn. Have no time to reply to your inquiries or to write home—Send this to the dear ones there with the assurance that I'll write when opportunity offers. Our late capture is composed of the finest set of horses I ever saw together. I am riding a magnificent animal called Bob Lee, who I bid off at $4100.

Have as many letters at Harrisonburg for me as you can when I return.

Yrs lovingly,
H. M.

Our loss in last fight was none other than three men severely hurt by falling off horses—

Harrisonburg Rockingham
Co. Va.
July 21 1864

Dearest—(who shall I say?)—Mother, I reckon, as it has been a long long time since I have written to her or indeed any body else at home. I am . . . struck when I refer to my memo & . . . that the 24th Apl is the last time I . . . T. M. J.–18th to Elvira & Fanny & 14th to Cally—but really since that time I have hardly had time . . . much less write—From what . . . present I have oftener failed to get . . . than otherwise. For a whole week together we would not sleep more than 3 or 4 hours of a night and so exhausted would we be during the day that altho' in spite of the enemy and expecting an attack at any minute we wo[uld] sleep while drawn up in line of battle, or leaning against a tree or if time permitted, throw ourselves on the grass relying on the first shot to arouse us. I came here seeking "active service" & have found it. But I've no reason for anything but thankfulness to a Kind Preserver who has enabled me to undergo it all without receiving any injury and in the finest of health. We had just returned from an expedition into the enemy's lines where with 80 men we attacked upwards of 100 of Averill's [Averell's] men all Western Virginians, killing 2 wounding 21—capturing 59—(a Capt & 2nd Lt) & 104 splendid . . . bridles etc complete without . . . a man—when we received . . . from Gen'l Early to strike the Rail . . . 60 miles West of his Army and after doing all the damage possible to join him in Md.[15] We celebrated the 4th July by burning an important bridge on the Balt. & O. R. R., and a considerable amt of property & being pursued by 260 mounted Infty We drove them back killing 3 & capturing three.[16] Our loss 1 man wounded & two or three horses killed & w[ounde]d. We were making forced marches for the first 6 days—succeeding in reaching Early's Army near Frederick City. He directed us to report to him for orders each day & closely employed did he keep us, too frequently day & night. He placed our comd–140 strong, to cover his rear as we approached Washington & in the advance coming out.[17] This was doing us honor—as it was from this . . . he expected Averill's [Averell's] & Hunter's . . . . We were skirmishing frequently . . . one day in the streets of Frederick City having a short fight the Yanks 250 strong charged us in town—the dust made it as dark as midnight & we were terribly mixed up for a while. Several hand to hand conflicts ensued—One of our Lts was struck across the nose with a sabre & killed three Yanks all of them in arms reach of him. We fell back on the reserve of inft & drew the Yanks into a trap—They losing between 40 & 50 killed & wounded and one prisoner—Our loss 5 missing 2 of whom known to be killed & one other wounded— together with several horses. But am sorry indeed time & paper is running short. Have been in full view of the city of Washington[.] Our troops skirmished along its breastworks for two days & then withdrew voluntarily—There is no question . . . that Genl Early could have . . . 1st & only line of fortifications . . . into the city if he had thought proper or been permitted by his orders—Report has it, that he was ordered by Genl Lee not to enter the city but simply to make demonstrations. There was certainly something other than the opposing forces wh[ich] prevented his doing it.[18] The battle of Monocacy Station, 3 miles from Fred[erick] City was a desperate one and a complete triumph of our arms.[19] Indeed every where that we met them we crushed them or drove them before us—And no wonder for never was a nation so surprised at the appearance of an invading army. They could not realize it till we knocked at the gate of Washington and then they were terror stricken throughout the land.

Rebel Brothers

An invasion from the land of spirits could not have surprised them more. And what is more, Genl Early is not done with them *yet*. I left the Army at Berryville 10 miles South of Winchester last Sunday & arrived here last night—Saddled my fresh horse & leave today to join my command near the B. & O.R.R. in Hampshire Co[unty].[20] I long to reach Penn. & show them what war is as carried on by the miserable wretch Genl Hunter.[21] I felt for the people of Md & simply took their horses & cattle, & grain because it was necessary for the welfare of our armies.

A part of our forces entered Baltimore & burned Ex-Gov Hick's house & also Gov Bradfords—leaving a note stating that it was done in retaliation for Gov Letcher's—Also burned PM Genl F. T. Blair's, in sight of Washington.[22] The whole movement has been a success from 1st to last. Have sent out some 12[00] or 1500 prisoners killed & w[ounde]d as many more—Supplied our forces with excellent clothing shoes etc & obtained thousands of horses & cattle. The Genl made a levy of so much money & so many outfits on every town & city thru wh[ich] we passed. Hagerstown $20,000 & 1500 outfits—etc—Have not been in one place long enough to hear from Chas for nearly two months. Hill's Corps was not with us. The last letters from Tex[as] are Cally's M[ar]ch 17. Fanny's 27th and A. T. T. Apl 21st. Will write when I return from this campaign. Pray for my welfare & daily growth in grace & blessings from Your own aff son, Dearest love to all—in much haste.

HMT

Hardy Co. Va.
July 26th 1864

Dear Chas

Yours of 27th ult. I found waiting for me when I arrived here, as also a packet of letters from Mother & Cally of various dates forwarded from the university by Mary Launcelot. Yours of 18th July was handed me yesterday. On the 21st inst. I wrote to Mother forwarding thro' Capt Cady & three or four lines to you. Had returned to Rockingham from near Winchester on a very lame horse, to procure a fresh one arriving at night on the 20th & leaving for this Co on the 21st to join my co[mman]d which had been ordered by Genl Early to strike the Balt. & O.R.R. again, but movements about Winchester have prevented the contemplated expedition & delayed it so that I have time to write you more fully than by the few lines before alluded to. I rather expected to meet you in Penn. then having reason to believe that Hill's Corps was on the m[a]rch to join Early. I am sorry to hear of your indisposition. What can you want with a horse to ride when you are behind fortifications in an invested city? If ever I get leisure enough to have two or three days to myself to look round and get . . . horses together etc I'll try to let you have one; but then you'll never be able to pay for it—for I have nothing less than a $4000. horse. So I suppose I had better lend or give him to you—if you can show good cause why you sho[uld] have another. If you had written me on the subject sooner I could have bro[ugh]t out an elegant one from Md. for you but as I was riding a very fine animal I didn't bother myself about another knowing that if I had a lead horse it threw me in the rear of our com[man]d & precluded my taking part in any scouts or other exciting scenes that might occur. We covered the rear going in & took the advance coming out—having good opportunities in the latter position to get fine horses—Don't think that our com[man]d of 140 men got more than 6 or 8—owing to the fact that we were mostly mounted on fresh horses out of a recent capture, to wh[ich] I think I have already alluded—and left the horses for those who needed them. In consequence of our absence at the time of Early's starting & the necessity for delivering a lot of prisoners at Harrisonburg whom we had just taken our comp[an]y was thrown behind two days and then found that we had been ordered to take the extreme left flank of the movement—striking the R R near Cumberland—some 35 miles to Westward of Genl Imboden—while he was the same distance from any support on his right. A company of Missourians who distinguished themselves very highly at the Newmarket fight—going in with 62 men & coming out with . . . —has been told by the Genl that they might attach themselves to any com[man]d they pleased, joined us with 35 men—whom we mounted—thus furnishing us with a most valuable reinforcement. On the 4th July we reached the R R at Patterson's C[ree]k station–6 miles from Cumberland—burning an important bridge—R R depot—large brick tank & machinery for filling it etc. Just as we had completed it we were attacked by 250 m[oun]t[ed] infty—fell back 5 miles to Frankfort Hampshire Co. in the direction of Imboden. They followed us when we formed and charged them killing three & capturing three Yanks & one horse—Wounded not known—Our loss one man slightly w[ounde]d & two horses killed. While we were pursued we drove off about 50 head of cattle turning them over to the Genl. We were then under forced

Rebel Brothers

~

marches all the time to overtake Early wh[ich] we did the night before the battle of "Monocacy Station." We reported to him in person & no rest did he give us day or night—hardly. Expecting Averill [Averell] & Hunter we were continually scouting & watching—sometimes 5 or 6 miles in the rear. Our com[man]d had quite a severe little fight in the streets of Frederick City on the 10th just after our army had left—being charged by . . . cavalry & getting terribly mixed up in the dense clouds of dust produced by the stir. Really you could not see more than a horses length, & that indistinctly. One of our Lts was struck across the nose with a sabre but instantly killed the Yank—He killed another just in the act of cutting at one of our men with his sabre and then another still. Our men now fell back some 200 or 300 yards on our infty rear guard drawing the Yanks close up—They poured in a volley wh[ich] terminated the affair & put the Yanks to flight. Our loss was one wounded & five missing—two of them known to be killed. Theirs was between 40 & 50 killed & wounded. The cavalry followed us at very respectful distance afterwards.[23] I was at the time on picket, two and a half miles on the Balt[imore] road. The fight at "Monocacy Station" I only saw from a distance—but rode over the field an hour afterwards & the dead & wounded told how heroically both parties fought. The Yankee dead & wounded were very numerous—Saw them in almost every position—stiff & cold—& in the agonies of death. Saw them stripped of almost every rag of clothing mutilated by shot & shell in every part. The wounded groaning & shrieking with pain. We buried no dead except our own & altho' we gathered up very many of their wounded and put them under the trees—gave them all the attention we could spare still I saw wounded Yanks 26 hours after the fight lying in the broiling sun with no water & no attention & so concealed that they might never [be] found. But at the time the Yank cavly was pressing us & we had no time to do anything for them. I was disappointed at the results of the campaign & have been unable to see why Early did not take Washington. It could have been done easily the first day and at small sacrifice from the best lights before me. I still correspond with . . . but am tired of doing so much the larger share . . . be very hard to get the boots or shoes either but . . . when I get a chance. Write to me often and address as before. . . .

Yours,
Henry.

Send this home.

... Co. Virginia
Aug ... 1864

Dear Chas

I notice on my memo book among "letters recd July 24th Chas—dated June 27" & also July 25—Chas—dated July 18th" but as I can't find the latter or recollect its contents I am forced to the conclusion that it is an imaginary entry. I remember writing to you on the 25th July from Hardy Co[unty] & by the by it was from the house of some of your old Rockbridge comrades viz: Mr. James Heiskell.[24] His son Isaac is disabled & now at home, & altho' Uncle John Minor had told me to make the acquaintance of the family—he having known & liked Isaac when at the University—I had forgotten all about it & just happened to drop in & make their acquaintance accidently. They are staunch old school Presbyterians and just as kind as they can be. But then the same as to the kindness may be said of all the people in the Moorefield Valley and very many in other portions of the county & Hampshire Co[unty] too—they never seem to know where to stop in their kindness ... a rebel soldier, & particularly ... McNeill's men. I am sometimes seriously embarrassed by importunate invitations to dine, etc. While at Moorefield a few days since I had spent an hour with an agreeable young lady & on rising to go was pressed to remain to dinner wh[ich] I declined but the lady of the house insisted that I must return & that if I was in sight she would call me—to wh[ich] I assented & left calling at another house on a different st[reet]. Her little son soon hunted me up with the announcement that dinner was waiting & I had to leave amid the many objections of the gentleman & lady at whose house I was. On my return a third gentleman called me across the street & insisted on my dining with him as "they were so crowded" at the first house—but there stood a sweet pretty young creature on the porch opposite making music by a frequent reiteration of my name & urging me to "come on"—My third friend seeing that he had the *sweet influences* to contend with invited my horse to dine at ... with fr[iend] No. 1 .... dinner as we sat down to w[oul]d make one's mouth water in the best of times & much more now to a poor hungry dirty & worn out rebel. I have met some accomplished & elegant women over here. While I think of it let me tell you of meeting a Mrs. Harper & 2 daughters at Romney who remembered & inquired for you very kindly. She sent for me on hearing my name to know if I was any kin to you. Also a Mrs. McSherry at Martinsburg.

Rebel Brothers

Relative to your boots let me tell you that I think the chances in Rockingham are bad—but that I have at last discovered the place where they can be had and have accordingly left your measure and engaged a pair of fine cavalry boots made of the best material and to be ready by the 14th of this month. Think you may rely on their being ready & as soon thereafter as possible I shall go down after them & either forward or bring over the ridge, as I am thinking of getting a furlough as soon as the active portion of the ca . . . absolutely need rest . . . about as much as mortal could stand. The bootmaker occupies a retired position in the woods near the Balt. & O. R. R. Bacon went over to Charlottesville some two weeks ago on a furlough & to make arrangements for a transfer to some other branch of the service[,] asserting that this partisan service would kill him—seeing rest neither day nor night. Shall be sorry to lose so pleasant a companion but believe I shall hang on to the "old concern." Relative to sending you a horse I fear I shall be unable to do so out of those I have on hand now. My $4100 horse—"Bob Lee," is laid up with a sore eye & lame foot leaving me only two horses in riding order. I own a half int[erest] in a fourth—but must sell this to keep me in funds. Can probably let you have one out of the next capture. Am sorry to find no letters for me on my arrival here. While at Romney rcvd one from Mother for[warde]d by you—& dated Feb 10th. Believe I alluded to the packet of letters from home dated in M[ar]ch, Apl & May & sent by the University & thence to me. Hope some more have come ere this. Am anxious to hear from you as you speak in your last of being unwell. In the regular army you can't get off to a private house when slightly indisposed—as we can. Thanks to Providence I have never been the least unwell. Tho' frequently broken down or nearly so—but am always just fool enought to want to go on every expedition & have never missed one while with the command. Do write as often as possible—directing as before.

Yours affecly,
Henry M.

Hardy Co Va
Sept 7th/64.

Dear Chas:

Nothing from you for a long time—Aug 7th was the last. Why don't you write more often? I wrote you Aug. 8th & 27th. Am now in charge of a squad of twenty men guarding a wagon train through a country infested with "Swamps" and will be absent some three or

Wild and Changeful Life
～

four days from the bal[ance] of the com[man]d—I see little news except through Yankee papers. Have been resting up our horses for a few days past—principally engaged for last 3 or 4 weeks in gathering cattle from the Allegheny Mts for the Govt.[25] Have sent over to the "Valley army" large numbers. Several days ago we had a grand picnic, given to our com[man]d by the ladies of Petersburg, Hardy Co[unty]. The grass was spread with all that the appetite c[oul]d crave—Upwards of 100 soldiers present & about same n[umber] of ladies—Altho' in a country where the Yanks might come upon us at any moment, I could not resist the temptation to hitch my horse to a buggy and wait on two lovely sisters—driving them eleven miles one day & staying all night in a country full of "Swamps"—who give no quarter—took them back next day.—Did I tell you that I had met with the *lovliest creature* on earth out here? I wish you c[oul]d have one view of her—your heart would melt under the influence! I may tell you her name some of these days.[26]

Look here! Tell me who Robt Coleman married?—Was it a Miss Breeden from Winchester? Be sure.

One pair of boots has been made for you in Hampshire but as I could not go down at the time appointed they were sold to keep them from falling into Yankee hands—He makes another pair which when I go on a scout I hope to get. No chance for a horse yet. Write to me often. Hope you all have cleared the R R of those troublesome Yanks. Nothing of interest here that you will not hear of ere this reaches you. You had better send even this little scrap home when you write, as I may not have a chance to write to them for several weeks. Am now sitting on the ground, writing on my knee.

> *Your loving Bro,*
> *Henry*

Hardy Co. Va.
Nov.br 8th 1864

Dear Chas:

Yours of the 29th ult. was recd last night and I use the sheet of paper you kindly sent to reply thus early. The "Enquirer" of 28th accompanied it. On 23d—finishing on the 30th—I wrote to you & Cally—ford'g to you enclosed letters wh[ich] had been recd direct from TM. & MMJ. of July 2d & 16th and on 4th an unfinished letter to Sister M. giving the result of a little fight we had on the Balt & O R R on morning of 1st inst & which epistle was cut short by

having to go with three other men on a scout to . . . road . . . another
. . . from which I just returned yesterday—having made in the 6
days & nights a distance of more than 200 miles traveling mostly at
night—You may judge how tired I was. On our return we met a force
of 300 or 400 Yankee cavalry with two pieces of artly but turning out
of the road let them pass on. They had made a forced march reaching Moorefield at night & succeeded in capturing four of our com[-
mand]d (one wounded) & stealing some 15 or 20 horses & double
that no. of cattle from the citizens—retreated after a stay of 5 hours.
Those captured were at citizen's houses. Our com[man]d fell back
across the Shenandoah Mts to Mt. . . . having been sent for to see
his father who was . . . of the officer in ch[ar]ge not feeling secure,
as he wd have been had he possessed the nerve to remain. Suppose
they will return in a day or two. In mean times I am at liberty. Last
night after having spent an agreeable evening at a house with 5 or 6
ladies & 7 or 8 gents. We were alarmed by a heavy banging at the
door & demands for entrance—producing considerable sh's . . .
were Yanks—but on making our escape at the back door—we found
it to be a man in terrible state of excitement who had riden two
miles at speed to let us know that the town was "full of Yanks"—
We caught horses & made for the woods—finding this morning "No
Yanks" near. It will render us more careful hereafter. Our affair at
Green Spring turns out to [be] better than we had reported–3
killed & 4 or 5 w[ounded]–24 prisoners & 45 horses—saddles etc.
Our loss one killed & one wounded. I was interested in your description of your "bomb proof" & could see the whole thing
plainly—but such spelling! You ought to take more pains—or your
"Prescriptions" & "Directions" will create many a smile when
you commence "practice." I'll name a few—"Missils" "faceing"
"leviled"—"boreing"—"Excelent"—"agreably" "assisible"—"ex-
treame" etc. I too look forward with pleasure to visiting you this
winter—Am sorry to say that thus far have been unable to procure
boots for you Comd has been in Hampshire . . . Balt. made cav'ly
boots at $25. . . but hadn't the needful—Can bring you 2 or 3
hndkfs. Will you have white linen or silk? Also have the hat—Can
get the gauntlets if I can get the money—Do undershirts. I have
two very worn wool undershirts—& made of fine white blanket &
the other a white flannel (Yankee obtained on field of Monocacy) a
little worn but good & warm—which I will bring you if you desire—
I have two knit ones—got in Md. Let me know. The leather is . . .
too but can be got only with Yankee money or specie. My only

chance is to capture some luckless Yankee who has it. They strip us—& we do them. Shall go to the Valley in a few days & sell a horse as I am already out of money. Recd a letter yesterday from Edlow Bacon who with his son is in the Rockbridge battery. Continue to for'd recent papers—& should be glad of a dozen "two cent" or paper stamps. I . . . send Yankee papers to Mary L. & Uncle Wm. O[verton] etc. On the last scout got "Balt" papers only one day old—today I am waiting on some young ladies—Tomorrow morng start again for the R.R.—Write often & send papers etc. Our old capt was reported very low several days since & his son sent for—but later accts since sent here as better. I fear there is little hope for him . . . what will become of his compy . . .

Hardy Co[unty]
Nov. 28th/64

Dear Chas.

Yours of 17th at hand with several papers—Yesterday had fighting with Yanks nearly all day—pursued them eleven miles & captured one piece artillery—Complimented by Genl Rosser who was nearby with two Brig's cavalry but none of his men took part as their presence was desired to be kept secret.

I am safe—our com[man]d behaved gallantly—will write more fully—

Yours,

H. M. T.

Near Petersburg, Hardy Co Va. December 3rd 1864.

Dear Chas:

Yours of the 17th ult. has been duly recv'd as acknowledged in a few penciled lines, written on 28th Nov. just to let you know that I was well & safe. We have had busy times here for the past few days. On Sunday the 27th we were lying quiet by grazing our horses near Petersburg when about an hour be-sun in the morning a dispatch reached us which produced great stir in camp & in less than two minutes we were on our way to Moorefield–11 miles distant—I was in the secret and immediately knew what was the cause of the movement which was no less than the sudden appearance of Genl Rosser with two Brigades cavly destined for the Balt. & O. R. R. & particularly New Creek station—a noted Yankee strong hold & one which has never been taken.[27] In less than two hours after reaching Moorefield we had our pickets driven in by the advancing Yanks &

feared that the whole of Rosser's plans would be defeated—He, however, remained quitely in camp some three miles above Moorefield & ordered Lt. McNeill to pitch into the Yanks & that if we could not whip them, he would reinforce us. We have since ascertained this force to be one of four columns sent out for the special purpose of destroying or driving from this region of country our little com[man]d.[28] Three columns 100 to 150 strong were to advance from the R. R. on three different roads & the "Swamps" some 250 strong to come down from the mountains in our rear & take possession of our usual road to the valley. All this has been clearly divulged by captured dispatches from Genl Kelly [Kelley], com[man]d[ing] this Dept. We immediately advanced towards the Yanks but under cover of the hills & woods—finding that 30 Yanks had crossed the S[outh] branch of the Potomac & were driving our pickets & would soon be sufficiently near to see Rosser's camp fires—Rosser sent us word to charge them. We did this in grand style driving them across the river at a deep & rocky ford. Just as we reached the river their whole force, occupying a bluff some 40 feet high rose & attempted to protect the crossing of the river pouring in a terrible fire of grape from a 12 lb. brass gun & making the air musical with the hiss & whiz of smaller missles. Our fellows stood it admirably & fought them for several minutes with only the river intervening say some 100 yards wide—and finding that it would be destruction to attempt to cross under such a fire, we moved rapidly down the river to another ford & crossed & charged them again putting the whole thing to flight & so fiercely did we pursue them that we drove them through a narrow defile in the mountains where 100 men ought to have held at bay a thousand & continuing the pursuit for 11 or 12 miles took their artillery—wagon—& ambulance 32 prisoners–50 horses & killed & wounded about 10 that fell into our hands and scattered the remainder in the mountains. Our loss three men wounded—Some of the Yanks were terribly cut up with sabres. It was a grand day for us[,] being the first piece of artillery we had ever captured. The Yankee force was 140. Ours about 100 effective men including 10 or 12 of Rosser's men. We reached Moorefield about 8 o'clk at night, and found Rosser's forces in motion for the R.R. In consequence of our chase and to guard the roads we were left. On the next morning, the second Yankee force destined to destroy us came into Moorefield knowing nothing of the fate of its cooperating force.[29] Before we could get at them they fled pursued by 6 or 7 of our men who captured one Yank. The third column hearing of the

having no chance to mail till I came over did so on the 9th (I think) adding a P.S. The extract you enclose is I suppose the production of Henry Allen. Chas I have a good horse 5 years old which I can bring you when I come over but he is not fat tho' in serviceable order. Say immediately if I shall bring him. Can you get a saddle, bridle etc? And will you have anything to feed with? But probably you will be better off in this than we are, since Rosser's cavly has gone over to Hardy & eaten us out. I heard yesterday that his cavly had been badly whipped over there & which was just what I expected for the Yanks won't permit any body but McNeill to occupy that country.

What "Uncle" is it whom you speak of as wishing to hear from & see me? Relative to your proposed transfer to the Engineer Corps I am sorry to be incapable of advising you. As regards my transfer from present command I must say that I have no idea of making any change at present. You are erroneously informed as to the character & efficiency of our command. We are rendering more service to the country than we could possibly do in any other capacity and altho' there is more exposure and hardship to undergo, than in the regular cavalry, still the wild and ever changeful life, the exemption from association with large bodies of troops all form attractions for me which I am unwilling to give up lightly. As to your remarks about promotion I reply that I am not fighting for promotion or glory but simply "to be let alone." And when this war is over, if I survive, it will be enough for me & my immediate friends to know that I have come as near the performance of my duty as men generally do. The remainder of mankind may think as they please.

Genl Early says that our "two companies have rendered more important service than any brigade of cavalry in his Army."[32] You must know that since Early's occupation of the Valley we have furnished him almost exclusively with meat obtained from inside the enemy's line. A good deal of it coming from Maryland and all obtained at much personal risk and hard labor. We are his scouts too constantly watching & dogging the every movement of the enemy, both by ordinary road & R.R. and at the same time have probably killed wounded & captured as many Yanks during the time as any other two companies in the service.

Let me hear from you immediately about the horse etc. If the weather continues this bad the busy season will soon be over & I shall come across the Ridge if I can raise money enough. Tell me of the probabilities of the closing of the campaign about Richmond when you write. It's getting to be a long long time since we heard

Wild and Changeful Life

~

CHAPTER 9

"*People Are* Blue, Blue," *1865*

Defences around Petersburg
Chesterfield Co, Virginia
January 16th 1865—

Dear John Overton:

I arrived here on the 13th passing the University where I spent two days, & Uncle Wm Overton's—staying one day—Had intended to stay another day there but found Uncle Wm & Polly gone to Richmond and all sorts of reports relative to preparation for the evacuation of Richmond & Petersburg in circulation & the citizens with whom I happened to talk so depressed by the military situation that there was little pleasure in seeing them and I hastened on where I might associate with *soldiers* who are not so much subject to these fits of despondency. The various operations tending to strengthen our works here abouts—the building of plank roads & R.R. s etc all give the lie to these reports.

I have spent the time here most pleasantly & have been much interested & instructed by the inspection of the works on this grand field of operation. Charles & myself went round to see Surg Henry A. Minor from whom & another of Chas' friends, we borrowed horses & spent the whole day in riding round & viewing the stupendous works protecting this immense line.

This whole country presents an intricate network of mines & countermines—"covered-ways" (ditches 6 1/2 or 7 feet deep) leading to the main works & picket lines & then others leading parallel with the works—enabling our troops to approach without being exposed to the fire of the enemy.[1] The many thousands of troops on and near the front line almost entirely underground. Of course their quarters are very dark. At one point we rode as near the front as was safe & leaving our horses tied under cover of a "Redoubt" walked to the main line of works, held by the bristling bayonets of a line of infantry 26 miles long. Reliefs are constantly on duty in the trenches & in case of an alarm thousands of brave men rush from their holes in the ground to the surface of the earth ready to repel the attack. The scene reminded me of an ant-bed. You see only a few stragglers around the entrance while all's quiet—but stir them up, and (to me) untold thousands rush to the surface. On reaching the main works we found that a sort of understanding existed between the men at that point not to shoot at each other—so we crossed the line & walked on the surface of the earth, 75 yards farther on to our picket line which here was only 35 yards from the enemy's picket line. This main line of works being about the same distance to the rear of his picket line, thus:

In front and on the right and left—I could see hundreds of Yanks standing in groups of 15 or 20—or running & playing—throwing clods of earth at each other—while others were busy in strengthening or repairing their picket-line so as to be better protected when sharp shooting recommenced. Our fellows with characteristic laziness were standing on the picket line or hovering over little fires—with their guns stuck bayonet deep in the ground & blankets spread from one to the other to keep off the wind. I asked them why they did not repair the washes in their lines. One of them replied that 'when sharpshooting recommenced, they would slip into that ditch & shoot through those little holes.' Then the ditch had mud & water ankle deep in it. It was not usual for officers to show themselves on the picket line & I was a little uneasy lest the Yanks might mistake me (with my long heavy beard & suit of gray rigged off with staff buttons etc) for some officer of high rank & shoot me. Particularly as I saw some of them slip behind their works and peep through the holes or over the top at us—and the group of 20 or 25 right in front of us all turned round & stared at us & a Yankee Sergt—a fine looking fellow ran & got a late Yankee paper & asked if 'we would not have it.' Our pickets assured us that he "didn't think they would shoot *at* us with out first shooting *over* us to give warning." We declined receiving the paper as it was contrary to or-

Rebel Brothers

ders. In my field of operations we never get that close to each other without shooting unless we are scouting & lying concealed from view & I felt considerably relieved when we got under cover again.[2]

At another point we approached the works where it was necessary to follow the "covered-way." Immediately in our front a truce was existing but had not been long made & the Yankees exhibited a good deal of shyness—never exposing the whole person—but only peeping over occasionally.

A hundred or two yards to our left the sharp shooting was going on continually. Many on both sides were killed in this way. A hat or tin cup held up on a stick is instantly riddled by the other side. Our men have little loop holes protected by iron or heavy oak—just large enough for the muskets to go through & splayed on the inside so as to admit of shooting to the right or left—they stand to one side or the other & shoot—at the flash of the gun a Yank immediately in front may even put a ball into the loop hole without hitting our man.

We also visited the "crater," the result of, and scene of the explosion by which Grant expected to attain his long-wished-for end.[3] Chas has no doubt described it to you. I forgot to tell you that our line of works is protected also by "abatis" (trees cut down & all the branches sharpened & pointing to the front) & for many miles of open country by "chevaux de frise." This is made of logs ten feet long and 8 or 10 inches in dia. through which holes are bored every 5 inches on two sides of the log and at right angle & sharpened heart pine spokes put through so as to extend 2 1/2 or 3 feet on each side. These are then fastened together by iron links & hooks. The enemy can pull them away—can't climb over, nor can he creep through. These are placed about 20 feet from the line. All of this the enemy can see—consequently there is no harm in speaking of it.[4] There is much that he don't see. I am glad to learn from Chas that you had written to us—He had fwded me the letter which I shall doubtless get on my return to my command. My dearest love to all at home. Accompanying this are letters from me to Fanny A. T. T. & Bow— of 21 Dec Jan 6th & Dec 30.

They had been much detained by want of opportunity to send them to the Valley & then he had not mailed them when I came down a day or two afterwards. I shall call on Capt Cady in passing thro Richmond. Saw Henry Allen yesterday. He was well. Remember me to Farish—Ballinger—League (& Jeff) Tucker, Mac. Mott, J. S. Sydnor & J. B. S. Andrews & Grover, B. C. Franklin, H. B. An-

People Are Blue, Blue

∽

drews, Aschoff, Mr. Frederick F. Flake & any other friends who inquire for me.

Yours affly,
Henry M.

Richmond, Va.,
January 18th, 1865.

A. C. Rose will probably be the bearer hereof. Have just seen Geo Branard, & Captain Cady—Yesterday heard of the fall of "Ft. Fisher."[5] People are *blue, blue.* A reaction must take place soon or we are ruined.

I am now on my way back to my command.

Henry

Epilogue

Thus, the Trueheart brothers' Civil War letters ended. General Lee's right flank was turned finally at Five Forks on April 1, 1865, almost eleven months after Grant had begun the effort. The ragged, gray remnants of the Army of Northern Virginia were forced to retreat painfully westward. On April 9, 1865, the guns fell silent at Appomattox Court House, Virginia.

The terms of surrender were generous. Receiving the surrender and stacking of arms for the Union was Maj. Gen. Joshua Lawrence Chamberlain, a former commander of the 20th Maine Infantry Regiment and a hero of Gettysburg. Leading the pitifully thinned Confederate ranks was Maj. Gen. John B. Gordon of Georgia. As the Confederates came abreast of the drawn up Federal ranks, General Gordon was startled to hear General Chamberlain bring his troops to "Present Arms," a military sign of respect. Drawing himself up in the saddle, Gordon returned the salute—a proud but sad moment, as the famed army marched past and into the gathering haze of military history. Afterwards, the soldiers went home.

New Orleans, La.
August 29th 1865.

Dear Tom [Joseph]

I am here staying with my kinsman, Dr. Lewis W. Minor, awaiting the departure of an U.S. Govt. transport. Shall not get- off probably till the last of this week.

Henry is in Virginia. Ere this I suppose you have had letters from him telling you all of his expected marriage in October to a Miss Cunningham, of Virginia. Both he and I have written frequently since the Surrender. His wife will of course come to Texas with him at once. He is anxiously awaiting the reception of some money from Texas. Raise for him by some means or other four or five hundred dollars, and transmit by check on New York; enclose the original to him care of Mr. W. M. Randolph—Moorefield, Hardy Co. West Va; the duplicate, care of Professor Jno. B. Minor, University of Virginia. Thus he will get either one or the other in a short time. He cant stir a pig till he gets the money; so hurry up your cakes. And never did famished Confederate[s] await with more longing eyes the coming of hot buckwheats swimming in fresh butter and molasses, than does he, poor fellow, the arrival of the much needed cash. Again I say, hurry up your cakes.

Please have the enclosed advertisement inserted *at once* in the Galveston News and Houston Telegraph. Do so without fail please and also without delay.

I might come over on the [*Haze*], but am out of money and traveling at the expense of my beloved "Uncle Sam," and hence have to wait for Uncle's ships.

Much love to Sister Mary and Mrs. "Joseph" & all at Mr. Howard's, and at home.

> *Affectionately your brother and friend,*
> *Chas. W. Trueheart*

To Mr. T. M. Joseph Galveston Texas

For the next several years after returning to Galveston, Charles practiced medicine there. In 1866, he married Mary Bryan of Brazoria County, Texas, a grandniece of Stephen F. Austin. She died the following year, 1867.

After Mary's death, Charles continued his medical education, first at Bellevue Medical College in New York, and then in Europe at Göttingen, Germany; Vienna, Austria; and Berlin. In 1870–71, he served with the Germans during the Franco-Prussian War as a surgeon in their military hospitals. At the close of the war, he returned to Galveston, where he resumed practice. "It is reputed that [he] brought the first fever thermometer to the United States upon his return from Germany."[1]

In 1872, Charles was wed again, this time to Miss Ella Street. The wedding took place in Tuscaloosa, Alabama. From this union, there were five children, all of whom were born in Galveston.[2]

During the following years, Charles was an active member of the Galveston County and Texas State Medical Associations. "He was a professor at the Galveston Medical College (1866), member of the

Epilogue

∾

Galveston County Board of Medical Examiners (1876), vice president of the trustees of the Texas Medical College and Hospital (1887), member of the John Sealy Hospital Board of Managers (1901–1902), and city health physician (1901–10). [He] encouraged George and Rebecca Sealy to establish the John Sealy Hospital and exerted considerable influence as an advocate for Galveston as the site of the University of Texas Medical Branch. He participated in extensive efforts to improve the water and sewerage systems of Galveston, and he assisted with plans for constructing a seawall and raising the city's grade after the hurricane of 1900."[3]

Former Confederate surgeon, Dr. Charles W. Trueheart, died in San Antonio, Texas, on December 14, 1914.

Petersburg, Hardy Co. Va.
Ap 24th/65.

My darling Mother:

Hearing that a gentleman has asserted his intention of trying to reach Texas via Yankeedom, I regard it as affording some vague hope of forwarding with success this letter & accordingly write—though there is nothing but disaster and ruin to the Confederacy to record. Before this reaches you you will have heard of the fall of Richmond & subsequently the surrender of the Army of Northern Virginia. The effect upon citizens & soldiers you may readily conjecture. Ere we heard of the surrender of Lee's army it was too late to retreat from this region of country with one hope in a hundred of joining Johnston & still less of reaching the Trans-Miss.

We are now surrounded on all sides by Yankees but continue to hold our own more from a sense of honor and duty however than from any hope that it will do any good. Many of the thousands who escaped from the A.N.V. are going in and taking the parole. The Yankees met us a few days since under flag of truce offering the terms accorded to Lee and also permit us to retain all private horses *arms* & accoutrements. Only one man from our command went forward for the parole—the remainder are determined to wait the orders or in the event receiving none, the action of our superior officers—Lomax, Rosser etc whose commands are disbanded & scattered over the country each taking care of himself—Since their escape from the A.N.V. Our meeting with Yanks a few days since was a strange sight—all fully armed, & many of us riding U.S.

Epilogue
~
217

horses, and all having U.S. arms, & saddles etc but under the white flag all went off quietly. My only hope for the Confederacy is in foreign intervention—without it we are whipped completely. The last intelligence from Charles is by letter dated 27th March. Have been totally cut off since & have no hope of seeing him soon unless he was among the captured & with the protection of his parole comes over to this country which I hope he may do.

The *noble fellow* wrote me on the 11th March that he could no longer remain in the medical department, when able bodied young men were so much needed in the front and that he had sent in his resignation & as soon as accepted, would return to the ranks in Artillery.

Can hear nothing about any body or anything except through Northern papers. I shall return to Texas as soon as the state of the country and my duty to my command here will permit—but when that will be nobody—at least I do not know. Don't know anything about any of our relatives or friends—*all mixed up I reckon.*

Shall spend most of our time in the mountains and woods untill we can learn the fate of the Confecy more fully. A pretty state of affairs—but it can't be helped now—

Don't know when I shall have an opportunity of writing again. I'll bid you all a long farewell, maybe—Kiss all the dear ones at home for me, Cally, Fanny, & Minny—Sister Mary and her flock and Elvira and hers—not failing to remember me affectionately to Father, T. M. J. & R. H. H., and retaining a large share for my own dear Mother. May a merciful God do better for us than we deserve and again permit us all to meet on earth and live happily together.

Your Loving Son,
[Unsigned—Henry]

In 1866, in Hardy County, West Virginia, Henry M. Trueheart was wed to Annie Van Meter Cunningham, the daughter of Mr. and Mrs. William Streit Cunningham. From their union came five children: Sally; Henry M., Jr.; Ann V.; Rebecca, and Elvira.

In the years following, Henry served his family and community in a number of ways. He "served as a member of the Galveston School Board for twenty-five years and was its President for four years."[4] He was "a member of the board of directors of Southern Cotton Press Company, the Galveston & Western R. R. Co., the Texas Trust & Guarantee Co., and the Galveston Land & Improvement Co., and for several years was a director and vice president of the Galveston Wharf Co."[5]

Henry M. Trueheart, "died at Grandview Sanitarium, Wernersville, [Pennsylvania], in his eighty-second year. He had gone to the mountains of Pennsylvania for the benefit of his health."[6]

In repose, side by side, the brothers' unremarkable surroundings belie their lives.

Notes

Preface

1. George R. Stewart, *Pickett's Charge* (Boston: Houghton Mifflin, 1959), xi.

2. Edwin B. Coddington, *The Gettysburg Campaign* (Dayton, Ohio: Morningside Press; 1979), xi.

3. Gerald F. Linderman, *Embattled Courage* (New York: Free Press, 1987), 23.

Introduction: The Truehearts of Galveston

1. Henry Martyn Trueheart, "Memoirs of Henry Martyn Trueheart, jotted down from time to time as they occurred to him for the amusement and information of his children. Begun Oct. 1898. The last written April 1912," Trueheart Collection, Rosenberg Library, Galveston, Tex. A typed copy of this document is in the Trueheart Collection and is the basis for much of the family background presented in this book. Some of the material in Henry Martyn Trueheart, "Memoirs," comes from the diary of James Lawrence Trueheart, John Overton Trueheart's brother and the uncle of Henry M. and Charles W. Trueheart; this was later published as Frederick C. Chabot, ed., *The Perote Prisoners* (San Antonio, Tex.: Naylor, 1934), 1–3. The diary relates James' experiences during the capture of San Antonio in 1842 by the Mexican Gen. Adrian Woll, and during the subsequent imprisonment of James and other unfortunate Texans in Perote Prison in Mexico. Apart from the family information contained in the diary and in Henry Martyn Trueheart, "Memoirs," scattered material concerning the family can be found in genealogical studies, census reports, newspaper articles, and other places. Research on various aspects of the family's history proved the material contained in Henry Trueheart's memoirs to be accurate. In the editor's opinion, the document is a reliable family history.

2. The trip took two or three months, with a stop at the home of Ann Minor Trueheart's brother, Dr. William T. Minor, in Huntsville, Ala. From that point, the trio took a flatboat down the Tennessee, Ohio, and Mississippi rivers. At the mouth of the Red River, they disembarked and completed the journey overland through Louisiana and into Texas. See Chabot, *Perote Prisoners*, 2.

3. Mrs. J. E. Warren, "Tompkins Family," *William and Mary Quarterly* 2d ser., vol. 10, no. 1 (Jan. 1930): 232.

4. Heale-Muscoe, *Genealogies of Virginia Families From the William and Mary College Quarterly Historical Magazine*, vol. 3 (Baltimore, Md.: Genealogical Publishing Co., 1982), 709.

5. Henry Martyn Trueheart, "Memoirs," 1.

6. Gifford E. White, *1840 Citizens of Texas* (St. Louis. Mo.: Ingimire Publications, 1983), 252. James L. Trueheart is listed also.

7. James K. Greer, *Colonel Jack Hays: Texas Frontier Leader and California Builder* (New York: E. P. Dutton, 1952), 25.

8. Francis T. Ingimire, *Texas Ranger Service Records, 1830–1846* (St. Louis, Mo.: Ingimire Publications, 1982), 150. James L. Trueheart is listed also under "Texas Ranger—Spies" and as being enlisted in Captain Hays' company in Jan.–May 1841. See n. 1 above and Chabot, *Perote Prisoners*.

9. Greer, *Colonel Jack Hays*, 41.

10. William S. Speer, *The Encyclopedia of the New West* (Marshall, Tex.: United States Biographical Publishing Co., 1881), 547–48. The biographical sketch of Dr. Charles W. Trueheart contained in this volume states that John O. Trueheart was a resident of San Antonio during the Mexican invasion of 1842, "doing good service in defence of the country."

11. Mrs. Marjorie Trueheart Williams McCullough and Mrs. Sally McCullough Futch, interview by Edward B. Williams, Galveston, Tex., 28 Apr. 1992. Mrs. McCullough is the granddaughter of Henry Martyn Trueheart, great-granddaughter of John Overton Trueheart, and niece of Dr. Charles W. Trueheart. At age 96, she remembered her grandfather and Uncle Charles well. It was her belief that, during his five years in Texas (1838–43), John Trueheart made trips back to Virginia to visit his family from time to time. Mrs. Futch is Henry M. Trueheart's great-granddaughter.

12. Henry Martyn Trueheart, "Memoirs," 2.

13. Ibid. Henry lists an Elvira Susan and a Caroling Hill as Trueheart children. Mrs. McCullough said that there were no children by those names. Nonetheless, both brothers addressed letters to their sister, Elvira (whom they sometimes referred to as "Bow"). There were Caroline and Mildred. The *Census of 1860* lists both Caroline and Mildred as members of the Trueheart family. Mrs. McCullough remem-

bered her aunts—particularly Mildred, whom she described as a "fisherman" who lived in a boarding house. By the time of the Civil War, Sister Mary was the wife of Thomas M. Joseph, mayor of Galveston, and Elvira was the wife of Robert H. Howard of Galveston.

14. Henry Martyn Trueheart, "Memoirs," 4.

15. David G. McComb, *Galveston: A History* (Austin: University of Texas Press, 1986), 42–43. Menard's associates were Thomas F. McKinney, Samuel May Williams, Mosely Baker, John K. Allen, Augustus C. Allen, William H. Jack, William Hardin, A. J. Gates, and David White. Gary Cartwright, *Galveston: A History of the Island* (New York: Atheneum, 1991), 72–75, gives primary credit for the survey to a local eccentric named Gary Borden. Borden is reported to have had, as his primary mode of transportation, a pet bull. He is also remembered, in the aftermath of his wife's death from yellow fever in 1844, for his efforts to prevent future yellow fever outbreaks by refrigerating Galveston's entire population. According to Cartwright, Borden proposed constructing a giant refrigerator building to house Galvestonians during the summer. Supposedly, he went so far as to construct a giant icebox using ether to cool the box's interior. His greatest invention, made some years later, after he had left Galveston, was condensed milk.

16. Ibid., 43.

17. McComb, *Galveston: A History*, 44.

18. Gary Cartwright, *Galveston: A History of the Island*, 72–73.

19. McComb, *Galveston: A History*, 44.

20. Cartwright, *Galveston: A History of the Island*, 85.

21. Bureau of the Census, *The Census of 1860*, Texas, Galveston County, City of Galveston, Fourth Ward, 155.

22. Henry Martyn Trueheart, "Memoirs," 5.

23. Ervin L. Jordan, Jr., *Charlottesville and the University of Virginia in the Civil War* (Lynchburg, Va.: H. E. Howard, 1988), 24–25.

24. Ibid.

25. William W. Blackford, *War Years with Jeb Stuart* (New York: Charles Scribner's Sons, 1946), 150.

26. Robert J. Driver, Jr., *The 1st and 2nd Rockbridge Artillery* (Lynchburg, Va.: H. E. Howard, 1987), 80.

27. Roger U. Delauter, Jr., *McNeill's Rangers* (Lynchburg, Va.: H. E. Howard, 1986), 124.

Chapter 1: "These Troublesome Times," 1861

1. Students of that era seem to have differed little from those of other eras in their likes and dislikes, except that sometimes they took direct action against their oppressors. In 1825, the students became so

disrespectful of the mostly British faculty that the faculty collectively threatened to resign. In 1835, the faculty chairman, Gessner Harrison, was horsewhipped before a crowd of students. In 1840, student Joseph E. Semmes of Georgia shot and killed Professor John A. G. Davis. See Jordan, *Charlottesville and the University*, 6.

2. Dr. James Lawrence Cabell earned his medical degree from the University of Virginia in 1833. He graduated from the University of Maryland in 1834 and served at hospitals in Baltimore, Philadelphia, and Paris, France, until 1837. He returned to the University of Virginia in 1837 and later served as faculty chairman. He was surgeon-in-charge of the Charlottesville Hospital during most of the war. Ibid., 47–48.

3. Socrates Maupin became faculty chairman in 1854. He was a native of Albemarle, Va., and held master's and medical degrees. He had taught at Hampden-Sydney College and at Richmond Medical College. Ibid., 22.

4. Dr. John Staige Davis served with Dr. Cabell at the Charlottesville Hospital throughout the war.

5. Galveston was evacuated by the Confederate authorities in Oct. 1862. See Allwyn Barr, "Texas Coastal Defense, 1861–1865," *Southwestern Historical Quarterly* 45 (July 1961): 1–31.

6. This key letter, unlike most of the others, has not withstood the ravages of time well. The edges have worn away and, with them, handwritten text. The editor has attempted to "fill in the blanks" wherever the missing text is fairly obvious. Otherwise, the text is fragmented, as is the original.

7. The unit was the 1st Rockbridge Artillery, a 2nd being organized later in the war. The First (Stonewall) Brigade, to which the battery was attached, included the 2nd, 4th, 5th, 27th, and 33rd Virginia Infantry Regiments. It became one of the most famous in the Army of Northern Virginia. The first battery commander, William Nelson Pendleton, graduated from the U.S. Military Academy, West Point, N.Y., in the class of 1830. He resigned from the army in 1833. In 1838 he was ordained a minister of the Episcopal Church. In 1853 he became rector of Grace Episcopal Church, Lexington, Va. He later became chief of artillery for the Army of Northern Virginia. To the men of the 1st Rockbridge Artillery, he was always known as "Old Penn." William T. Poague, *Gunner with Stonewall* (1957; reprint, Wilmington, N.C.: Broadfoot Publishing Co., 1987), 5, 7.

8. John M. Goul graduated from Washington College in the class of 1853, and from the Union Theological Seminary in 1854. He enlisted in the 1st Rockbridge Artillery at Winchester, Va., on 15 June 1861. He was appointed the unit's chaplain on 10 May 1862. He died of typhoid fever in a Lexington hospital on 9 Aug. 1862. Robert J. Driver, *The 1st and 2nd Rockbridge Artillery* (Lynchburg, Va.: H. E. Howard, 1987), 66.

9. At this time Charles presumably is referring to Capt. William McLaughlin and 1st Lt. John B. Brockenbrough. Both were lawyers. Ibid., 72, 76.

10. Governor Letcher told the troops present that they "had a long and bloody war before [them]." John O. Casler, *Four Years in the Stonewall Brigade* (1906; reprint, Marietta, Ga.: Continental Book Co., 1951), 56.

11. On 4 July 1861, Jackson received word of his promotion to brigadier general, effective 17 June. In late Oct., he was promoted to the position of major general. James I. Robertson, Jr., "Stonewall Jackson: Molding the Man and Making a General," *Blue and Gray Magazine* 9 (June 1992): 19. On 4 Nov. 1861, Major General Jackson was ordered to leave the army at Centreville and proceed to Winchester to take command of the Shenandoah Valley District. He left by the first available train, arriving in Winchester that same evening. U.S. War Department (comp.), *War of the Rebellion: A Compilation of the Official Records of the Union and Confederate Armies*, ser. 1, vol. 5, ch. 14, p. 937. Before leaving, he delivered an emotional farewell speech to his beloved "Stonewall" Brigade. Rising in his stirrups, "Old Jack," as he was affectionately called by the men, concluded: "In the Army of the Shenandoah you were the First Brigade! In the Army of the Potomac you were the First Brigade! In the Second Corps of the army you are the First Brigade! You are the First Brigade in the affections of your general, and I hope by your future deeds and bearing you will be handed down to posterity as the First Brigade in this our second War of Independence. Farewell!" G. F. R. Henderson, *Stonewall Jackson and the American Civil War*, vol. 1 (1936; reprint, Seacaucus, N.J.: Blue and Grey Press, 1987), 167. In little more than a month, the brigade was reunited with its first commander when ordered to the Shenandoah Valley as part of reinforcements for the beleaguered area. It served under "Old Jack" for the time that remained of his life.

12. The battery arrived in Winchester on 10 Nov., moved on to near Kernstown, and several days later moved to another bivouac west of Winchester. Driver, *1st and 2nd Rockbridge Artillery*, 10.

13. Throughout the "Stonewall" Brigade, the lament was much the same. Members of the 27th Virginia Infantry forced their way through the militia pickets set up outside Winchester and indulged in a "spree," most landing in the guardhouse as a result. Casler, *Four Years in the Stonewall Brigade*, 60.

14. In a letter dated 5 Nov. 1861, to Secretary of War Judah P. Benjamin, General Jackson requested that Lt. Daniel Truehart, Jr., or some other good artillery officer be ordered to Winchester to take charge of the heavy ordinance. Later, in his report of operations from 4 Nov. 1861 to 21 Feb. 1862, he mentioned Maj. D. Truehart, Jr., chief of artillery,

as being "successful in the work assigned to him." U.S. War Department, *War of the Rebellion: Official Records*, ser. 1, vol. 5, ch. 14, p. 389.

15. This was the beginning of General Jackson's winter campaign of Dec. 1861–Jan. 1862. For details of the campaign, see Henderson, *Stonewall Jackson*, vol. 1, 185–98; Douglas Southall Freeman, *Lee's Lieutenants: A Study in Command*, vol. 1 (New York: Charles Scribner's Sons, 1942), 122–30; and Robert G. Tanner, *Stonewall in the Valley* (Garden City, N.Y.: Doubleday, 1976). In a letter to Secretary of War Benjamin, General Jackson acknowledged the difficulties of a winter campaign: "I deem it of very great importance that Northwestern Virginia be occupied by Confederate troops this winter. At present it is to be presumed that the enemy are not expecting an attack there, and the resources of that region necessary for the subsistence of our troops are in greater abundance than in almost any other season of the year. Postpone the occupation of that section until spring, and we may expect to find the enemy prepared for us and the resources to which I have referred greatly exhausted. I know that what I have proposed will be an arduous undertaking and cannot be accomplished without the sacrifice of much personal comfort; but I feel that the troops will be prepared to make this sacrifice when animated by the prospects of important results to our cause and distinction to themselves" (U.S. War Department, *War of the Rebellion: Official Records*, ser. 1, vol. 5, ch. 14, pp. 965–66).

16. These were rifled Parrott guns captured at Manassas.

17. Lieutenant Poague reported to Col. Turner Ashby at Charlestown about 7 Dec. 1861. Reaching there sometime in the night, he located Ashby in a local hotel. There, Poague "found him sitting up in his bed with nothing but a red flannel shirt on. He was a slender, swarthy man with long black mustache and whiskers. He was very kind in his greeting and was sorry I had to make the march by night. He directed that we find a camp and make ourselves as comfortable as possible, saying he would want us next day." Poague, *Gunner with Stonewall*, 12.

18. The canal spoken of was the Chesapeake and Ohio Canal, extending from Cumberland, Md., to Washington, D. C. It paralleled the Potomac River and was a major transportation artery between Washington, D.C., and the West. A series of dams along its length formed locks. Canal boats carried various types of vital cargo, coal among them. The expedition was one of several in Dec. 1861 aimed primarily at destroying Dam No. 5, not Dam No. 4, as Charles says in his letter. Although the dam was damaged by Jackson's force in the next attempt of 17–18 Dec., it was repaired by the Federal forces guarding it and continued in operation. For a detailed description of these operations launched from Charlestown and Martinsburg, Va., see James I. Robertson, Jr.,

The Stonewall Brigade (Baton Rouge: Louisiana State University Press, 1963), 56–57.

19. According to Lieutenant Poague, the Union force was sent across the river to capture Colonel Ashby, who was known to patrol the area on a regular basis. See Poague, *Gunner with Stonewall*, 13.

20. A description of the recklessly gallant Ashby is given by a young member of Jackson's staff, Henry Kyd Douglas: "[He] was a man of striking personal appearance, about five feet ten inches tall, with a well-proportioned figure, graceful and compact, black eyes, black hair, and a flowing black beard. His complexion was of the darkest brunette, so dark that a Federal scout whom he once shot with a pistol declared he had been shot by a Negro. His face was placid and stern; even his smile was shadowed with a tinge of melancholy.... His face did not flush in battle or under excitement; only the melancholy passed away and his countenance, alive, determined, was still calm. He often smiled, rarely laughed. His eye was gentle, peaceful; in battle it did not sparkle fitfully but burned steadily beneath his dark brows.... Riding his black stallion, he looked like a knight of the olden time; galloping over the field on his favorite war horse, his white one, eager, watchful, he was facinating, inspiring. Altogether he was the most picturesque horseman ever seen in the Shenandoah Valley—he seemed to have been left over by the Knights of the Golden Horseshoe." Henry Kyd Douglas, *I Rode with Stonewall* (Chapel Hill: University of North Carolina Press, 1940), 81–82.

21. Ashby's command had a reputation for indiscipline and bravery to the point of recklessness.

22. Holmes Conrad, Jr., and his brother, Tucker Conrad, were members of the 33rd Virginia Infantry. Killed at their side was their cousin, Payton Harrison. See Robertson, *Stonewall Brigade*, 43.

23. This attempt to destroy Dam No. 5 occurred in mid-Dec. 1861, about ten days after Ashby's capture of the Federal party.

24. This material was not found in the Trueheart Collection.

25. This letter recounts the same events as the preceding two letters, except that it gives more detail regarding General Jackson's participation.

Chapter 2: "A Band of Southerners," 1862

1. In that era, military operations customarily were suspended during the inclement winter months. Unpaved roads were unsatisfactory for the transportation of heavy, horse-drawn military equipment and supplies in cold, wet weather. Also, troops were not clothed to with-

stand extreme weather conditions. Armies usually went into semi-permanent "winter quarters" roughly from November through March. Jackson's winter encampment of late Jan. to Mar. 1862 was named Camp Zollicoffer. Various attempts at conducting winter campaigns were made during the Civil War, but generally they were less than successful.

2. The objectives of the campaign were to drive Union forces from northwestern Virginia and to deny them use of the Baltimore and Ohio Railroad and the Chesapeake and Ohio Canal. See Driver, *1st and 2nd Rockbridge Artillery*, 11.

3. The command included: Garnett's brigade; McLaughlin's [1st Rockbridge Artillery], Carpenter's, and Water's batteries; Loring's division, including Anderson's, Gilham's, and Taliaferro's brigades; Shumaker's and Marye's batteries; and Meem's militia command. See U.S. War Department, *War of the Rebellion: Official Records*, ser. 1, vol. 5, ch. 14, p. 390. Bath, Va., is now Berkeley Springs, W.Va.

4. "Old Jack" reported four wounded—one lieutenant and three privates. Ibid.

5. Jackson shelled Hancock "after having demanded the surrender of the Federal force occupying it, and giving two hours in which to remove women and children. It was Sunday and our battery did the bombarding." Poague, *Gunner with Stonewall*, 16.

6. The destruction of this and several other bridges severed communications between Union forces at Hancock, Md., and at Romney, Va. Jackson next turned his attention toward Romney.

7. Poague remembered: "[W]e had a most dreadfully disagreeable time at Romney. Our large company was quartered in a small church, Methodist I think, and had to do our cooking in the graveyard, which nearly surrounded the church. It rained and snowed almost the whole time. Horses tied to the hitching rope had to eat what little feed they got in the mud. No boxes or nosebags were to be had. The mud was so deep that they could with difficulty change their position. The men soon became infested with vermin. We officers escaped by occupying the high pulpit. The situation was disgusting." Poague, *Gunner with Stonewall*, 17.

8. Due to the inefficiency of the supply organization and the increasing shortages of all commodities as the war wore on, Confederate soldiers often had to fend for themselves. As Bell Wiley notes, "The most reasonable source from which troops might purchase foodstuffs, and the one patronized most frequently, was the producer himself. Sometimes farmers came to camp with their provisions, and on other occasions soldiers sought out the countrymen." Bell I. Wiley, *The Life of Johnny Reb: The Common Soldier of the Confederacy* (New York: Bobbs-Merrill, 1943), 100.

Mess 19 consisted of Robert Frazer; Charles Minor; Norborne Henry; William Wilson; Robert E. Lee, Jr.; Abner Arnold; Carter Minor; Arthur Robinson; Hugh McGuire; and Charles Trueheart. See "Old Mess XIX, Poague's Battery," Trueheart Collection, Rosenberg Library, Galveston, Tex. Robert E. Lee, Jr., was the commanding general's youngest son. Hugh McGuire was the brother of Dr. Hunter McGuire of General Jackson's staff. Dr. McGuire attended General Jackson after his mortal wounding at Chancellorsville in May 1863.

9. Each man would have contributed about $1.88 per month to defray the cost of the cook. The approximate pay for a private was $13.00 per month; pay frequently was six months or more in arrears.

10. It seems that General Loring may have been persuaded by some of his brigade and regimental commanders to go over Jackson's head. See their letter addressed to him, in U.S. War Department, *War of the Rebellion: Official Records*, ser. 1, vol. 5, ch. 14, pp. 1046–47. Judah P. Benjamin, the affable Confederate secretary of war, wishing to please everyone, readily gave in to Loring's demands that his troops evacuate Romney. Under the circumstances, Jackson had little choice but to submit his resignation. As a result, "Governor Letcher [of Virginia] went into an uproar at the prospect of losing one of Virginia's leading commanders, while both Benjamin and President Jefferson Davis hastened to revoke the order and issue their apologies to Jackson." Robertson, *Stonewall Brigade*, 67.

11. These troops were under the command of Maj. Gen. Nathaniel P. Banks and numbered about 25,000 men.

12. Maj. Gen. James Shields' troops numbered about 9,000.

13. "Near nightfall on March 11 Jackson summoned the five regimental colonels of the Stonewall Brigade for a council of war. Heeding their advice, he ordered his army with all its supplies to move southward. Jackson's plan was to turn sharply at Newtown, race back down the pike, and deliver a night attack on Banks. But through misinterpreted orders the army moved through Newtown and continued so far southward as to make a night assault at Winchester completely out of the question. Jackson was furious." Robertson, *Stonewall Brigade*, 69. Jackson never again held a council of war.

14. Jackson's army had retreated through Strasburg to Mt. Jackson, where it had gone into bivouac to await further developments. Shields' division had pursued as far as Strasburg. On 21 Mar., Ashby informed Jackson that Shields had abandoned Strasburg and retreated toward Winchester. Jackson quickly pursued and late on Sunday, 23 Mar., launched an attack against Shields at Kernstown. The attack was a mistake; Jackson's army, exhausted from the march and outnumbered, was forced to retreat. Shields later boasted that he was the only Union general ever to defeat Jackson on the field of battle.

15. This was Maj. Gen. Richard S. Ewell's division. It was left behind by Lt. Gen. Joseph E. Johnston as he moved his army from Manassas Junction to the peninsula formed by the York and James rivers southeast of Richmond. The move by Johnston was to meet the threat posed by a Union army landed at Fortress Monroe and moving against Richmond from that quarter. This Union force was commanded by Maj. Gen. George B. McClellan, the so-called "Young Napoleon."

16. According to figures compiled from U.S. War Department, *War of the Rebellion: Official Records*, Union losses at Kernstown were 118 killed, 450 wounded, and 22 missing—a total of 590. See "The Opposing Forces in the Valley Campaigns," *Battles and Leaders of the Civil War*, edited by Robert U. Johnson and Clarence C. Buel (New York: Thomas Yoseloff, 1956), 2:299–301.

17. Ibid. Jackson's losses were placed at 80 killed, 375 wounded, and 263 missing—a total of 718.

18. Soon after Sharpsburg (Antietam), in Sept. 1862, Charles was sent to the hospital with scurvy. Later, he was detailed to hospital duty—not in Charlottesville, however, but first in Winchester and later in Lynchburg.

19. "Conscription was a response to crisis, the kind of response possible only from a man who grew with experience. [Jefferson] Davis [president of the Confederate States of America] learned the changing nature of the war and realized more clearly than others that traditions and values were fast diminishing in the battle smoke. To persist at all the government must mobilize and use every resource according to rigid national plan. It was not pleasant for a natural states-righter, not easy for a man appalled by centralization. But centralization was vital to survival, and the President worked diligently to build a powerful central government. Conscription was the first essential—it would give the administration control over manpower." Frank E. Vandiver, *Their Tattered Flags* (College Station: Texas A&M University Press, 1970), 130.

20. "A good many men who lived along the base of the Blue Ridge, who were liable to military duty, and some deserters, had taken refuge in the mountains and fortified themselves, and defied the conscript officers to arrest them. General Jackson sent some infantry and cavalry to capture them, when an old lady living nearby remarked that 'The deserters had mortified in the Blue Ridge, but that General Jackson sent a foot company and a critter company to ramshag the Blue Ridge and capture them.'" Casler, *Four Years in the Stonewall Brigade*, 70.

21. "As the army watched from a hillside on an April day, the dust of a Federal advance appeared, with Union cavalry driving at top speed. Just a few yards in front of them, on a white horse, was the figure of Ashby, firing at his pursuers, and himself under fire. It was clear that he

would not have time to burn the covered bridge in front of him, as he had been ordered to do in case of an enemy advance. Nevertheless he reined at the bridge as if to set fire to the brush piled against its timbers. The Yankees were upon him. One of the enemy fired, narrowly missing Ashby, striking his stallion in the side. Ashby cut the Federal from the saddle with his saber and disappeared into the bridge. Confederate officers thought he would never reappear; but he dashed out and, joining his troops, he got to the ground and stood over his dying horse, oblivious to the scattered fire of the engagement he had brought to the camp." Burke Davis, *They Called Him Stonewall: A Life of Lt. General T. J. Jackson, C.S.A.* (New York: Fairfax Press, 1988), 174–75.

22. Jackson's intention was to drive away the Federal force under General Milroy confronting Edward Johnson and then to attack Maj. Gen. Nathaniel Banks' army at Winchester. Freeman deems this engagement of 8 May 1862 tactically unimportant. It stands, however, as a prime example of the lengths to which Jackson would go to "mystify and mislead" his enemies. According to Freeman, "The advance had been more spectacular than the engagement. Jackson had turned off at Port Republic [and after an incredibly difficult march] had crossed the Blue Ridge at Brown's Gap. By way of White Hall, he had reached Mechum River Station on the Virginia Central Railroad and had moved his little Army by train to Staunton. Thence he had marched out the Parkersburg Turnpike, had joined [Maj. Gen. Edward (Allegheny)] Johnson and had repulsed a Federal attack. Milroy had retreated after the action. . . . Jackson had started in pursuit but had been able to accomplish little. The roads were incredibly bad; his transport was feeble." Freeman, *Lee's Lieutenants*, 1:354. Actually, the terrain was too rough for artillery work and the Rockbridge Artillery was not engaged.

23. Jackson now began to turn his attention to the army of Maj. Gen. Nathaniel Banks, centered around Strasburg. It became his purpose to tie up all Federal forces in the valley and prevent them from going to the aid of Maj. Gen. John Pope's army around Fredericksburg or Maj. Gen. McClellan's army gathered on the peninsula southeast of Richmond. The legend of Jackson's "foot cavalry" was being born. After defeating Milroy at McDowell and pursuing him as far as Franklin, Jackson "retraced his steps by way of McDowell, Lebanon Springs, off to Bridgewater where he quietly spent Sunday [May] 18th, and then on to Harrisonburg. Thence with no delay he moved down the Valley pike to New Market, crossed to the eastern side of the Massanutton Mountain and united with General Ewell who had moved down from near Conrad's Store. . . . On the 22nd of May he began his march, with Ewell in front, down through the Luray Valley to Front Royal. . . . In the early afternoon of the next day Ewell struck the pickets of the enemy within sight of and negligently near to Front Royal. They were

driven in and the small body of infantry supporting them easily routed." Douglas, *I Rode with Stonewall*, 49, 51.

Ten miles west at Strasburg, Banks received news of the rout and was put into a state of near panic. "Not only was [Jackson] not in his front, he was making for Banks' only route out of the Valley. Now Banks began a dash for Winchester to extricate himself from the closing jaws of Jackson's army." Robertson, *Stonewall Brigade*, 92. Banks' army narrowly escaped annihilation at Winchester and was driven across the Potomac in a state of complete disarray.

24. The battle Charles speaks of is the second battle of Kernstown.

25. After defeating Banks at Winchester, Jackson moved back up the valley, narrowly escaping the armies converging on Strasburg—Fremont's from the west and Shields' from the east. The hard-marching Army of the Valley squeezed through. The outmarched Federal armies pursued, only to have Jackson turn upon and defeat them at Cross Keys (Fremont) and Port Republic (Shields). These battles ended the Shenandoah Valley campaign of 1862 and established Jackson's reputation as one of history's true military geniuses.

With the valley clear of Federal armies, Jackson responded to Lee's call for his army's presence in front of Richmond. More hard marching was in store for the weary but willing "foot cavalry." This incomplete letter tells of some experiences of the 1st Rockbridge Artillery in what are called the Seven Days Battles.

26. Maj. Gen. Ambrose Powell Hill was a Virginian and a West Point graduate. He commanded a division in Jackson's army. In their dying moments, both Jackson and Lee, reliving the war in their delirium, called out for him to "come up." Ironically, while in the "old army," Hill and McClellan both had been suitors for the hand of Miss Ellen Marcy in marriage. McClellan had won that engagement. Maj. Gen. Daniel Harvey Hill was a North Carolinian, a West Pointer, and Jackson's brother-in-law.

27. The Seven Days Battles, beginning on 25 June 1862, included Oak Grove, 25 June; Mechanicsville, 26 June; Gaines' Mill, 27 June; Savage Station, 29 June; Frayser's Farm, 30 June; and Malvern Hill, 1 July. The sterling reputation earned by Jackson and his Army of the Valley was tarnished somewhat by their lackluster performance during the Seven Days. Many explanations have been offered for Jackson's uncharacteristic lethargy during the period. The most likely explanation is that he and his army were on the verge of total physical collapse after the rigors of the Shenandoah Valley campaign and the subsequent march to join General Lee before Richmond.

28. Each day General Lee skillfully made plans that, if properly executed, should have cut off McClellan's army and resulted in its destruction. Lee's frustration grew as, each day, his plans miscarried due

to faulty execution by his subordinates. Finally, as McClellan's troops were completing their retreat to the James River and fortifying Malvern Hill, Lee joined a group of senior officers observing the field. Included in the group were Maj. Gens. John B. Magruder, D. H. Hill, and James Longstreet. The usually composed commander could hardly conceal his impatience. "When a newly arrived brigadier came up to the group and expressed concern lest McClellan escape, the gray-bearded commander's patience snapped. 'Yes, he will get away,' Lee said bitterly, 'because I cannot have my orders carried out!'" Shelby Foote, *The Civil War: A Narrative* (New York: Vintage Books, 1986), 1:509.

29. At the beginning of the Peninsula campaign, McClellan established a main base of supply at White House on the York River. During his retreat to the James River at Harrison's Landing, he referred to the movement frequently as a "change of base." This euphemism for "retreat" was the subject of a great deal of derision in both the North and the South.

30. In the aftermath of the Seven Days, Jackson's command was sent northwest to oppose the combined forces along the Rappahannock River commanded by Maj. Gen. John Pope.

31. This letter was written three days after the last battle of the Seven Days campaign at Malvern Hill.

32. Ashby's death occurred late on the afternoon of 6 June 1862. According to Henry Kyd Douglas:

> In the afternoon of the 6th Fremont closed in cautiously upon Harrisonburg, and took possession, Ashby retiring. . . . As the sun was going down, Ashby, desirous of catching a party of the enemy who were in his front, ready to follow if he retired and retreat if he advanced, requested General Ewell to furnish him several regiments of infantry. The First Maryland, Colonel Bradley T. Johnson, and Colonel John Letcher's Virginia Regiment were sent to him. Skirmishing soon began, and the Federals, having been reinforced with infantry, drove the Confederate skirmish line back upon its support. Just then Ashby had his horse shot under him—the same, by the way, upon which Jackson was wounded at Bull Run. Thus suddenly dismounted, he placed himself at the head of the Virginia regiment, which was wavering under the hot fire, and waving his sword in the air moved forward and called upon them to follow him. At the same time General Ewell rode up and ordered the First Maryland to charge. The order was handsomely obeyed and in a few minutes the enemy was driven from the field.
>
> But Ashby was dead, shot through the heart. He never spoke, but calmly breathed his last in the arms of Lieutenant Jim Thomson, who loved him as only a fearless young soldier can love his hero, and whose love was fully rewarded by Ashby's love for him. . . . The

body of General Ashby was taken to Charlottesville by his Assistant Adjutant General, Captain Sturgis Davis, for burial. . . . Their captured foes, standing by as the hearse passed along the road, as if in sympathy for their bereavement and in respect for their great enemy, stood in respectful silence and many of them with uncovered heads. . . . In October, 1866, General Ashby's remains were removed from Charlottesville and on the 25th of that month were buried in the Stonewall Cemetary at Winchester with many services and ceremonies, in the presence of a great concourse of people. (Douglas, *I Rode with Stonewall*, 78–80; 81; 83)

33. This was the opening of the battles of Cross Keys and Port Republic. The Army of the Valley was confronted by a Federal army under Fremont advancing upon them from the west and another Federal army under Shields coming from the east. These battles were fought on Sunday, 8 June, and Monday, 9 June 1862, respectively. Jackson's plan was to divide his force and strike Fremont a blow at Cross Keys and then turn on Shields near Port Republic. It was a close thing, but in the end he succeeded admirably.

34. "At about 10 a.m. of today [Sunday, 8 June 1862], while some of us were quietly in our tents and the General [Jackson] and a portion of the staff were on the point of going over to the army across North River [Shenandoah], the Yankee cavalry and flying artillery, from down the river, made a dash upon Port Republic, our picket running away but some few coming through the town. The enemy appeared opposite Port Republic, across South River [Shenandoah] and began firing at such of our men as they could see, and especially at the bridge guard, while a portion of them crossed near the factory. As soon as the firing began the General started down toward it, on foot, as his horse was not ready, and went into the town, and when the others came on. Capt. A. S. Pendletown, Col. Wm L. Jackson, Lt. J. K. Boswell, Lt. Edward Willis and Col. S. Crutchfield, and some one brought his horse, he mounted and they all rode rapidly towards and through the bridge; but the enemy caught Willis and Crutchfield who were in the rear of the party." Jedediah Hotchkiss, *Make Me a Map of the Valley*, ed. Archie P. McDonald (Dallas, Tex.: Southern Methodist University Press, 1973), 53.

35. Following his narrow escape,

. . . [a] confused artillery duel raged about the town, and there was some skirmishing. The enemy soon pulled back . . . [and Jackson] brought up two infantry brigades to guard the bridge and the affair was almost over. . . . Some of his artillerymen had recently got new uniforms; and when Jackson saw a cannon pull into position by the bridge below him, he could not be sure whether the artillerymen serving the gun were the enemy or his own men; he had just ordered

Captain W. T. Poague toward the bridge with one of the Rock-bridge guns.

Poague, seeing the new and mysterious gun himself, turned to Jackson: "That can't be my gun, sir. They've not had time to set it up yet. It may be one of Carrington's."

Jackson studied the cannon's crew, and as he sat his horse by one of Poague's guns, he shouted to the men at the bridge, his womanish voice carrying through the town: "Bring up that gun! Bring it up here!" There was no reply. He stood in his stirrups. "Bring that gun up here, I say!"

The strange gun crew then moved, but only to turn the mouth of the cannon so as to bear on Poague, Jackson and the artillery piece at their side. They were Federals. Jackson's reaction was immediate. "Let 'em have it."

His own gun blasted at the enemy crew, driving it from the bridge. Jackson sent infantrymen down the hill with bayonets. As the troops rushed ahead of him, Jackson threw up his hands, posing as if in prayer. The men shouted and soon cleared the enemy from the village [Port Republic]. (Burke Davis, *They Called Him Stonewall*, 76–77)

36. The Confederate troops at Cross Keys were under the overall direction of Maj. Gen. Richard S. Ewell.

37. This does not square exactly with another account of what presumably is the same incident that Charles speaks of. According to Freeman, at one point the Federals of Shields' command put the Stonewall Brigade to flight. Trying to rally the faltering troops, "Winder and the regimental officers rode across the field, again and again. They wheeled and veered; they pleaded and shouted, they cut and commanded—all was futile. To the left and front, pursuing Federals now were visible. They came on so fast and so persistently that Winder ordered one of Poague's pieces halted. It must be turned on the Unionists. They must be held off till the scattered infantry could be rallied. The gunners stopped in perfect order; they loaded; they sent their charge where the pursuing Federals most threatened." U.S. War Department, *War of the Rebellion: Official Records*, ser. 1, vol. 12, pt. 1, pp. 714, 715, 729, 741, 763, 789; qtd. in Freeman, *Lee's Lieutenants*, 1:456. According to Charles' account, it does not appear that they were able to fire their fieldpiece.

38. "Federals were now pouring down the hill in a counterattack. [Brig. Gen. Charles] Winder saw at once that they must be held back until his troops could be rallied. He sent a courier to Poague, instructing the artillery officer to halt his withdrawal and to hold the Federals at bay as long as possible. The Rockbridge Artillery wheeled about handsomely and raked the advancing blue ranks. But the tide could not be

checked. Faced with completely envelopment, Poague hastily hitched his guns and started off. Not hearing his order, the crew of one six-pounder was left in a forward position. Federal shells pounded the area, killing an officer and two horses, and forcing the gun to be abandoned." U.S. War Department, *War of the Rebellion: Official Record,* ser. 1, vol. 12, ch. 24, pt. 1, pp. 715, 741, 750, 763; qtd. in Robertson, *Stonewall Brigade,* 111–12. Robertson mentions one officer killed; Charles mentions one officer, Lieutenant Davis, shot. See Driver, *1st and 2nd Rockbridge Artillery,* 64. The only Davis listed is 2nd Lt. James Cole Davis, wounded in action at Port Republic with a musket ball through the right side on 9 June 1862. He made his way from the battlefield and later recovered.

39. On 24 Sept. 1862, seven days after Sharpsburg (Antietam), Charles left the "fighting department," assigned to duty at the hospital in Winchester.

40. According to the records, Charles was appointed hospital steward on 18 Feb. 1863, and transferred to the hospital in Lynchburg. Driver, *1st and 2nd Rockbridge Artillery,* 80. However, this letter dated 26 Dec. 1862 places him in Lynchburg already.

41. Originally, the Texans were brigaded with the 18th Georgia Infantry and Hampton's South Carolina Legion. After the reorganization of the Army of Northern Virginia following Sharpsburg, the Texas Brigade was composed of the 1st Texas, 4th Texas, and Fifth Texas Infantry Regiments and the 3rd Arkansas Infantry Regiment. This remained the composition of the brigade throughout the remainder of the war. It was a singularly distinguished fighting unit.

Chapter 3: "This Fearful War," 1863

1. The exact location of their refuge is unknown. In other letters, such places as Double Bayou, Clear Creek, and Houston are referred to.

2. Considering the date of this letter, Charles must be speaking of Grant's first attempt to capture Vicksburg in Dec. 1862. With 40,000 men, Grant advanced down the Mississippi Central Railroad from Memphis in an attempt to capture the river bastion from the rear. In concert, Maj. Gen. William T. Sherman with 32,000 men advanced down the Mississippi River and attacked Vicksburg via Chickasaw Bluff up the Yazoo River. Grant established his base of operations at Holly Springs, Miss., and advanced on to the vicinity of Grenada. There he encountered 20,000 entrenched Confederate troops from the Vicksburg garrison under the command of Maj. Gen. John C. Pemberton. Confederate cavalry raids in his rear by Maj. Gens. Nathan Bedford Forrest and Earl Van Dorn resulted in the destruction of the Holly Springs base.

Sherman's failed assault on Chickasaw Bluffs ended any hope of success. Grant was forced to retreat.

3. The battle of Murfreesboro, or Stone's River, was fought in central Tennessee from 31 Dec. 1862 to 2 Jan. 1863. It was a two-day engagement; there was a lull on 1 Jan. The Union Army of the Cumberland, commanded by Maj. Gen. Williams S. Rosecrans, and the Confederate Army of Tennessee, commanded by Gen. Braxton Bragg, fought to a bloody stalemate. On 3 Jan., Bragg withdrew his army from the field.

4. On 13 Dec. 1862, Gen. Ambrose E. Burnside threw his Army of the Potomac across the Rappahannock River at Fredericksburg, Va., to assault an impregnable position held by Gen. Robert E. Lee's Army of Northern Virginia. The result of the attack was a bloody Union defeat.

5. Charles must be speaking of the raid against Kinston and Goldsboro by Union forces under the command of Gen. J. G. Foster. By all accounts, these raids were successful. However, the port at Wilmington remained open. See Hal Bridges, *Lee's Maverick General: Daniel Harvey Hill* (Lincoln: University of Nebraska Press, 1961), 163.

6. Gen. James Ewell Brown Stuart had first gained widespread fame by taking his cavalry command in a spectacular ride around Gen. George B. McClellan's Army of the Potomac during the Seven Days campaign in June 1862. He relished the fame his exploits brought and continually sought opportunities to expand his reputation.

7. Apparently a shortage of doctors had resulted in Charles' being appointed an assistant surgeon, even though at that point he had not received his medical degree. Dr. George K. Turner is listed as serving in General Hospital No. 2 as of June 1863. See Peter W. Houck, *Confederate Surgeon: The Personal Recollections of E. A. Craighill* (Lynchburg, Va.: H. E. Howard, 1989), 90–91.

8. Their refuge could have been along the banks of Clear Creek, which flows into Galveston Bay between Galveston and Houston.

9. Charles is probably speaking of the Second Presbyterian Church, located on the corner of Ninth and Church Streets. See Susan L. Foutz and George G. Morris, *Lynchburg in the Civil War* (Lynchburg, Va.: H. E. Howard, 1984), 4.

10. Apparently, the disease had made its first appearance earlier, for, "[O]n October 1, the city was shocked to learn that a soldier in one of the hospitals had died of smallpox. Few diseases were more dreaded, since only a few people had been vaccinated. Senior surgeons of the hospitals appointed medical officers as vaccine physicians whose duty was to vaccinate all persons in the immediate vicinity." Ibid., 25–26. Considering the number of vaccinations Charles mentions giving, he must have been one of those appointed a vaccine physician. In re-

sponse to fears of a possible epidemic, a smallpox hospital was established behind the city cemetery. Charles writes in a letter to Henry, dated 10 Mar. 1863, that he was in charge of the smallpox hospital.

11. "Since Lynchburg's founding in 1786, tobacco had given the city its financial base. . . . In 1860 there were also eighteen tobacco factories . . . processing the leaf for smoking or chewing. . . . The use of these factories changed drastically in the coming years as the ravages of war turned them into hospitals." Foutz and Morris, *Lynchburg in the Civil War*, 1–2.

12. Lee's Army of Northern Virginia and Burnside's Army of the Potomac went into winter quarters in their respective positions around Fredericksburg following the bloody affair of 13 Dec. 1862. In Jan. 1863, Burnside attempted offensive operations, but they bogged down in the mud that Charles mentions; in Civil War history, the effort is called "the Mud March."

13. A number of hospitals were established in Lynchburg, among them College Hospital; General Hospitals 1, 2, and 3; the Ladies Relief Hospital; Langhorne Hospital; Pratt Hospital; and the Wayside Hospital.

14. Erysipelas is an infection of the skin or mucous membranes. It was common during the Civil War period.

15. "Magruder's victory was complete. Union losses included two gunboats mounting at least 12 heavy guns and approximately 400 killed, wounded or captured. Confederate losses were 26 killed and 117 wounded." Kenneth J. Magee, "Most Disgraceful Affair," *America's Civil War*, 5 (Jan. 1993): 56.

16. Freeman describes Maj. Gen. John Bankhead Magruder as "handsome, perfectly uniformed, insistent, impatient and theatrical, and he always appears at a gallop. Despite a slight lisp, he loves to talk and he writes ceaselessly to his superiors. A certain aptitude for independent command he possesses, and with it ability to bluff an adversary." Freeman, *Lee's Lieutenants*, 1:xxxiv. During the Peninsula campaign early in summer 1862, Magruder did not measure up to expectations; hence his presence in Texas.

17. "The Red River was the Confederacy's chief supply route from the West. Tucked in between the Confederate strongholds of Port Hudson and Vicksburg, it was relatively secure from Union forces. [Adm. David Dixon] Porter had tried to remedy that situation in February [1862]. He ran two vessels (*Indianola* and *Queen of the West*) past Vicksburg, but both were captured before they could seriously threaten the Red River route." William M. Fowler, Jr., *Under Two Flags: The American Navy in the Civil War* (New York: Avon Books, 1990), 219.

18. Dr. John W. Minor is listed as serving in General Hospital No. 1 in Lynchburg as of June 1863. See Houck, *Confederate Surgeon*, 90–91.

19. Apparently, Hospital No. 1 and Claytor Hospital were the same.

20. Dr. G. A. D. Galt is listed as serving in Hospital No. 1 as of June 1863. Houck, *Confederate Surgeon*, 90–91.

21. "[T]his Confederate hospital was the largest military hospital in the history of the world. In the three years from April 1862 to April 1865 it treated 76,000 patients, 17,000 of them battle casualties, with an overall mortality of 'a little over 9 percent.'" Frank S. Johns and Anne Page Johns, "Chimborazo Hospital and J. B. McCaw, Surgeon-in-Chief," *Virginia Magazine of History and Biography* 62 (Apr. 1945): 190.

22. "The divisions of this immense hospital were five, or five hospitals in one, and five surgeons, each one of the five in charge of a division; also a number of assistants and acting assistant surgeons (forty-five to fifty), each in charge of several wards or buildings, and subject to surgeons of division, and all subject to Surgeon James B. McCaw, in charge of executive head." John R. Gildersleeve, "History of Chimborazo Hospital, C.S.A.," *Southern Historical Society Papers* 36 (1908): 87. The Fifth Division was the South Carolina Division, headed by Surgeon E. M. Seabrook of Charleston, S.C. Ibid., 91.

23. The Reverend Thomas Moore was pastor of the First Presbyterian Church during the war. The present site of the church in Richmond is on the east side of Tenth between Broad and Capitol. See Samuel J. T. Moore, Jr., *Moore's Complete Civil War Guide to Richmond* (n.p., 1978), 43.

24. Dr. Moses Drury Hoge was pastor of the Second Presbyterian Church and a lecturer of some note. "Stonewall" Jackson worshipped in this church when in Richmond. The present site of the church is 13 North Fifth Street. Ibid.

25. Surgeon Gen. Samuel Preston Moore was appointed to his post on 30 July 1861 and served for the duration of the war. "A native of Charleston, South Carolina, he ... was graduated from the Medical College of South Carolina in 1834. The next year he was appointed an assistant surgeon in the regular army. . . . He saw service in the Mexican War and received his surgeoncy while at Jefferson Barracks, Missouri, immediately after that conflict. On duty in New Orleans as medical purveyor when South Carolina enacted its secession ordinance, Moore resigned his commission and practiced medicine in Little Rock, Arkansas, for a short time before he was called in to take charge of the Confederated Medical Department." H. H. Cunningham, *Doctors in Gray: The Confederate Medical Service* (Baton Rouge: Louisiana State University Press, 1958), 28. Despite Charles' disdain, Surgeon General Moore performed with great distinction in his post. He "soon had the Medical Department operating efficiently. Examinations were prescribed to weed out incompetent personnel, the competent were assigned to key positions, and a reporting system intended to inform the Surgeon Gen-

eral of all pertinent medical facts and problems was instituted." Ibid., 28–29.

It is unclear why Charles was unable to return to the University of Virginia to complete his medical education, since there were military hospitals in Charlottesville. Since Richmond became the major medical center, probably there were more opportunities there. "In spite of all its attendant hardships, the war was a boon to certain Southern medical colleges, especially the Medical College of Virginia. The records of the College show that the attendance continued high through the war period except for the year 1861–62, when enrollment dropped to 67. The exigencies of the war and the presence of military hospitals in Richmond made medical education a very definite need." William F. Norwood, *Medical Education in the United States Before the Civil War* (Philadelphia: University of Pennsylvania Press, 1944), 275.

26. Presumably this is the wife of James Mason of Virginia, known for his involvement in the *Trent* affair. He was the Confederacy's envoy to London.

Chapter 4: "That Much Dreaded Place—The Field," 1864

1. The law, approved 28 Dec. 1863, provided that "no person liable to military service shall hereafter be permitted or allowed to furnish substitute for such service, nor shall any substitute be received, enlisted, or enrolled in the military service of the Confederate States." "Order Enrolling Principals Who Have Put in Substitutes," *Richmond Daily Dispatch,* 12 Jan. 1864.

2. Following the Gettysburg campaign in July 1863, the Army of Northern Virginia returned to Virginia and took up a generally defensive position behind the Rapidan River. The Bristoe and Mine Run campaigns, in fall 1863, were inconclusive campaigns of maneuver. There was a sharp action at Bristoe Station, but not at Mine Run. Afterwards, both armies went into winter quarters to await the return of suitable campaigning weather the following spring (1864).

3. After the retreat from Gettysburg, Brig. Gen. John D. Imboden was appointed by General Lee to command the Shenandoah Valley District. According to General Imboden, "In December, 1863, General Averell made a daring raid from New Creek with about four thousand cavalry. We prevented his getting into the Shenandoah Valley to strike at Staunton. But in 'shying' him off from that point we caused him to sweep on behind the North Mountain range, where he struck the Virginia and Tennessee Railroad sixty odd miles west of Lynchburg, and destroyed the army stores accumulated there, and then made his escape back to his base." John D. Imboden, "The Battle of New Market, Va., May 15th,

1864," in *Battles and Leaders of the Civil War*, ed. Robert U. Johnson and Clarence C. Buel (New York: Thomas Yoseloff, 1956), 4:480.

4. The Medical College of Virginia "was the eleventh medical school established in the United States. During the war between the States it was the only medical school open in the South, and ran two sessions yearly. It was the school to which all the Southern men, then studying medicine in the North, came at the beginning of the war, and it furnished many medical officers who ministered to the loved ones who were away in the field, wounded, sick or diseased." Christopher Tompkins, M.D., "Medical Education in the South," *Southern Medical Journal* 3 (1910): 326.

5. Charles completed his medical studies in Mar. 1864. See "Medical College Commencement," *Richmond Enquirer*, 11 Mar. 1864. Charles W. Trueheart, Galveston, Tex., is listed as one of the recent graduates.

6. "The Eighth Alabama infantry regiment . . . was the first Confederate regiment to be enlisted for the war. Its first service was at Yorktown. It fought in the battle of Williamsburg, May 5th, and at Fair Oaks, May 31 and June 1, 1862, in both of which engagements it took an important part and its losses were very severe. It was then transferred to the brigade of Gen. Cadmus M. Wilcox and was greatly distinguished at Mechanicsville, June 26th. Two days later it was prominent in the assault upon the enemy at Gaines' Mill and on June 30th was again in the midst of the conflict at Frayser's Farm. It was present, though not severely engaged, at Manassas and Harper's Ferry, and was in the thickest of the fight at Antietam, September 17th. It fought with its usual bravery at Gettysburg, July 2, 1863; the Wilderness, May 5, 6, and 7, 1864; Spotsylvania, May 8th to 18th; Salem Church, Cold Harbor, June 1 to 12, 1864. It formed a portion of the troops engaged at the Weldon railroad, June 22 and 23, 1864; was distinguished at the capture of the Crater, July 30th, and was also warmly engaged in the battle on the plank road below Petersburg." Clement A. Evans, ed., *Confederate Military History* (Atlanta, Ga.: Confederate Publishing Co., 1899), 79. The regiment surrendered at Appomattox Court House as a part of Forney's Brigade, Mahone's Division, Third Army Corps, Army of Northern Virginia; see "The Opposing Forces in the Appomattox Campaign," in *Battles and Leaders of the Civil War*, Johnson and Buel, eds., 4:752. A roster of regimental officers lists "Assistant Surgeon Charles W. Trueheart: From 4–23–64. Transferred to an Engineer's Corps, 12–64. Present from the battle of the Wilderness, 5–6–64 through the battle of Burgess' Mill, 11–64." Hilary A. Herbert, "History of the Eighth Alabama Volunteer Regiment, C.S.A.," ed. Maurice S. Fortin, *Alabama Historical Quarterly* 39 (1977): 203.

7. Lt. Col. Hilary A. Herbert was in command of the regiment at that time.

8. Each infantry regiment generally had assigned to it a surgeon and an assistant surgeon.

The duties of the assistant surgeon were to assist or relieve the surgeon in caring for the sick and wounded in camp or on the march. On the field of battle he was expected to be close up in the immediate rear of the center of his regiment accompanied by the infirmary detail, and to give primary attention, first aid to the wounded—this consisting in temporary control of hemorrhage by ligature, tourniquet, or bandage and compress, adjusting and temporarily fixing fractured limbs, administering water, anodynes, or stimulants, if needed, and seeing that the wounded were promptly carried to the field-hospital in the rear by the infirmary detail or ambulance.

The duties of the surgeons, in addition to caring for the sick in camp and on the march, were to establish a field-hospital as soon as they could learn that the command to which they were attached was going under fire, at some convenient and, if possible, sheltered spot behind a hill or in a ravine, about one-half to one mile in rear of the line of battle, which was done under direction of a brigade or division surgeon. Here the combined medical staff of a brigade or division aided one another in the performance of such operations as were deemed necessary, as the wounded were brought from the front by the infirmary detail on stretchers or in the ambulance. Amputations, resections of bone, ligatures of arteries, removals of foreign bodies, adjusting and permanently fixing fractures, and all minor and major operations and dressings were made when deemed best for the comfort and welfare of the wounded men. . . .

The uniform worn by the medical corps was similar to that of the rank and file with only a slight difference. While the cloth and cut were the same, the facings of the coat collar and cuffs and stripe down the sides of the trousers were black, while those of the infantry were light blue, the artillery, scarlet, and cavalry, buff; on the front of the cap or hat were the letters "M.S." embroidered in gold, embraced in two olive branches. On the coat sleeve of the assistant surgeon were two rows of gold braid, with three gold bars on the ends of the coat collar extending back about one and a half inches; while the surgeon had three rows of braid on the coat sleeves, and a single star on each side of the coat collar about an inch and a half from the end. (Deering J. Roberts, "Organization and Personnel of the Medical Department of the Confederacy," in *The Photographic History of the Civil War*, edited by Francis T. Miller [New York: Thomas Yoseloff, 1957], 7:350)

9. Charles is referring to the opening of the Wilderness campaign on Thursday, 5 May 1864. The Union Army of the Potomac was under the command of Maj. Gen. George G. Meade. Accompanying Meade's

army was the newly appointed lieutenant general in charge of all Union armies in the field, Ulysses S. Grant. After the bloody affair in the Wilderness on 5–6 May, the Army of the Potomac broke precedent by pushing forward instead of retreating, as it had tended to do in the past. In Grant, President Lincoln had found the man who could "face the arithmetic"—that is, accept the terrible losses necessary to wear Lee's army down. In order to protect the Confederate capital at Richmond, Lee was forced to retreat to Spotsylvania Court House, arriving there just before the vanguard of the Army of the Potomac appeared. The fighting in that area continued until Saturday, 21 May, and was among the fiercest of the war. Charles' command was on the left of the Confederate line of battle.

10. Charles is referring to the fight at the "Bloody Angle," "the longest sustained hand-to-hand combat of the Civil War." Noah Andre Trudeau, *Bloody Roads South* (New York: Fawcett Columbine, 1989), 171. See also William D. Matter, *If It Takes All Summer: The Battle of Spotsylvania* (Chapel Hill: University of North Carolina Press, 1988).

11. The weather was foul, with rain and fog. The Federal attacking column was from Maj. Gen. Winfield Scott Hancock's II Corps. Brig. Gen. Francis C. Barlow's division led the assault, and the other II Corps divisions aligned their movements on it. The initial success of the attack was attributable to the withdrawal of the Confederate artillery just prior to the action, General Lee being under the impression that the Federals were retreating toward Fredericksburg. This allowed the Federals to breach the line and capture Maj. Gen. Edward Johnson and a large part of his division, including Brig. Gen. George H. Steuart. The artillery was returned piecemeal, and eventually the Confederate line was restored, but only after some of the most terrible carnage of the entire war had ensued.

12. Effective Union strength at the beginning of the campaign is estimated at 118,000. Estimated Union casualties in killed, wounded, captured or missing from 5 May through 15 June are 54,929. See "The Opposing Forces at the Beginning of Grant's Campaign Against Richmond," in *Battles and Leaders of the Civil War,* Buel and Johnson, eds., 4:182. Confederate strength is estimated at about 61,000, with another 30,000 near Richmond and Petersburg. Casualty figures are only partially reported but must have been substantial.

13. Charles is describing the fighting at Cold Harbor. At one stage of the carnage, some 7,000 attacking Union soldiers were shot down in about ten minutes.

14. Actually, Grant, with more manpower reserves available than Lee had, was waging a war of attrition. His target was Lee's army, not Richmond.

15. Grant's army began crossing the Rapidan River on 5 May 1864.

16. This was the battle of the Wilderness.

17. According to General Grant, "Lee's position was now so near Richmond, and the intervening swamps of the Chickahominy so great an obstacle to the movement of troops in the face of an enemy, that I determined to make my next left flank move carry the Army of the Potomac south of the James River." E. B. Long, ed., *The Personal Memoirs of U.S. Grant* (Cleveland, Ohio: World Publishing, 1952), 446. "In his heart, Robert E. Lee knew that Grant's move across the James marked the beginning of the end for the Confederacy. Only a week earlier, he had made this point to Jubal Early: 'We must destroy the Army of Grant's before he gets to the James River. If he gets there it will become a siege, and then it will be a mere question of time.'" Trudeau, *Bloody Roads South*, 320–21.

18. The Army of the James, commanded by Maj. Gen. Benjamin Butler, had been moving up the James River from Fortress Monroe in conjunction with Grant's movements south of the Rapidan.

19. From these movements evolved the siege of Petersburg that lasted some ten months. Grant continued his established practice of extending his left flank until finally turning the Confederate right flank at Five Forks in early April 1865.

20. According to Theodore F. Rodenbough:

> Wilson's small division had been engaged in the varied and thankless duties of an infantry auxiliary until June 20th, when his command was swelled to 5000 effective men by the addition of Kautz's division (of Butler's army) of four regiments.
>
> On the 22d Wilson started under orders from Meade to cut the Weldon and Southside [rail]roads, and to continue the work of destruction "until driven from it by such attacks of the enemy as you can no longer resist." This was carried out to the letter. (Rodenbough, "Sheridan's Trevilian Raid," in *Battles and Leaders of the Civil War*, ed. Robert U. Johnson and Clarence C. Buel [New York: Thomas Yoseloff, 1956], 4:236)

Richmond newspapers referred to the raid as "the thieving and plundering of Wilson's gang in the counties of Dinwiddie, Nottaway, and Lunenburg." See "Depredations of the Raiders," *Richmond Daily Dispatch*, 1 July 1864. Among the items reputedly plundered were Negroes, money, silver plate, and cotton bales.

21. As Archer Jones notes:

> When, in June 1864, Lee detached a corps westward, it aimed at recovering the Shenandoah Valley, the scene of operations intended to distract Lee. In May, Grant's distracting force under General Sigel had advanced into the valley from the Baltimore & Ohio railroad. It had met defeat in battle and retreated so precipitously that soldiers who had said they fought with Sigel later said they ran with

him. But a Union army quickly returned under David Hunter, an adequate general, and overwhelmed the small rebel force left in the valley. Just after Cold Harbor, Lee sent the capable and resourceful General Jubal A. Early to the valley with his corps, one of the three composing Lee's army.

Acting with admirable dispatch and effectiveness, Early drove Hunter from the valley and acted to help peace partisans in the North's coming elections. (Archer Jones, *Civil War Command and Strategy* [New York: Free Press, 1992], 197–98)

See also Benjamin F. Cooling, III, *Jubal Early's Raid on Washington: 1864* (Baltimore, Md.: Nautical & Aviation Publishing Co. of America, 1989).

22. Henry Trueheart was a member of McNeill's command at that time.

23. This action took place during Grant's movement of the Army of the Potomac to the south side of the James River.

At daybreak [Monday, 13 June 1864], Robert E. Lee learned that Grant's army had slipped away during the night. According to Eppa Hunton, one of George Pickett's brigadiers, "It was said that General Lee was in a furious passion—one of the few times during the war. When he did get mad he was mad all over." . . .

Lee was calm enough by evening, when he informed War Secretary John Seddon of the facts. In the same message, he also passed along good news. Wade Hampton's cavalrymen had caught up with Sheridan's column near a place called Trevilian Station, and Hampton was claiming that he had "defeated the enemy's cavalry . . . with heavy loss."

(Grant's report on the Trevilian fight was very different from Lee's. According to Grant, the combat of June 11–12 had resulted in a repulse of the Confederate attackers and the successful completion of Sheridan's primary mission, the destruction of the Virginia Central railroad. Sheridan, Grant said, had then determined that a link-up with Hunter in the Shenandoah would not be possible, and on June 12 had started back for the Army of the Potomac.) (Trudeau, *Bloody Roads South*, 316–17)

24. The Confederates had been on the defensive since the begining of the campaign in early May, when

[O]n the 22nd of June General Grant suddenly found that Lee was on the offensive. The Divisions of Anderson, Wilcox and (Major General) Bushrod Johnson, with Mahone's had been ordered to march into a gap left between the [Federal] 2nd and 6th Corps stretched towards the Weldon Railroad. The fighting seems largely to have been done by the Alabama, Georgia, and Virginia Brigades of Mahone's Division, as it was the troops of these Brigades that captured all the flags taken from the enemy. The Alabama Brigade was on the left in the attack, and the 8th Alabama was on the left of our Brigade. The Alabamians marched through the woods and the 8th was halted and laid down in front of the enemy's breastworks, where it was subjected to a terrific fire. . . .

In the meantime, the other four regiments of the Alabamians, together with the Georgians and Virginians, moved on the extreme left flank of Grant's army and then all advanced together. The enemy fled in great confusion, losing 1,600 prisoners and ten flags. . . .

As soon as we had occupied the works of the enemy, our men expecting an attack provided themselves each with two guns of those captured from the enemy, and loaded them, every man of the 8th (and it is probably true of the other regiments) had not only his own, but two loaded guns besides. Soon the enemy were reinforced and made a gallant attack to recapture their works, but they were disastrously repulsed.

That night our troops returned to their stations with the spoils. The loss of the 8th in this battle was twenty-seven killed, wounded, and missing. (Herbert, "History of the Eighth Alabama," 144)

25. "On the 29th of June our Brigade with the Florida, now [Brig. Gen. Joseph] Finegan's Brigade, and with two pieces of artillery, and [Maj. Gen.] Fitz[hugh] Lee's Cavalry, intercepted the enemy's raiders at Stony Creek Depot sometimes called Ream's Station, on the Weldon Railroad, captured 198 men, seven officers, twenty-three ambulances, fifty-three wagons and fourteen pieces of artillery. The loss of the regiment here was five killed, wounded and missing." Ibid., 145.

26. After being dispatched to the valley by General Lee, General Early drove General Hunter's Union forces from the area. He then advanced down the valley and into Maryland, the strategy being to force General Grant to detach troops from in front of Petersburg to oppose him. At Monocacy, Md., on 9 July 1864, General Early defeated a Union force, hastily assembled under Maj. Gen. Lew Wallace, that was sent to oppose him. Early's advance then continued to the very gates of Washington, D. C. In the meantime, General Grant had dispatched two divisions of the VI Corps from Petersburg to help defend the capital. These troops arrived in the nick of time to turn Early back into Virginia. For details of this campaign, see Jubal A. Early, *Jubal Early's Memoirs* (1912; reprint, Baltimore, Md.: Nautical & Aviation Publishing Co. of America, 1989), 371–98.

27. For Governor Letcher's account of the burning of his home, see "The Burning of Gov. Letcher's Dwelling," *Richmond Sentinel,* 20 July 1864.

28. General Early makes no mention in his memoirs of the burning of Maryland Governor Bradley's home. However, in a footnote, he does mention and disclaim responsibility for the burning of U.S. Postmaster

General Montgomery Blair's home: "On the night of the 13th the house of Postmaster General Blair near Silver Spring was burned, and it was assumed by the enemy that it was burned by my orders. I had nothing to do with it and do not yet know how the burning occurred. Though I believed that retaliation was justified by previous acts of the enemy, yet I did not wish to incur the risk of any license on the part of my troops and it was obviously impolitic to set the house on fire when we were retiring, as it amounted to notice of our movement." Early, *Jubal Early's Memoirs*, 395.

29. The Texas Brigade remained with the Army of Northern Virginia for the rest of the war.

30. Charles is referring to the detonation of a giant "mine" tunneled under the Confederate line by Union sappers of the 48th Pennsylvania Infantry Regiment. The Union objective was to breach the opposing line and then exploit the breakthrough. The mine was detonated on 30 July 1864, tearing a great gap in the Confederate line. However, a poorly coordinated Federal assault was beaten back with considerable loss to both sides. Charles' regiment was heavily involved in the action. For one of many accounts of the battle of the Crater, see William H. Powell, "The Battle of the Petersburg Crater," in *Battles and Leaders of the Civil War*, ed. Robert U. Johnson and Clarence C. Buel (New York: Thomas Yoseloff, 1956), 4:545–60. For the part played by the 8th Alabama, see Herbert, "History of the Eighth Alabama," 143–72.

31. "So outstanding was [Girardey's] performance at the battle of the Crater, in organizing and timing Mahone's counterattack after the explosion of the Federal mine, that four days later he was jumped to the grade of brigadier general with temporary rank from July 30. This was the only instance in the Confederate Army of such a promotion. On August 16, 1864, only thirteen days after he had received his commission, while commanding the brigade of which he had formerly been adjutant, General Girardey was killed near Fussell's Mill on the Darbytown Road, while resisting a Federal assault on the east end of the Richmond defenses." Ezra J. Warner, *Generals in Gray* (Baton Rouge: Louisiana State University Press, 1959), 106.

32. The order of battle of opposing forces at Petersburg and Richmond lists the 8th Alabama as a unit in A. P. Hill's Corps, Mahone's Division, Sanders Brigade. Wright's Brigade is not listed, maybe having been commanded by Brig. Gen. G. Moxley Sorrell at the time. See Robert U. Johnson and Clarence C. Buel, "The Opposing Forces at Petersburg and Richmond," in *Battles and Leaders of the Civil War*, Johnson and Buel, eds., 4:590–94.

33. Apparently, Charles is relating his experiences in the action near Globe Tavern on the Weldon Railroad, 18 Aug. 1864. See Orlando B. Wilcox, "Actions on the Weldon Railroad," in *Battles and Leaders of the*

Civil War, Johnson and Buel, eds., 4:568–71. Also see Herbert, "History of the Eighth Alabama," 173–75.

34. For another view on the conduct of the Negro troops in the Crater fight, see Henry G. Thomas, "The Colored Troops at Petersburg," in *Battles and Leaders of the Civil War,* Johnson and Buel, eds., 4:563–67.

35. Casualty figures for the Federal IX Corps and one division of the X Corps that participated in the action are given as 3,798. Confederate losses are given as "not fully reported." See Powell, "Battle of the Petersburg Crater," in *Battles and Leaders of the Civil War,* Johnson and Buel, eds., 4:560.

36. Grant established his base and headquarters at City Point on the James River. The former base is known today as Hopewell, Va.

37. Atlanta had fallen to Federal armies commanded by Maj. Gen. William T. Sherman on 2 Sept. 1864.

38. For a description of the medical problem, see George W. Adams, "Confederate Medicine," *Journal of Southern History* 6 (May 1940): 151–66.

39. For a description of the "beefsteak raid," see the excellent biography of Wade Hampton by Manley W. Wellman, *Giant in Gray* (New York: Charles Scribner's Sons, 1949), 156–59.

40. On paper at least, a brigade composed of four regiments numbered about 4,000 men.

41. The only record of a wound suffered by Charles is that of his being shot in the finger at High Bridge, 7 Apr. 1865, during the retreat to Appomattox. See Col. T. M. R. Talcott, "Parole List of Engineer Troops, Army of Northern Virginia, Surrendered at Appomattox C. H., April 9th, 1865," *Southern Historical Society Papers* 32 (1904): 56.

42. The partisan leader, John Hanson McNeill, was mortally wounded at Meem's Bottom on 3 Oct. 1864. He died on 10 Nov. 1864, at Hill's Hotel in Harrisonburg, Va. See Delauter, *McNeill's Rangers,* 78–87.

43. In Dec. 1864, Charles transferred to the Confederate Engineers, commanded by Col. T. M. R. Talcott. For a history of the Confederate Engineers, see James L. Nichols, *Confederate Engineers* (Tuscaloosa, Ala.: Confederate Publishing Co., 1957)

Chapter 5: "That All Important Arm of the Service," 1865

1. Col. W. W. Blackford was a Trueheart kinsman, the same one who, as a member of Maj. Gen. Stuart's staff, mentioned seeing Charles at Sharpsburg on 17 Sept. 1862. For his description of this phase of the war, see Blackford, *War Years with Jeb Stuart.* Col. T. M. R. Talcott was

the son of Col. Andrew Talcott. The elder Talcott was a lifelong friend of Robert E. Lee and had been his commander at Fortress Monroe in the 1830s. For Col. T. M. R. Talcott's reminiscences, see T. M. R. Talcott, "From Petersburg to Appomattox," *Southern Historical Society Papers* 32 (1904): 67–72.

2. "There was at the time only one ray of light—the possibility of a negotiated peace.... Three leading Southerners, Vice President Stephens, Judge J. A. Campbell [assistant secretary of war], and Senator R. M. T. Hunter, had gone to Federal lines on the 29th [Jan. 1865] and ... had proceeded to Hampton Roads. There they conferred unofficially with President Lincoln. The ... meeting ... however, ended ... with no apparent possibility of an understanding." Douglas Southall Freeman, *R. E. Lee* (New York: Charles Scribner's Sons, 1935), 4:2. Confederate President Jefferson Davis was still insisting on the recognition of Southern independence, which, of course, President Lincoln had no intention of granting.

3. Apparently, Charles is speaking of Charles Minor, who was a member of Mess 19, Rockbridge Artillery, and is listed as surrendering at Appomattox as a 2nd lieutenant of the 1st Engineer Regiment, Company "A." See Talcott, "Parole List," 51. The reason his presence enhanced Charles' position is obscure.

4. "Indeed, [Jefferson Davis] ... thought that in the failure of the Hampton Roads conference he could find a tool to lever the people of the Confederacy into greater commitment. The very day after the commissioner's report reached his hands, he allowed it to be published in the Richmond press, thinking that this new proof of Lincoln's intention to accept nothing but subjugation might stiffen the all-but-flaccid resolve of his people.... For once in his career, Jefferson Davis had engineered a stunning public relations victory. The release of the Hampton Roads material showed everyone exactly what the Confederacy faced, seemingly crystallizing what remained of their spirit of independence." William C. Davis, *Jefferson Davis: The Man and His Hour* (New York: Harper Collins, 1991), 592–93.

5. Throughout the Petersburg campaign, General Grant's strategy was to extend his left, ceaselessly attempting to turn the Confederate right. Eventually, the plan paid off at Five Forks on 1 Apr. 1865, as General Lee was forced to abandon his works and begin the retreat that ended at Appomattox Court House a week later.

6. In Aug. 1864, Maj. Gen. Philip Sheridan took the Union command in the Shenandoah Valley. In Oct. 1864, Sheridan defeated Early's army at Cedar Creek and, in effect, ended Confederate hopes in that region. Sheridan's army wintered at Kernstown in 1864–65, launching raids against various objectives, principally the Virginia Central Railroad. These raids failed in their objective.

After the failure of these expeditions no further movements were attempted in the Valley, and most of the infantry of Sheridan's army was sent either to the Army of the Potomac at Petersburg, or elsewhere where it was needed. In February Sheridan made arrangements to march from the Valley with the cavalry with a view to interrupting and destroying, as far as possible, the lines of supply through central Virginia. After accomplishing this it was intended that he should either move west of Richmond and join Sherman's army, or return to the Valley, or join Meade's army in front of Petersburg, as might be most practicable. February 27th the movement commenced, the command consisting of two superb divisions of cavalry which had been recruited and remounted during the winter, under [Merritt], as chief-of-cavalry. The march to Staunton was made without noticeable opposition. On the morning of March 2d Early was found posted on a ridge west of Waynesboro. The veteran soldier was full of pluck and made a bold front for a fight, but his troops were overcome, almost without even perfunctory resistance, by the advance regiments of the column, and Early, with a few general officers, barely escaped capture by flight. All Early's supplies, all transportation, all the guns, ammunition and flags, and most of the officers and men of the army were captured and sent to the rear.

From this point Sheridan moved unmolested to the Virginia Central Railroad, which was destroyed for miles, large bridges being wrecked, the track torn up, and the rails heated and bent. The command was divided and sent to the James River Canal, which was destroyed as effectually as the railroad. This done, the cavalry proceeded to White House, on the Pamunkey River, where it arrived on March 19th, 1865. (Wesley Merritt, "Sheridan in the Shenandoah Valley," in *Battles and Leaders of the Civil War*, Robert U. Johnson and Clarence C. Buel, eds., 4:521)

7. The Confederacy was so short of men that an amnesty was offered in an attempt to entice deserters to rejoin their units. Estimates of the number of deserters ranged as high as 200,000 men.

8. Charles was not transferred to the artillery and finished the war with the Engineer Corps.

9. This is the only mention in the brothers' letters of McNeill's Rangers' most remarkable wartime exploit, the capture of Federal Major Generals Crook and Kelley. In his memoirs, Henry recounted the adventure:

During the very cold spell of weather, on February 25, 1865, the command under Lieut. Jesse McNeill, including a few volunteers, and numbering about sixty-six men, disguised in blue overcoats, went about one hundred and twenty miles in advance of all Confederate troops, entered Cumberland, Md., a city of four thousand inhabitants, fortified and garrisoned by seven thousand Federal troops, and guarded by three lines of pickets, and took Major General Kelly [Kelley] and Maj. Gen. George Crook out of their beds, and carrying them close by their infantry camp, delivered them as prisoners at Richmond, Va.

Such a raid with its results seems almost incredible, but as things turned out it was easy of accomplishment. A spy who had been sent into the city, met us some six miles from Cumberland, and reported the conditions and exact rooms occupied by each General. We cross[ed] the North Branch of the Potomac at an unused ford, leaving a Yankee picket undisturbed a half mile to the West; outran and captured the next picket, forced the countersign from him, "Bull Run"; placed him under care of two Confederates with instructions to shoot him if "Bull Run" failed to pass us at the reserve post, and under these circumstances he naturally told the truth. On reaching the reserve post, the "countersign" insured us a friendly reception, and upon getting nearer we covered them with our pistols, and they surrendered. They were paroled to remain in their tent until morning, we telling them that Gen'l Fitzhugh Lee was close by with ten thousand Cavalry. Taking their arms from them, later throwing them away in the snow, we proceeded down the pike to the city, arriving about three a.m. Detachments were sent East and West to cut the wires, to the livery stables, and to the Headquarters of each General.

I happened to be with the squad sent to Gen. Crook's quarters at the "Revere Hotel," where we found a sentinel at the door. One of the men dismounted presumably to deliver dispatches from Newcreek, but instead of dispatches, presented a pistol with one hand, and seized his gun with the other, and put him under guard. Joseph W. Vandiver and Joseph W. Kuykendall and I were dismounted, the two former going to Gen. Crook's room and I standing sentinel at the door.

About this time a train rolled in from the West over the B & O R. R. stopping within a hundred feet of the hotel. Several R.R. men came along and asked, "What's the news, boys?" etc.—they were seized and pushed inside the cordon of mounted men to be held until we were ready to depart. The other squads had performed their duties in their several directions, one capturing Gen. Kelly [Kelley] at the "Barnum House," and also his Adjutant General, and others taking charge of all the good horses that could be found.

Probably fifteen or twenty minutes covered our stay in the city, and then the detachments having all re-united, the column moved down the pike, and crossed the Potomac, a mile or more below town, where the reserve pickets were posted, and at the point where the R.R. embankment and trestle over the river met. Private Kuy-

Notes to Page 144

◞

kendall was at the head of the column marching by twos, and the Captain and other officers protecting the rear. Gen. Crook, mounted on a bare back horse, came next, with a guard on either side; then Gen. Kelly [Kelley] with John Cunningham on one side and I on the other. The sentinel called, "Halt, who comes there?" Kuykendall replied, "Friends, with the countersign." "Dismount one and advance with the countersign," called the sentinel. Kuykendall hesitated only a second, then cool and self-possessed, turned to the column and in a clear, loud voice gave the order, "Column forward, march!"—then turning to the officer in command of the Reserves, said, smiling, "We have no time to go through with that nonsense; Fitzhugh Lee is reported outside of town with ten thousand Cavalry, and we are ordered out on a scout." The embankment was now swarming with reserves, each with his gun at "ready"; but the bluff had its effect, and when the head of our column was within sixty or eighty feet of the Yankees, the Officer replied, "All right boys, come on," and our command thus passed within twenty or thirty feet of the reserves, laughing and talking with them; some saying, "You fellows will come tearing back here after a while with the Rebs after you," and our boys assuring the Yanks "we are not afraid of the Rebs."

Of course the Generals had been warned that the slightest alarm or attempt to escape would mean instant death, and they evidently believed it for they were as quiet as lambs.

We then passed along the pike within one or two hundred feet of the Yankee infantry camp, embracing hundreds, if not thousands of tents, and the sentinels keeping watch, but as we came from town and wore the loyal Blue, we were supposed to be all right.

Gen. Crook, later distinguished as an Indian fighter[,] sat erect upon his barebacked horse with his arms folded across his breast, and was the picture of dignified resignation. Several miles from town we stopped and pressed a saddle from a farmer, and thus made him as comfortable as possible. The weather was very cold, every breath freezing on the men's mustaches, and as we rode at a gallop the sweat on the horses formed a frost work around each hair making it stand out and thus presenting a weird spectacle. A small favor shown Gen. Crook brought cordial appreciation and thanks. I stopped his horse long enough to pull down his underdrawers which had worked up to the knee, and he said "Young man, if I can ever be of service to you, call on me."

We were followed by a hundred Federal Cavalry which skirmished with our rear guard for some twenty miles, but were easily held in check along the narrow mountain roads; also by two hundred and fifty Cavalry from Newcreek (later called Keyser), which was ten miles nearer Moorefield than was Cumberland, and they attempted to intercept us, and when they got to the South Branch of the Potomac, thirty-seven miles from Newcreek, we were one mile ahead of them, and on their left flank. Five hundred Cavalry were sent from Winchester to intercept us from the East, but arrived several hours after we had passed the stated point.

With our prisoners, the two Generals, and Gen. Kelly's [Kelley's] Adjt. Gen'l, Thayer Melvin, we went into camp eight or ten miles above Moorefield on the South Fork where we enjoyed much needed rest, having ridden near a hundred miles in thirty hours, and only one man wounded in our command. The next day the prisoners were sent on to Richmond. Gen. Kelly's [Kelley's] fine horse, "Phillippi," and a fine race mare were captured by John Arnold. This horse was presented to Kelley [Kelley] by the people of Phillippi after the fight there, and of which Kelly was the hero. (Henry Martyn Trueheart, "Memoirs," 14–16)

See also "Capture of Generals Crook and Kelly of the Federal Army," *Southern Historical Society Papers* 19: 186–88; and Darrell Cochran, "Confederates Brilliant Exploit," *America's Civil War* 4 (Sept. 1991): 41–45.

Chapter 6: "Prepare Quietly to Evacuate the Place," 1862

1. The battle of Shiloh, in south-central Tennessee, was fought on 6–7 Apr. 1862.

2. According to one source, the Federal frigate *Santee*, commanded by Capt. Henry Eagle, demanded the surrender of Galveston on 17 May 1862. Barr, "Texas Coastal Defense," 10. The article also outlines the evolution of Confederate and Federal command and military organization along the Texas coast in general and in Galveston in particular.

3. President Lincoln declared a blockade of the southern coast on 19 Apr. 1861. In July, the first blockader, *South Carolina*, with Comdr. James Alden in charge, appeared off Galveston. From among his first captures, Alden armed the schooners *Dart*, *Shark*, and *Sam Houston*, to help in the blockade operation. Ibid., 6.

4. The general was Brig. Gen. Paul O. Hebert, at that time the newly appointed Confederate commander in Texas. Col. Cook was Joseph J. Cook, a U.S. Naval Academy graduate, commander of the 3rd Battalion, Texas Artillery.

5. Clear Creek flows into Galveston Bay between Houston and Galveston. In one of his letters, Charles mentions that the family had a house on Clear Creek.

6. By the time this letter was written, Galveston was in Union hands, having fallen in early Oct. 1862. For an account of the bloodless event, see Magee, "Most Disgraceful Affair," 50–56.

7. Virginia Point is on the mainland from which location the railroad from Houston connected with Galveston Island.

8. Like many well-to-do southerners, the Truehearts were slave-owners.

Chapter 7: "A Texan and Possessing 'Winning Ways,'" 1863

1. Undoubtedly, the "General" referred to was Hebert's replacement, Maj. Gen. John B. Magruder, who arrived on the scene in Nov. The scout was part of preparations made to recapture Galveston from the occupying Federal force.

2. The only Federal troops readily available for the defense of Galveston were Companies G, D, and I of the 42nd Massachusetts Infantry, under Col. Isaac S. Burrell.

3. Colonel Cook was Col. Joseph Cook, the Confederate island commander. Henry's knowledge of the city and his surveying experience were being put to good use.

4. Maj. Van Harten was John Van Harten, commanding the artillery troops participating in the attack.

5. The Strand is the street running along the waterfront. In recent years, the area has been restored and is a popular tourist attraction.

6. The Confederate troop disposition began on the evening of 31 Dec. 1862. The attack began with artillery preparation against the Federal vessels lying close to shore within the port of Galveston, followed by an infantry assault against the 42nd Massachusetts holding Kuhn's Wharf at the foot of 18th Street.

7. The Confederate gunboats were two improvised river steamers, the *Bayou City* and the *Neptune*. Both had been armored with cotton bales in Houston; the *Bayou City* was armed with a 32-pounder fieldpiece, and the *Neptune* had two 24-pounder fieldpieces. They were accompanied by the tenders *Lucy Gwin* and *John F. Carr*. The plan was for the two gunboats to act as rams against the six Federal vessels anchored off the Galveston wharves. These were: the flagship *Westfield*, with Commodore William B. Renshaw commanding; the *Clifton;* the *Sachem;* the *Owasco;* the *Corypheus;* and the *Harriet Lane*.

8. Fort Point is located on the eastern end of Galveston Island and overlooks the entrance to Galveston Bay. Eagle Grove is where the railroad bridge from the mainland connects with the island.

9. Both the captain of the *Harriet Lane*, Comdr. J. M. Wainwright, and the executive officer, Lt. Comdr. Edward Lea, were found on

board, mortally wounded. Commander Wainwright was the grandfather of Gen. Jonathan M. Wainwright, the defender of Bataan and Corregidor in the Philippines during the early, dark days of World War II.

10. Nicaragua Smith was a Galvestonian who had deserted to the Federal blockading squadron in the summer of 1861. Prior to his execution he tapped his foot to music provided by a local band, and he went to his death without benefit of a blindfold. See McComb, *Galveston: A History*, 79.

11. For a concise description of the battle of Galveston, see Fowler, *Under Two Flags*, 225–27.

12. For an interesting account of the fight between the *Alabama* and the *Hatteras*, see Raphael Semmes, *Memoirs of Service Afloat* (1869; reprint, Seacaucus, N.J.: Blue and Grey Press, 1987), 540–50. "290" was the hull number of the CSS *Alabama*.

13. Capt. Raphael Semmes was master of the CSS *Alabama*.

14. Henry had decided to go to the fighting department in Virginia, for among other reasons, to be near Charles.

15. Gen. Edmund Kirby Smith was in command of the Confederate Department of the Trans-Mississippi.

16. Vicksburg fell to General Grant's besieging Federal forces on 4 July 1863.

17. Henry was mistaken. Maj. Gen. Ambrose E. Burnside was not at Vicksburg during that campaign.

18. Lt. Gen. Joseph E. Johnston was sent to Jackson by President Davis to take charge of the Confederate troops there and thence to go to the aid of Lt. Gen. Pemberton's command, besieged at Vicksburg by Maj. Gen. Grant's Union army. Johnston did not go to Pemberton's aid, and the Vicksburg garrison was forced to surrender on 4 July 1863. For General Johnston's views on the subject, see Joseph E. Johnston, *Narrative of Military Operations During the Civil War* (1874; reprint, New York: Da Capo Press, 1990), 174–204.

19. J. B. Polley listed the three men as members of Company L, First Texas Infantry, killed at Gettysburg. See J. B. Polley, *Hood's Texas Brigade* (1910; reprint, Dayton, Ohio: Morningside Press, 1988), 314.

20. Listed as 1st Lt. D. U. Barziza, Company C, 4th Texas Infantry, wounded at Gettysburg. Ibid., 319.

21. There is no original of this letter in the Trueheart Collection, only a transcript. Mr. Greene, assistant archivist at the Rosenberg Library, speculates that the original was probably retained by some unnamed family member.

22. The regiment was the 7th Virginia Cavalry of Maj. Gen. J. E. B. Stuart's cavalry division. The regiment was raised by Col. Angus W. McDonald, Sr., of Winchester, Va. He was a 62-year-old attorney, a West Point graduate, and a militia colonel. The regiment began operations

on 17 June 1861. Henry Trueheart was a member of Company F, the Hampshire Rifles. See Richard L. Armstrong, *7th Virginia Cavalry* (Lynchburg, Va.: H. E. Howard, 1992), 1–2.

23. Brig. Gen. William E. "Grumble" Jones was a Virginian and a graduate of West Point, class of 1848. He had distinguished himself earlier in the war, but a dispute with Maj. Gen. Jeb Stuart had resulted in his reassignment to command of the Department of Southwest Virginia and East Tennessee. He was killed at the battle of Piedmont on 5 June 1864. See Warner, *Generals in Gray*, 166–67.

24. Sterling Price, "Old Pap," was born in Virginia and educated at Hampden—Sydney College. He was a veteran of the Mexican War and thereafter became a lawyer and politician in Missouri. Ibid., 246–47. Sam Jones was a Virginian by birth and was a graduate of the United States Military Academy, class of 1841. Ibid., 165–67.

25. There is no original letter with this transcript.

26. 2d Lt. Charles Vandevender (Vandiver) was from Hampshire County, W.Va. "W[ounded] Culpepper C[ourt] [House], 9/13/63, right side, just above pants pocket (also as through the body). His saber strap took the worst of it." Armstrong, *7th Virginia Cavalry*, 238.

27. On 12 Sept. 1863 the Bristoe campaign began.

> During the Bristoe Campaign, the brigade received orders to picket and scout in the vicinity of Madison Court House. Part of its duty was to screen Lee's advance and to distract the enemy.
>
> On September 13, 1863, the brigade encountered Generals Kilpatrick and Buford near Culpepper Court House and a severe fight took place. Colonel Lomax, commanding the brigade, held the Federals at bay for about two hours before being forced to retire. General W. H. F. Lee's Brigade soon arrived, and together they drove the Federals away. (Ibid., 58)

28. Polley lists Cady as a private in Company L, 1st Texas Infantry. Polley, *Hood's Texas Brigade*, 313.

29. Louis T. Wigfall, born in South Carolina, was a former U.S. senator from Texas. He was a leader of the secession movement, first commander of the Texas Brigade in Virginia, and a Confederate States senator representing Texas. He was a close friend of President Jefferson Davis in the beginning but became his bitter critic and opponent in the later stages of the war. Wigfall is buried in Galveston, not far from the final resting places of Henry and Charles Trueheart.

30. Henry must be speaking of Col. R. H. Dulany. See Blackford, *War Years with Jeb Stuart*, 236–37; and Armstrong, *7th Virginia Cavalry*, 139.

31. For a biographical sketch of Thomas A. Marshall, see Armstrong, *7th Virginia Cavalry*, 191.

32. For biographical sketches of Kuykendall, Parker, and Vandiver, see Ibid., 179, 204, and 238–39, respectively.

33. This action is described thus:

General Stuart met the Federals under Buford at Jack's Shop at about 4 p. m. on September 22, 1863. While Stuart engaged Buford, Kilpatrick attacked his rear, nearly cutting him off. Jone's Brigade, now commanded by Colonel Funsten, moved to the rear to check Kilpatrick. Two squadrons of the 7th Virginia Cavalry, led by Colonel Marshall, charged the enemy. After reaching the crest of a hill, Marshall discovered the Federals drawn up in the woods some distance in his front. The Federals were dismounted and poured a deadly fire into the ranks of the 7th Regiment as they charged. As Marshall drew near the Federals, he saw that his men were strung out and only a few were close at hand. Turning his column to the left into a thick pine forest, Marshall halted to allow his men to close up.

At this point General Stuart came up and urged Marshall to charge again. Captain John B. Magruder, Company B, immediately led his men in a charge, resulting in his death. The 11th and 12th Regiments then charged and drove the enemy back. In the fighting at Jack's Shop, the 7th Virginia Cavalry had one man killed, three wounded, and one captured. (Armstrong, *7th Virginia Cavalry*, 58–59)

34. Brother Charles had studied under Drs. Cabell and Davis while a medical student at the University of Virginia before the war.

35. General Meade had been in command of the Union Army of the Potomac since shortly before Gettysburg. General Rosecrans commanded the Union Army of the Tennessee in central Tennessee. Two corps, the XI and XII, were sent to Rosecrans under overall command of Maj. Gen. Joseph Hooker.

36. Lieutenant General Longstreet's corps, minus Pickett's Gettysburg-decimated division, was sent to reinforce Lt. Gen. Braxton Bragg's Army of Tennessee, the movement beginning about 9 Sept. 1863. Only parts of the two divisions reached Bragg in time to participate in the Confederate victory at Chickamauga on 19–20 Sept. 1863.

37. Bragg should have emulated Lee. Had he pursued Rosecrans' badly beaten army, he truly could have won a glorious victory. Within two months his army was driven from Missionary Ridge overlooking Chattanooga by the same Union army that had been driven from the field at Chickamauga. Now, however, it was commanded by Rosecrans' successor, Maj. Gen. Ulysses S. Grant.

38. For a brief account of the battle of Sabine Pass, see Barr, "Texas Coastal Defense, 1861–1865," 23–24.

39. The Confederate Conscription Act exempted, among others,

certain publicly elected officials, such as the Truehearts' brother-in-law, Thomas M. Joseph, mayor of Galveston. Henry Trueheart was the elected tax assessor—collector of Galveston County, even though absent in Virginia serving in the 7th Virginia Cavalry. Later, his service with McNeill's Partisan Rangers was made possible by this exemption from the terms of the Conscription Act. Only exemptees were allowed to serve in partisan units.

40. "On September 24, 1862, Hanse [McNeill's] company was formally mustered into the Confederate service as Company I, 1st Regiment Virginia Partisan Rangers." Delauter, *McNeill's Rangers*, 22.

41. President Davis was in Chattanooga dealing with a command crisis within the Army of Tennessee, commanded by Lt. Gen. Braxton Bragg. Bragg's staff was insisting he be replaced because of his poor leadership of that army and his failure to follow up the victory at Chickamauga. See William C. Davis, *Jefferson Davis*, 518–25. See also Thomas L. Connelly, *Autumn of Glory: The Army of Tennessee, 1862–1865* (Baton Rouge: Louisiana State University Press, 1971), 241–47; and Judith L. Hallock *Braxton Bragg and Confederate Defeat*, vol. 2 (Tuscaloosa: University of Alabama Press, 1991), 98–99.

42. The Army of Northern Virginia and the Army of the Potomac battled sporadically after the retreat from Gettysburg and before the opening of the spring campaign of 1864. The action took place mainly along the Rappahannock River.

43. Gen. John D. Imboden was born in Virginia and attended Washington College in Lexington. He was a lawyer and politician before the war. See Warner, *Generals in Gray*, 147.

44. Philip Edloe Bacon was born on 7 Nov. 1847 and thus was only sixteen at the time. In Jan. 1865, he transferred to the Rockbridge Artillery, Charles' old unit, with which he surrendered at Appomattox Court House. See Delauter, *McNeill's Rangers*, 117.

Chapter 8: "The Wild and Ever Changeful Life," 1864

1. Henry is speaking of a foraging expedition undertaken by Maj. Gen. Fitzhugh Lee into northwestern Virginia during late 1863 and early 1864. Afterward, Lee said that his entire command came back more or less frostbitten. See U.S. War Department, *War of the Rebellion: Official Records*, ser. 1, vol. 33, ch. 45, pp. 7–8.

2. Desertion was a serious problem in the Confederate armies, particularly after 1863. It was hoped that granting furloughs during the winter months, when campaigning was reduced, would reduce the growing number of desertions.

3. There seems to be some confusion about the nature of the charges against Capt. Hanse McNeill.

> Recalled to the Shenandoah Valley by General Imboden, Hanse hastily prepared to answer charges placed against him by his former commander. At Harrisonburg on April 12, Hanse stood trial for violating the 3rd Section of the 3rd Article of the Confederate Army Regulations. While extant court martial records do not specify Hanse's exact infraction, the article itself specifies the procedures to be followed in the dispersal of public property and funds upon a change of command. Apparently General Imboden was dissatisfied with the partisan captain's accounting of the Rangers' numerous captures while operating under regular army officers. The court found Hanse innocent of this charge but the Ranger captain's judicial ordeal was not over.
>
> Only three days after being acquitted of the first charge, Hanse was brought to trial for a second infraction. Unlike his first trial the charge on this occasion was explicitly clear: "Knowingly receiving and entertaining a deserter from other than his own company and refusing to deliver him up." Once again the court found Hanse innocent. The final act in this drama occurred in Richmond which determined the future of the entire Ranger command. On April 21 the Confederate Secretary of State [James A. Seddon] exercised the authority granted to him in the repeal of the Partisan Ranger Act. Called upon to approve the recommendation of Major Melton of the Adjutant and Inspector General's Office for the disbanding of all the partisan ranger commands . . . Seddon replied, "Mosby's and McNeill's commands I prefer to have retained as partisan rangers. In respect to the others Major Melton's suggestions are approved." The daring exploits of Mosby's and McNeill's Rangers during the final year of the war would fully justify Secretary Seddon's decision to retain these two commands as the only legally authorized partisan organizations remaining in the Confederate service. (Delauter, *McNeill's Rangers*, 65)

The disbanding of the partisan commands came about as a result of a minor argument between McNeill and Brig. Gen. Thomas Rosser over the treatment of horses in the field. Rosser became incensed that a non—West Pointer such as McNeill should admonish a West Pointer, such as himself, about anything military. Rosser gained Major General Stuart's and Lieutenant General Lee's ear, and the deed was done.

4. "The Spring of 1864 would see the war become a gruelling test of endurance. . . . The romance and glory of war now became a day-to-day fight for survival as General Grant hammered the beleaguered Southerners on all fronts. An integral part of Grant's strategy called for

a thrust into the Shenandoah Valley, where McNeill's Rangers would learn first-hand the grim reality of a war of attrition." Ibid., 64.

5. "About this time the people of the City of Richmond, to show their esteem . . . desired to present him with a home. General Lee, on hearing of it, thus wrote to the President of the Council: ' . . . I assure you, sir, that no want of appreciation of the honor conferred upon me by this resolution—or insensibility to the kind feelings which prompted it—induces me to ask, as I most respectfully do, that no further proceedings be taken with reference to the subject. The house is not necessary for the use of my family, and my own duties will prevent my residence in Richmond. I should therefore be compelled to decline the generous offer, and I trust that whatever means the City Council may have to spare for this purpose may be devoted to the relief of the families of our soldiers in the field, who are more in want of assistance, and more deserving it, than myself.'" Capt. Robert E. Lee, Jr., *Recollections and Letters of General Robert E. Lee* (1904; reprint, Seacaucus, N.J.: Blue and Grey Press, n.d.), 116.

6. See Delauter, *McNeill's Rangers*, 66–67, for an account of this raid. See also John D. Imboden, "The Battle of Piedmont," *Confederate Veteran* 31 (Dec. 1923): 459–61.

7. Henry apparently is speaking of the battle of New Market, fought on 15 May 1864. It was in this engagement that the Virginia Military Institute cadet corps participated valiantly.

8. "The partisans were subjected to long-range cannon fire from the Maryland shore for more than a mile before finally reaching a position beyond the range of the Federal guns. Amazingly the only casualties suffered during this ordeal were two horses wounded by exploding shells. Unfortunately three Hampshire County residents were not as lucky. A stray Federal shell overshot the rebels and went screaming into a nearby home instantly killing a young mother and two of her children." Delauter, *McNeill's Rangers*, 67.

9. After the defeat at New Market, General Sigel was replaced by the more aggressive Maj. Gen. David Hunter. Hunter advanced up the Shenandoah Valley as far as Lynchburg. In the meantime, General Lee, recognizing the danger, detached Gen. Jubal Early's corps from the Army of Northern Virginia to the valley. Hunter was defeated at Lynchburg on 18 June 1864 and driven from the area. Early's advance continued to the gates of Washington, D.C., in July 1864.

10. This would be Gen. William Edmondson "Grumble" Jones, sent to intercept Hunter. He was killed at Piedmont on 5 June 1864. See Warner, *Generals in Gray*, 166–67.

11. This would be Gen. John Crawford Vaughn. Ibid., 316–17.

12. "During the next two weeks [about 10–24 June 1864] the parti-

sans operated in the upper Shenandoah Valley harrassing Hunter's supply lines. During this period McNeill's Rangers were the only organized rebel force operating in the northern Shenandoah Valley. The Rangers' constant maneuvering served the dual purpose of annoying the Federals while simultaneously gathering information on enemy strength and deployment." Delauter, *McNeill's Rangers*, 71.

13. During this period, the Rangers, or elements thereof, were being shifted back and forth between northwestern Virginia and the Shenandoah Valley, to meet dual threats. The "Swamp Dragons" were a western Virginia Union home guard unit and an archenemy of McNeill's command. "In an attempt to keep their enemy off balance in northwestern Virginia, McNeill's Ranger's rendezvoused in Hardy County for a hit-and-run strike on the Swamp Dragons. As the Union Home Guards were returning from New Creek on June 19 the partisans ambushed the Unionists' supply train near Petersburg. In the ensuing bitterly contested skirmish the Rangers killed or wounded more than a dozen of their mortal enemies. The victory came at a high price, however, as Lt. B. J. Dolan was mortally wounded while leading a charge against the Home Guards. Embittered by the death of their popular leader[,] the Rangers invaded the predominantly pro-Union region of the Smoke Hole community of Hardy County the next day to avenge their lieutnant's death. Several additional Home Guards were killed in retaliation for Lieutenant Dolan's death before the Rangers sullenly withdrew north toward Moorefield." Ibid.

14. "As they silently approached the hamlet of Springfield early in the morning of June 27 [according to Henry, it was the 26th] the Rangers were startled to see a detachment of the 6th West Virginia Cavalry enjoying a swim in the South Branch River. The Federals had turned their horses out to graze in the nearby meadow while they cavorted in the stream. The Rangers galloped up to the river bank and ordered their highly embarrassed enemies to come ashore. The Federals were caught literally with their pants down; 54 enlisted men and 3 officers surrendered without firing a shot. The rebels also confiscated more than 100 excellent cavalry mounts." Ibid., 71–72.

15. In conjunction with Early's advance down the Shenandoah Valley, General Imboden struck out west from Staunton on 28 June for a raid on the Baltimore and Ohio Railroad. Upon his arrival in northwestern Virginia, Imboden called upon McNeill's Rangers to cooperate with his [Northwestern] Brigade in an attack on the vital Union supply line to the west. On 4 July, the Northwestern Brigade attacked the strongly fortified railroad bridge at the mouth of the South Branch River. As their comrades fought the Federals at the South Branch, McNeill's Rangers were engaged farther to the west at the railroad bridge which

spanned Patterson's Creek. The Confederates were frustrated in their designs on both bridges. Large Union garrisons and the arrival of heavy Federal reinforcements forced the rebels to retire with both bridges still standing." Ibid., 72.

16. Henry's account differs from that of Delauter in that the latter says the bridges were not burned successfully.

17. Henry's account conflicts seriously with that of Delauter. According to Delauter, McNeill did not accompany Early into Maryland. Thus, "frustrated in their attempt to destroy the South Branch bridge, the Northwestern Brigade moved east on July 5 to join General Early. For the next two weeks Imboden's command played a key role in Early's Maryland campaign. The departure of the Northwestern Brigade permitted McNeill's Rangers to resume their independent actions. During their comrades' absence the partisans kept constant pressure on the Union army's supply lines. Unable to mount a serious offensive against their numerous foes, the Rangers were forced to rely upon hit-and-run tactics to keep the Federals in a continuous state of alarm. Hovering near the Baltimore and Ohio Railroad[,] the partisans would dash upon unguarded stretches of railroad, tearing up track and destroying small bridges. . . . The Rangers' lonely vigil finally came to an end in mid-July when General Early returned to the Shenandoah Valley." Delauter, *McNeill's Rangers*, 72–73.

18. As he indicates in his memoirs, General Early had every intention of entering the city. Only the untimely arrival of two divisions of the Union Sixth Corps dispatched by General Grant from the Petersburg lines prevented him from doing so.

19. For a first-hand account of the battle of Monocacy, see Early, *Jubal Early's Memoirs*, 387–88.

20. "In yet another underestimation of the Confederate's offensive capability the Federal commander [Grant] recalled a portion of the two infantry corps he had temporarily dispatched from Petersburg for the defense of Washington. The departure of Grant's veteran infantrymen permitted General Early to resume the offensive. Moving rapidly north, Early soundly defeated the conglomerate Federal Army of West Virginia on July 24 at the Second Battle of Kernstown. The overwhelming Confederate victory at Kernstown placed the entire Shenandoah Valley under rebel control. Taking immediate advantage of this situation, Early marched his command down the Valley Pike to Martinsburg where they dedicated two full days to the systematic destruction of the Baltimore and Ohio Railroad." Delauter, *McNeill's Rangers* 73.

21. In late July and early Aug. 1864, Gen. Early sent Gen. John McCausland and 4,000 troopers on a raid into Pennsylvania. On 30 July 1864, they burned Chambersburg, Penn., having failed to receive a de-

manded ransom. This was in retaliation for the destruction wreaked in the Shenandoah Valley by Gen. David Hunter, including the burning of both the Virginia governor's home and the Virginia Military Institute at Lexington. For an account of the raid, see Liva Baker, "The Burning of Chambersburg," *Civil War Chronicles* 3 (Summer 1993): 41–46.

22. Henry was wrong in several respects. The "F. T. Blair" to whom he refers was Francis Preston Blair, the father of Union postmaster general Montgomery Blair. Although Confederate forces did deplete the elder Blair's fine wine cellar, they did not burn his mansion at Silver Spring. However, ". . . the retreating Rebels fired son Montgomery Blair's place since he was a member of Lincoln's cabinet." Benjamin F. Cooling, "Monocacy: The Battle That Saved Washington," *Blue and Gray Magazine* 10 (Summer 1993): 56.

23. Neither Delauter nor Early mentions this action.

24. James Heiskell was the father of Isaac P. and Jacob C. Heiskell, both of whom served in the 1st Rockbridge Artillery. See Driver, *1st and 2nd Rockbridge Artillery*, 67.

25. While absent attending to these duties, the Rangers were unaware of the appointment of Maj. Gen. Philip H. Sheridan to the Union valley command and his subsequent defeat of Early's army both at the third battle of Winchester and at Fisher's Hill. These victories once again opened the valley to Union forces as far south as Harrisonburg.

26. Undoubtedly, this was Ann Van Meter Cunningham, who was to become Mrs. Henry M. Trueheart shortly after the war's end.

27. "Stung by his defeats at Winchester and Cedar Creek in September and October, Jubal Early once again turned his attention to northwestern Virginia. In the hope that he would repeat his successful performance of the preceding January, General Thomas L. Rosser was selected to lead the rebel expedition into Hampshire and Hardy counties. On November 26, Rosser departed from his camp near Staunton to begin his raid into Federally occupied territory. Prior to leaving the Shenandoah Valley, Rosser dispatched a courier to Jesse McNeill [Hanse's son and successor following his death] with detailed instructions concerning the Rangers' role in the upcoming Confederate invasion." Delauter, *McNeill's Rangers*, 88.

28. The Union command was the 6th West Virginia Cavalry, led by Lt. Col. R. E. Fleming. His second-in-command was a Major Potts.

29. This force was commanded by Major Potts.

30. New Creek was a large Federal supply base. Rosser, by clothing his lead troopers in the blue uniforms taken from Fleming's captured men, was able to overpower the Federal pickets and take the place with practically no bloodshed. The supply base then was put to the torch. That destruction completed, Rosser advanced to Piedmont and its Fed-

eral maintenance and repair facilities. It had been rebuilt after the destruction by McNeill's Rangers the previous May. Rosser destroyed it again, the second time in seven months.

31. After the destruction of New Creek and Piedmont, Rosser's command returned to the Shenandoah Valley.

32. In his memoirs, General Early, in speaking of Capt. John McNeill, said he had "performed many daring exploits during the war, and had accompanied me into Maryland, doing good service." Early, *Jubal Early's Memoirs*, 461.

Chapter 9: "People Are Blue, Blue," 1865

1. Forty years thence, in 1914–18, this could have been a description of the works wending their way from the North Sea across northern France to the Alps—the Western Front.

2. Informal truces, such as this one described by Henry, were not uncommon during this war. An unwritten code of honor demanded that fair warning be given before hostilities were resumed.

3. Actually, Lt. Gen. Grant was not enthusiastic about the project that produced the Crater. He felt it had little chance of accomplishing its goal. He was right.

4. The purpose of these devices, which were supplanted by concertina wire during World War I, was to slow and to make vulnerable to defensive firepower an attacking force as it approached the frontline.

5. Fort Fisher was the Confederate bastion guarding the approaches to the Cape Fear River. Upriver lay Wilmington, N.C., the last Confederate port not effectively in Federal hands. Fort Fisher fell on 15 Jan. 1865.

Epilogue

1. Rick Cox, "Charles Trueheart Weaves True Tales of Civil War," *North San Antonio Times*, 11 Mar. 1982, p. 2.

2. There were four daughters (Bessie, Ann, Titelle, and Lella) and one son (Charles, Jr.). Chester R. Burns, "Charles William Trueheart," unpublished paper, 2. A copy of this paper was furnished by Mrs. Edward Futch, Galveston, Tex.

3. Ibid., 1.

4. "Charles Martyn Trueheart," *Confederate Veteran* 22, no. 1 (Nov. 1914): 521.

5. John Henry Brown, *Indian Wars and Pioneers of Texas* (Austin, Tex.: State House Press, 1988), 258–60.

6. "Charles Martyn Trueheart," 521.

Selected References

Adams, George W. "Confederate Medicine." Journal of Southern History 6 (May 1940): 151–66.

Armstrong, Richard L. *7th Virginia Cavalry.* Lynchburg, Va.: H. E. Howard, 1992.

Baker, Liva. "The Burning of Chambersburg." *Civil War Chronicles* 3 (Summer 1993): 41–46.

Barr, Allwyn. "Texas Coastal Defense, 1861–1865." *Southwestern Historical Quarterly* 45 (July 1961): 1–31.

Blackford, William W. *War Years with Jeb Stuart.* New York: Charles Scribner's Sons, 1946.

Bridges, Hal. *Lee's Maverick General: Daniel Harvey Hill.* Lincoln: University of Nebraska Press, 1961.

Brown, John Henry. *Indian Wars and Pioneers of Texas.* Austin, Tex.: State House Press, 1988.

Cartwright, Gary. *Galveston: A History of the Island.* New York: Atheneum, 1991.

Casler, John O. *Four Years in the Stonewall Brigade.* 1906. Reprint, Marietta, Ga.: Continental Book Co., 1951.

Chabot, Frederick C. *The Perote Prisoners.* San Antonio, Tex.: Naylor, 1934.

"Charles Martyn Trueheart." *Confederate Veteran* 22, no. 1 (November 1914): 521

Coddington, Edwin B. *The Gettysburg Campaign.* Dayton, Ohio: Morningside Press, 1979.

Connelly, Thomas L. *Autumn of Glory: The Army of Tennessee, 1862–1865.* Baton Rouge: Louisiana State University Press, 1971.

Cooling, Benjamin F., III. *Jubal Early's Raid on Washington: 1864.* Baltimore, Md.: Nautical and Aviation Publishing Company of America, 1989.

Cox, Rick. "Charles Trueheart Weaves True Tales of Civil War." North San Antonio Times. 11 Mar. 1982, p. 2.

Cunningham, H. H. *Doctors in Gray: The Confederate Medical Service.* Baton Rouge: Louisiana State University Press, 1958.

Davis, Burke. *They Called Him Stonewall: A Life of Lt. General T. J. Jackson, C.S.A.* New York: Fairfax Press, 1988.

Davis, William C. *Jefferson Davis: The Man and His Hour.* New York: Harper Collins, 1991.

Delauter, Roger U., Jr. *McNeill's Rangers.* Lynchburg, Va.: H. E. Howard, 1986.

Douglas, Henry Kyd. *I Rode with Stonewall.* Chapel Hill: University of North Carolina Press, 1940.

Driver, Robert J. *The 1st and 2nd Rockbridge Artillery.* Lynchburg, Va.: H. E. Howard, 1987.

Early, Jubal A. *Jubal Early's Memoirs.* 1912. Reprint, Baltimore, Md.: Nautical & Aviation Publishing Company of America, 1989.

Evans, Clement A., ed. *Confederate Military History.* Atlanta, Ga.: Confederate Publishing Co., 1899.

Foote, Shelby. *The Civil War: A Narrative.* 3 vols. New York: Vintage Books, 1986.

Foutz, Susan L., and George G. Morris. *Lynchburg in the Civil War.* Lynchburg, Va.: H. E. Howard, 1984.

Fowler, William M., Jr. *Under Two Flags: The American Navy in the Civil War.* New York: Avon Books, 1990.

Freeman, Douglas Southall. *Lee's Lieutenants: A Study in Command.* 3 vols. New York: Charles Scribner's Sons, 1942–44.

———. *R. E. Lee.* 4 vols. New York: Charles Scribner's Sons, 1934–35.

Gildersleeve, John R. "History of Chimborazo Hospital, C.S.A." *Southern Historical Society Papers* 36 (1908): 86–94.

Greer, James K. *Colonel Jack Hays: Texas Frontier Leader and California Builder.* New York: E. P. Dutton, 1952.

Hallock, Judith L. *Braxton Bragg and Confederate Defeat.* Vol 2. Tuscaloosa: University of Alabama Press, 1991.

Heale-Muscoe. *Genealogies of Virginia Families.* Baltimore, Md.: Genealogical Publishing Co., 1982.

Henderson, G. F. R. *Stonewall Jackson and the American Civil War.* 1936. 2 vols. Reprint, Seacaucus, N.J.: Blue and Grey Press, 1987.

Herbert, Hilary A. "History of the Eighth Alabama Volunteer Regiment, C.S.A." Edited by Maurice S. Fortin. *Alabama Historical Quarterly* 39, nos. 1–4 (1977): 5–321.

Hotchkiss, Jedediah. *Make Me a Map of the Valley.* Edited by Archie P. McDonald. Dallas, Tex.: Southern Methodist University Press, 1973.

Houck, Peter W. *Confederate Surgeon: The Personal Recollections of E. A. Craighill.* Lynchburg, Va.: H. E. Howard, 1989.

Imboden, John D. "The Battle of Piedmont." *Confederate Veteran* 31 (December 1923): 459–61.

Ingimire, Francis T. *Texas Ranger Service Records, 1830–1846*. St. Louis, Mo.: Ingimire Publications, 1982.

Johns, Frank S., and Anne Page Johns. "Chimborazo Hospital and J. B. McCaw, Surgeon-in-Chief." *Virginia Magazine of History and Biography* 62 (April 1945):190–200.

Johnson, Robert U., and Clarence C. Buel, eds. *Battles and Leaders of the Civil War.* 4 vols. New York: Thomas Yoseloff, 1956.

Johnston, Joseph E. *Narrative of Military Operations During the Civil War.* 1874. Reprint, New York: Da Capo Press, 1990.

Jones, Archer. *Civil War Command and Strategy.* New York: Free Press, 1992.

Jordan, Ervin L., Jr. *Charlottesville and the University of Virginia in the Civil War.* Lynchburg, Va.: H. E. Howard, 1988.

Lee, Capt. Robert E., Jr. *Recollections and Letters of General Robert E. Lee.* 1904. Reprint, Seacaucus, N.J.: Blue and Grey Press, n.d.

Linderman, Gerald F. *Embattled Courage.* New York: Free Press, 1987.

Long, E. B., ed. *The Personal Memoirs of U.S. Grant.* Cleveland, Ohio: World Publishing Co., 1952.

McComb, David G. *Galveston: A History.* Austin: University of Texas Press, 1986.

McCullough, Mrs. Marjorie Williams McCullough, and Mrs. Sally McCullough Futch. Interview by Edward B. Williams. Galveston, Texas, 28 April 1992.

McWhiney, Grady. *Braxton Bragg and Confederate Defeat.* Vol. 1. Tuscaloosa: University of Alabama Press, 1969.

Magee, Kenneth J. "Most Disgraceful Affair." *America's Civil War* 5 (January 1993): 50–56.

Matter, William D. *If It Takes All Summer: The Battle of Spotsylvania.* Chapel Hill: University of North Carolina Press, 1988.

Miller, Francis T., ed. *The Photographic History of the Civil War.* 3 vols. New York: Thomas Yoseloff, 1957.

Moore, Samuel J. T., Jr. *Moore's Complete Civil War Guide to Richmond.* N.p., 1978.

Nichols, James L. *Confederate Engineers.* Tuscaloosa, Ala.: Confederate Publishing Co., 1957.

Norwood, William F. *Medical Education in the United States Before the Civil War.* Philadelphia: University of Pennsylvania Press, 1944.

Poague, William T. *Gunner with Stonewall.* 1957. Reprint, Wilmington, N.C.: Broadfoot Publishing Co., 1987.

Polley, J. B. *Hood's Texas Brigade.* 1910. Reprint, Dayton, Ohio: Morningside Press, 1988.

Richmond (Va.) Daily Dispatch. 1861–65.

Richmond (Va.) Enquirer. 1861–65.

Richmond (Va.) Sentinel. 1861–65.

References

～

Robertson, James I., Jr. *The Stonewall Brigade*. Baton Rouge: Louisiana State University Press, 1963.

———. "Stonewall Jackson: Molding the Man and Making a General." *Blue and Gray Magazine* 9 (June 1992): 8–26, 52–55.

Semmes, Raphael. *Memoirs of Service Afloat*. 1869. Reprint, Seacaucus, N.J.: Blue and Grey Press, 1987.

Southern Historical Society Papers. 1876. Reprint, Millwood, N.Y.: Kraus Reprinting Co., 1977.

Speer, William S. *The Encyclopedia of the New West*. Marshall, Tex.: United States Biographical Publishing Co., 1881.

Stewart, George R. *Pickett's Charge*. Boston: Houghton Mifflin, 1959.

Tanner, Robert G. *Stonewall in the Valley*. Garden City, N.Y.: Doubleday, 1976.

Tompkins, Christopher. "Medical Education in the South." *Southern Medical Journal* 3 (1910): 325–27.

Trudeau, Noah Andre. *Bloody Roads South*. New York: Fawcett Columbine, 1989.

U.S. Bureau of the Census. *Census of 1860*. Texas, Galveston County, City of Galveston, Fourth Ward.

U.S. War Department (comp.). *War of the Rebellion: A Compilation of the Official Records of the Union and Confederate Armies*. 128 vols. Washington, D.C., 1880–91.

Vandiver, Frank E. *Their Tattered Flags*. College Station: Texas A&M University Press, 1970.

Warner, Ezra. *Generals in Gray*. Baton Rouge: Louisiana State University Press, 1959.

Warren, Mrs. J. E. "Tompkins Family." *William and Mary Quarterly* 2d ser., vol. 10, no. 1 (January 1930): 221–238.

Wellman, Manley W. *Giant in Gray*. New York: Charles Scribner's Sons, 1949.

White, Gifford E. *1840 Citizens of Texas*. St. Louis, Mo.: Ingimire Publications, 1983.

Wiley, Bell I. *The Life of Johnny Reb: The Common Soldier of the Confederacy*. New York: Bobbs-Merrill, 1943.

Index

Alabama, CSS, 163–64
Albemarle Rifles, 9, 24
Alden, Comdr. James, 253 n3
Allen, B. W., 18
Allen, Henry Lownes, 123, 140–41
Antietam, battle of, 10, 69
Appomattox Court House, CW at, 10
Army of Northern Virginia. *See indi-*
vidual unit names and sites of battles.
Army of the Potomac. *See individual*
unit names and sites of battles.
Army of the Valley. *See individual unit*
names and sites of battles.
artillery battalion, CW's attempt to re-
cruit, 28
Ashby, Col. Turner: character, 35–38,
226–27 n17, n20–21; death of, 63–
64, 233–34 n32; escape, 54, 227
n19, 230–31 n21
atrocities: Confederate, 116, 132;
Union, 44–47, 60, 96–97, 196, 244
n20
Austin, Stephen F., 216
Averell, Bvt. Maj. Gen. William W.,
87, 240 n3

Bacon, Philip Edloe, 181, 185, 192,
258 n44
Baltimore and Ohio Railroad, battles
near, 42–43, 192–93, 198–200,
206–207, 228 n2, 261–62, n15, n17
Banks, Gen. Nathaniel P., CW's impression of, 62
Barlow, Brig. Gen. Francis C., 243
n11

Bath, Va., battle at, 41–42
battle fatigue, 62, 105, 110, 197
battlefield scenes, descriptions of,
92–93, 110–12, 114–16, 172–76,
201
Bayou City, CSS, 160–61, 254 n7
Benjamin, Judah P., 229 n10
Berkley, Robert, 80
Blackford, Charles, 28, 76
Blackford, Col. W. W., 10, 136–37,
248 n1
Blackford, Eugene, 35–36, 69, 76
Blackford, Launcelot ("Lanty"), 28,
35, 56, 59, 76
Blackford, Lewis, 28, 76
Blackford, Mary, 76–77, 80, 93, 169
Blackford, William ("Willie"), 28, 76
blacks: conduct at the Crater, 115–16;
flight from Confederates, 60; pro-
posal for Confederate arming of,
135. *See also* slaves
Blair, Francis Preston, 199, 263 n22
Blair, Montgomery, 246–47 n28, 263
n22
"Bloody Angle," battle of, 90–91, 98,
243 n10–11
Borden, Gary, 223 n15
Bragg, Lt. Gen. Braxton, 180, 257
n36–37
Bristoe campaign, 87, 172–78, 240 n2,
256–57 n27, n33
Brockenbrough, Lt. John B., 28
Brooklyn, USS, 162–65
Bryan, Maj. G. M., 166
Bryan, Mary, **17**, 216

Bulkley, Kate, 50–51
Burk (CW's professor), 20
Byars, Lucy, 163

Cabell, James Lawrence, 18, 53, 178,
    224 n2
Cady, Capt. D. C., 175, 256 n28
casualties, horror of, 110–12, 114–16,
    172–76, 201
Chamberlain, Maj. Gen. Joshua Law-
    rence, 215
Chambodout, Father, 159
Charlottesville and University Battal-
    ion, 9, 24
Chesapeake and Ohio Canal dam,
    34–39, 226–27 n18, 228 n2
Chickamauga, battle of, 179–80, 257
    n35–37
Chimborazo Hospital, 79, 81, 239
    n21–22
civilian attitudes toward Confederate
    presence, 53, 61, 69, 72, 185, 191,
    202
Civil War, origins and inception, 8–9
Clear Creek, Tex., 156, 165, 253 n5
Clifton, USS, 160–61, 180, 254 n7
Cold Harbor, Va., battle of, 92–93,
    243 n13–14
Comanches, as threat to Texas set-
    tlers, 4
Confederate Army. See individual unit
    names; morale: military
Confederate Congress: Conscription
    Act, 53–54; substitutes bill, 87,
    240 n1
Confederate Engineers. See 1st Regi-
    ment Engineers
Confederate Peace Commission to
    Washington (1865), 140, 142, 249
    n2, 4
Confederate States of America: estab-
    lishment of, 8, 145; weakness of,
    15–16
Conrad, Holmes, 37–38
Conrad, Holmes, Jr., death of, 37–38,
    227 n22
Conrad, Tucker, death of, 37–38, 227
    n22

Conscription Act: effects, 104–105,
    180, 257–58 n39; reasoning for,
    230 n19; soldiers' reaction, 53–54
Cook, Col. Joseph J., 154, 253 n4
Corypheus, USS, 160–61, 254 n7
courtship rituals: in artillery regi-
    ment, 33–35; at college, 20, 24; for
    CW, 72, 77, 82, 87, 120–21, 185;
    for HM, 86–87, 109, 183, 185,
    204, 215
Crater, battle of, 105–106, 110–16,
    213, 247–48 n30–31, n33–35
Crook, Maj. Gen. George, capture of,
    11, 144, 250–53 n9
Cross Keys, battle of, 58, 64–65, 234
    n33
Culpepper Court House, Va., battle
    at, 172–76, 256 n27
Cunningham, Annie Van Meter, 204,
    215
Cunningham, Sally, 11
Cunningham, William Streit, 218

Dabney, Cornelia, 80
Davis, Jefferson, 82–83, 230 n19
Davis, John Staige, 18–19, 53, 178,
    224 n4
Dolan, Lt. B. J., 197, 261 n13
Dulany, Col. R. H., 176, 256 n30

Eagle, Capt. Henry, 253 n2
Eagle Grove, Galveston, Tex., 160
Early, Maj. Gen. Jubal A.: assault on
    Washington, 198–99, 246–47
    n26–28, 260 n9, 262 n18; Shenan-
    doah Valley (1863–64), 97, 99–
    100, 244–45 n21, 249–50 n6
education for women, importance of,
    138
8th Alabama Volunteer Infantry: his-
    tory, 241 n6; organization, 88–89,
    247 n32; Wilderness campaign,
    89–96, 98, 242–44 n9–18. See also
    Petersburg, Va.
Engineers, Confederate. See 1st Regi-
    ment Engineers
Ewell, Maj. Gen. Richard S., 58–59,
    230 n15

Index

∽

field conditions: Bristoe campaign, 170–71; Fredericksburg, 74, 238 n12; Petersburg, 110, 139–40, 212–13; Shenandoah Valley (1863–64), 186; Wilderness campaign, 89; Winter campaign (1861–62), 33–49, 227–28 n1, n7
1st Regiment Engineers, 133–34, 139–42, 248 n43
1st Rockbridge Artillery: battle preparations, 30–31; CW's induction, 27–28; Kernstown (1862), 55–56; Napoleon guns, **30**; organization of, 29, 224 n7; Seven Days Battles, 56–57, **149,** 232 n27; Shenandoah Valley campaign (1862), 48–56, 58–67, 229–32 n13–17, n22–25, 234 n33, 235–36 n37–38; Winter campaign (1861–62), 33–49, 225–26 n12, n15–21, 227–28 n1, n5–7
Five Forks, Va., battle at, 215
Fort Point, Galveston, Tex., 160
Fort Sumter, surrender of, 24
42nd Massachusetts Regiment, surrender of, 161, 254 n6
Franco-Prussian War, CW's role in, 216
Frederick City, Va., battle at, 198, 201
Fredericksburg, Va., battle at, 71, 237 n4
Fremont, Gen. John C., 62, 65
Front Royal, battle at, 59, 231–32 n23

Galveston, Tex.: battle of (1863), 73, 75, 158–66, 254 n2, n6–10; blockade of, 153–54; evacuation of Truehearts, 38, 71, 224 n8, 237 n8; hurricane of 1900, 217; occupation of, 26, 31, 154–57, 254 n6; origin and development, 6–7
Girardey, Brig. Gen., 106, 111, 247 n31
Gordon, Maj. Gen. John B., 215
Goul, Rev. John M., 29, 224 n8
Grant, Gen. Ulysses S.: Petersburg

siege, 95–97, 114, 118–19, 122, 129, 244 n19, 245–46 n24, 249 n5; Wilderness campaign, 89–96, 242 n9, 243–44 n17–18
Gray, Peter W., 175
Green Spring, Va., skirmish at, 205

Hampton, Wade, "The Beefsteak Raid," 124
Hampton Roads conference, 140, 142, 249 n2, n4
Hancock, Maj. Gen. Winfield Scott, 98, 243 n11
Hancock, Md., battle at, 42–43, 228 n5–6
Hanover County, Virginia, origins of family, 4–6
Harper's Ferry, Va., battle at, 9, 24–25
Harriet Lane, USS, 160–62, 254 n7, 9
Hatteras, USS, 163–64
Hays, John Coffee, 5
Hebert, Brig. Gen. Paul O., 153–54, 253 n4
Heiskell, James and Isaac, 202, 263 n24
Hill, Elizabeth, 22
Hill, Maj. Gen. Ambrose Powell, 56, 232 n26
Hill, Maj. Gen. Daniel Harvey, 56, 232 n26
Hoge, Rev. Moses, 81, 239 n24
hospitals, establishment of, 238 n13, 239 n21–22. *See also* medical duties: Confederate hospital
Howard (CW's professor), 16–17
Howard, Elvira Trueheart, 5–6, 156, 165, 222–23 n13
Howard, Robert H., 156, 165, 223 n13
Hunter, Maj. Gen. David, 196, 260 n9
Hurlbut, S. B., 8, 20

Imboden, Gen. John D., 183, 195, 258 n43, 261–62 n15

Jack's Shop, battle at, 257 n33
Jackson, Gen. Thomas J. ("Stone-

Index

～

Jackson, Gen. Thomas J. (*cont.*)
wall"): Chesapeake and Ohio dam
strategy, 38–39; conflict with Gen.
Loring, 48, 229 n10; conscription
rebellion reaction, 54, 230 n20;
farewell to "Stonewall" Brigade,
225 n11; Kernstown retreat,
51–52; Port Republic escape, 64,
234 n34–35; seen in review, 30;
Seven Days Battles, 56–57, **149**,
232 n27. *See also* Shenandoah Valley campaign: (*1862*); Winter campaign (1861–62)
Jefferson and Washington Literary
Society, 20, 24
Johnson, Maj. Gen. Edward, capture
of, 90, 98, 243 n11
Johnston, Gen. Joseph E., 9, 166–68,
230 n15
Jones, Brig. Gen. William E.
("Grumble"), 170, 195, 256 n23,
260 n10
Jones, Gen. Sam, 171, 256 n24
Joseph, Mary Minor Trueheart, 5–6,
27, 223 n13
Joseph, Thomas M., 27, 163, 165,
223 n13

Kelley, Maj. Gen. Benjamin F., 45,
144, 250–53 n9
Kemper, Mary, 182
Kernstown, Va., battles at, 51–52, 58,
229–30 n14, n16–17, 262 n20
Kimbrough, Lucy, 178
Kuykendall, Capt. Isaac, 176

Lea, Lt. Comdr. Edward, 161–62,
254–55 n9
Lea, Maj. (father of Edward), 161–62
League, Jeff, 158–59
Lee, Gen. Robert E.: amnesty proclamation, 143, 250 n7; character, 85,
106–107, 110–12, 123–24, 191,
260 n5; Seven Days Battles frustration, 232–33 n28; on Wilderness
campaign, 243–44 n11, n17
Lee, Robert E., Jr., 8, 9, 26

Letcher, Gov. John, 9, 30, 100, 225
n10, 246 n27
Lincoln, Abraham: blockade of
Galveston, 253 n3; derision for,
60–62; election (1864), 130; Inaugural Address reaction, 21–22
Longstreet, Gen. James, 179–80, 257
n36
Loring, Gen., conflict with Gen. Jackson, 48, 229 n9
Lynchburg, Va., CW's medical duty
at, 10, 69–70, 74, 77–78, 236 n40

Magruder, Maj. Gen. John B., 10, 75,
158–61, 238 n15–16, 254 n1
mail delivery problems, 54, 66–67,
79, 81–82, 84, 99, 103–104,
168–69
Manassas, second battle of, 10
Manly, Col. (Confederate officer at
surrender of Galveston), 153–54
Marshall, Col. Thomas A., 176, 256
n31
Martinsburg, Va., battle at, 61
Mason, James, 82–83, 240 n26
Maupin, Socrates, 18, 59, 224 n3
Maury, Commodore Matthew Fontaine, 4
Maury, Diana Minor, 4
Maury, John, 27
Maury, Richard, 4
McClellan, Gen. George Brinton,
56–57, 232–33 n26, n29
McDowell, W.Va., battle at, 55, 59,
231 n23
McLaughlin, Col. William, 28
McNeill's Rangers: capture of Union
generals (1865), 11, 144, 250–53
n9; and Conscription Act, 104–
105; CW's opinion of, 132; HM's
induction into, 181; importance
of, 209; Partisan Ranger Act, 189,
259 n3; Shenandoah Valley campaign (1863–64), 190–201, 203–
208, 260–62 n7–17, 263–64
n30–32; winter foraging expeditions, 186

Index

McNeill, John Hanson, 127, 181–82, 188–89, 248 n42, 259 n3
McNeill, Lt. Jesse, 208, 263 n27
Meade, Maj. Gen. George, 179–82, 242 n9, 257 n35
Medical College of Virginia, 241 n4
medical duties: Confederate hospital, 66, 69–70, 74, 77–78, 80, 236 n39–40, 237 n7; regimental, 89, 106–108, 110–12, 122–23
Melhousen, Theodore, death of, 168
"Memoirs of Henry Martyn Trueheart," origin, 221
Menard, Michel B., 6
Mexican government, relations with Texas settlers, 4, 6
Mexican War (1846–48), 5
Minor, Ann Tompkins, 4, 6, 157, 163–65
Minor, Berkeley, 20, 27, 55–56, 59
Minor, Charles, 4, 20, 43
Minor, Charles, Jr., 30, 59, 141, 169, 249 n3
Minor, Clara, 80, 178
Minor, Col. Launcelot (grandfather), 4
Minor, Diana (Mrs. R. Maury), 4
Minor, Elizabeth ("Lizzy") (Mrs. Fontaine), 77–78
Minor, Fanny C. (Mrs. R. Berkley), 28, 80, 126, 178
Minor, Henry, 89, 125, 211
Minor, John, 4, 18, 31, 69–70, 78, 80, 202
Minor, John W., 76, 77, 165, 238 n18
Minor, L. C., 28
Minor, Launcelot (uncle), 4, 20, 28, 74, 76, 78, 80, 81
Minor, Lewis W., 215
Minor, Livy, 77, 80
Minor, Lucian (cousin), 80
Minor, Lucian (uncle), 4, 6
Minor, Lucius, 81
Minor, Mary Ann, 80
Minor, Mary L., 31, 121
Minor, "Nannie" (aunt), 31, 76
Minor, Peter, 89

Minor, William (cousin), 20
Minor, William (uncle), 4
Monocacy Station, battle at, 198–99, 201
Monticello Guards, 9, 24
Moore, Rev. Thomas, 81, 239 n23
Moore, Samuel Preston, 81, 239 n25
Moorefield, Va., skirmish at, 205, 207–208
morale: civilian, 169, 211, 214; military, 53–54, 135, 143–44, 187, 191, 250 n7
Murfreesboro, Tenn., battle at, 71, 237 n3

Napoleon guns, **30**
Neptune, CSS, 160–61, 254 n7
New Creek, battle at, 206–208, 263–64 n28–31
New Market, battle at, 193–95, 260 n7–9
North Carolina, raids in, 71, 237 n5

Overton, Polly, 81
Overton, William, 28, 31, 81
Overton, William, 5, 28, 144, 211
Owasco, USS, 160–61, 254 n7

Parker, Lt. Thornton, 176
Partisan Ranger Act, 189, 259 n3
Payne, Capt. John, 160–62
Pendleton's Battery. *See* 1st Rockbridge Artillery
Pendleton, William Nelson, 9, 27, 224 n7
Petersburg, Va.: Grant's strategy, 244 n19, 249 n5; siege of, 95–103, 118–27, 129–31, 142, 211–13, 245–46 n24–25. *See also* Crater, battle of
Piedmont, Va., battle at, 195–96
Piedmont, W.Va., battle at, 192–93
Port Republic, Va., battles at, 63–67, 234–35 n33–35, n37–38
Price, Gen. Sterling, 171, 256 n24
Princeton College, 4
prisoners of war, 37, 162, 250–53 n9

Index

〜

provisions, obtaining. *See* supply problems

Rapidan River, maneuvers near (1863–64), 87, 172–76, 240 n2, 256 n27
Rappahannock River, battles near, 181–83
real estate business, family, 7–8
"Rebel Monster," CSS, 166–67
Red River, battle at, 75, 238 n17
Richmond, Va.: CW's studies at, 8, 10, 15–28, 79–85, 223–24 n1–4, 239–40 n21–22, n25; Seven Days Battles, 56–57, **149,** 232 n27
Rinaldo, USS, 163
Rockingham Militia, mutiny of, 53–54
Romney, Va., 43–46, **148**
Rosecrans, Maj. Gen. William, 179–80, 257 n37
Rosser, Gen. Thomas L., 206–208, 263–64 n27, n30
Royal Yacht, CSS, 163

Sabine Pass, Tex., battle at, 180
Sachem, USS, 160–61, 180, 254 n7
Sam Houston, USS, 153, 253 n3
San Antonio, Tex., 4, 5–6
Santee, USS, 156, 253 n2
Scurry, Gen., 160
secession: criticism of, 15–16; reaction to Lincoln's inaugural address, 21–22; student sympathy, 23
Semmes, Capt. Raphael, 163, 255 n13
Seven Days Battles, 56–57, **149,** 232 n27
7th Virginia Cavalry: Bristoe campaign, 170–78, 256–57 n27, n33; organization, 255–56 n22
Shenandoah Valley campaigns, **147;** (*1862*), 48–56, 58–67, 229–32 n13–17, n22–25, 234–36 n32–38; (*1863–64*), 190–201, 203–208, 259–62 n4, n7–17, 263 n25–31. *See also* Winter campaign (1861–1862)

Shenandoah Valley militias, 9
Sheridan, Gen. Philip, 97, 143, 244–45 n20, n23, 249–50 n6
Sherman, Maj. Gen. William T., 134–35, 236 n2
Shields, Gen. James, 48, 64–65, 229 n14
slaves: arming of, 135; Truehearts' sale of, 157, 164–65
smallpox outbreak at Lynchburg, 72–73, 237 n10
Smith, Gen. Edmund Kirby, 166–67, 255 n15
Smith, Mrs. Gen. E. Kirby, 175
Smith, Nicaragua, 162, 255 n10
Sons of Liberty, 8–9, 19
South Battery, Galveston, Tex., 162–63
South Carolina, USS, 253 n3
Southern Guards, 8–9, 19, 23–25
Southwick, J. W., death of, 168
Spotsylvania Court House, battles at, 90–95, 98, 243 n10–11
Steger, Overton, 80
"Stonewall" Brigade, 39, 47–48, 224 n7, 225 n11. *See also* 1st Rockbridge Artillery; Jackson, Gen. Thomas J. ("Stonewall")
Street, Ella, marriage to CW, 216
Stuart, Maj. Gen. J. E. B., 71–72, 78, 177, 237 n6, 257 n33
supply problems: CW, 32–33, 47, 108–109, 131, 138, 228–29 n8–9; HM, 170–71, 179, 191, 200, 203–205
surveying, dangers of, 4–5
"Swamp Dragons," 197, 207–208, 261 n13
Swan, William, 80

Talcott, Col. T. M. R., 136–37, 248 n1
tax collection. *See* Trueheart, Henry Martyn: assessor and collector of taxes
Texas Brigade: CW's transfer plans, 104, 117; organization of, 236 n41, 247 n29, 256 n29
Texas Ranger, John O. as, 3–5

Index

〜

Texas Revolution of 1836, 4

trench warfare, 90–96, 100–103, 121–22, 126–27, 131, 211–13. *See also* Petersburg, Va.

Trevilian Raid, 97, 244 n20, 245 n23

Trueheart, Annie Cunningham, 204, 215

Trueheart, Ann Tompkins Minor, 4, 6, 157, 163–65

Trueheart, Caroline Hill ("Cally"), 5–6, 164

Trueheart, Charles William, **17**; attempted artillery transfer (1865), 144, 250 n8; attempted transfer of HM to regular army, 131–33; at battle of the Crater, 105–107, 110–13, 213, 247–48 n30–31, n33–35; on blacks, 60, 135; on character of Union soldiers, 92–93; children of, 264 n2; on Confederate atrocities, 116, 132; on conscription, 53; courtship of, 22–23, 72, 77, 82, 87, 120–21, 185; on courtship rituals, 24, 33–35; death of, 217; on death of colleagues, 37–38; on education of women, 138; Franco-Prussian War duty, 216; glories of the fighting life, 28–29, 68, 73; at Harper's Ferry, 9, 24–25; health of, 53, 57, 127, 230 n18, 248 n41; Henry's injury, 78–79; homesickness, 50–51; hospital duties, 66, 69–70, 74, 77–78, 80, 236 n39–40, 237 n7; hostility to Unionists, 23; human cost of war, 68; impressions of Gen. Lee, 85, 106–107, 110–12, 123–24; lodging for Henry, 82–83; medical career in Texas, 216–17; medical duties on battlefield, 89, 106–108, 110–12, 122–23; medical studies, 8, 10, 15–28, 79–85, 178–79, 216, 223–24 n1–4, 239–40 n21–22, n25, 241 n5; military training, 24, 26; military units, 19, 27–28, 88, 133 ; morale of, 26, 71, 75, 87, 130, 134–35, 142; need for horse, 108–109, 200, 203, 209; at Petersburg, 95–

103, 118–27, 129–31, 142; on pillaging, 88; religious fervor, 69, 72, 88, 107, 130; on returning to Texas, 19–20, 26–27, 104, 117; Richmond living conditions (1864), 187; on secession, 15–16, 21–22; Seven Days Battles, 56–57; in Shenandoah Valley (1862), 48–56, 58–67, 232 n24, 235 n37; supply problems, 32–33, 47, 108–109, 131, 138, 228–29 n8–9; tobacco critique, 31–32; traveling to Texas, 5–6, 215–16; on Union atrocities, 44–47, 60, 96–97; in Wilderness campaign, 89–96, 98, 242–43 n9–10, n13 ; in Winter campaign (1861–62), 33–49, 225–26 n12, n15–21 227–28 n1, n5–7; youth, 7

Trueheart, Daniel, Jr., 33, 225–26 n14

Trueheart, Ella Street, marriage to CW, 216

Trueheart, Elvira Susan ("Bow") (Mrs. R. Howard), 5–6, 156, 165

Trueheart, Fanny Overton, 5–6, 137–38, 165

Trueheart, Henry Martyn, **155**; assessor and collector of taxes, 8, 169, 178, 180, 186; battle of Galveston, 158–66; cattle business of, 7–8; children of, 218; conscription status, 104–105; courtship of, 86–87, 109, 183, 185, 204, 215; criticism of CW's writing, 188; dairy of, 7; death of, 219; defense of cavalry honor, 182; homesickness, 184; horse dealing with CW, 200, 203, 209; impressions of Gen. Lee, 191; injury to, 78–79, 81, 176–81; lodging with CW, 82–83; on McNeill's Rangers, 209; memoirs of, 221; military units, 170, 181; need for prenuptial money, 215–16; at Petersburg, 211–13; possible transfer to regular army, 131–33, 136–37, 139–42, 208–209; postwar activities, 217–19; prewar activities, 7–8; in Shenandoah Val-

Index

Trueheart, Henry Martyn (*cont.*)
ley (1863–64), 190–201, 203–208,
260–62 n7–17, 263–64 n30–32;
supply problems, 170–71, 179,
191, 200, 203–205; travel to Virginia, 166–68; on Union atrocities,
196
Trueheart, James Lawrence, 4
Trueheart, John Overton, 3–7, 165,
222 n10
Trueheart, Lucian Minor, 5–6
Trueheart, Mary Bryan, **17**, 216
Trueheart, Mary Minor (Mrs. T. Joseph), 5–6, 27, 223 n13
Trueheart, Mildred ("Minnie"), 5–6,
222–23 n13
Trueheart, Washington, 4
typhoid fever, 31

Union soldiers, trading with, 170
University of Virginia: CW's medical
studies at, 8, 10, 16, 18–19,
223–24 n1–4; faculty of, 16, 18–
19, 223–24 n1–4
University Volunteers, 9

Vandevender ("Vandiver"), Lt.
Charles, 172, 176, 256 n26
Van Harten, Maj. John, 159, 254 n4
Vaughn, Gen. John Crawford, 196,
260 n11

Vicksburg, Miss., battles at, 71, 166–
68, 236 n2, 255 n18
Virginia, **146–49**. *See also individual
cities and towns*
Virginia Military Institute, 9, 19
Virginia Point, Tex., 156, 160, 254 n7
Virginia, Western, dissent on seces-
sion, 22

Wainwright, Comdr. J. M., 161–62,
254–55 n9
War Years with Jeb Stuart (W. W. Black-
ford), 10
Washington, D. C., skirmishes near,
198–99
Waters, J. D., death of, 168
Weldon Railroad, Petersburg, Va.,
battle at, 113, 247 n33
Westerlage, John, 156
Wharton, Gen. John A., 175
Wigfall, Louis T., 175, 256 n29
Wilderness campaign, 89–96, 98,
242–44 n9–18
Winchester, Va., battle at, 48–49, 55–
56, 59, 229 n13, 232 n23
Winder, Brig. Gen. Charles, 66,
235–36 n38
Winter campaign (1861–62), 33–49,
225–26 n12, n15–21, 227–28 n1,
n5–7

TEXAS A&M UNIVERSITY

MILITARY HISTORY SERIES

★ 44 ★

Rebel Brothers gathers the remarkable letters written by Charles and Henry Trueheart to their family, friends, and each other. As members of a prominent Galveston family, both men bring to their correspondence the breeding, education, and class attitudes regularly associated with Old South genteel society. Yet, their widely diverse wartime experiences offer a multiple perspective rarely found in Civil War-era letters and journals.

Charles, who entered the war as an infantryman in a company composed of University of Virginia students, eventually served as an artillerist in the 1st Rockbridge Artillery with the legendary "Stonewall Brigade" and as an assistant regimental surgeon, 8th Alabama Infantry, with Gen. Robert E. Lee's Army of Northern Virginia. He ended the war at Appomattox Court House as an assistant surgeon with the 1st Regiment Confederate Engineers. Henry's letters include a firsthand account of the Battle of Galveston and of his experiences riding with the 7th Virginia Cavalry and McNeill's Partisan Rangers. Offering the reader a rare glimpse into the life of a Confederate cavalryman, the letters also chronicle Henry's participation in McNeill's famous raid on Cumberland, Maryland, in which Union Generals George Crook and Benjamin Kelley were captured.

The correspondence shows two men who possessed a keen understanding of Confederate military tactics and strategy, as well as of the political